Val Morsman

PAINTING IN HER TRUE COLOURS

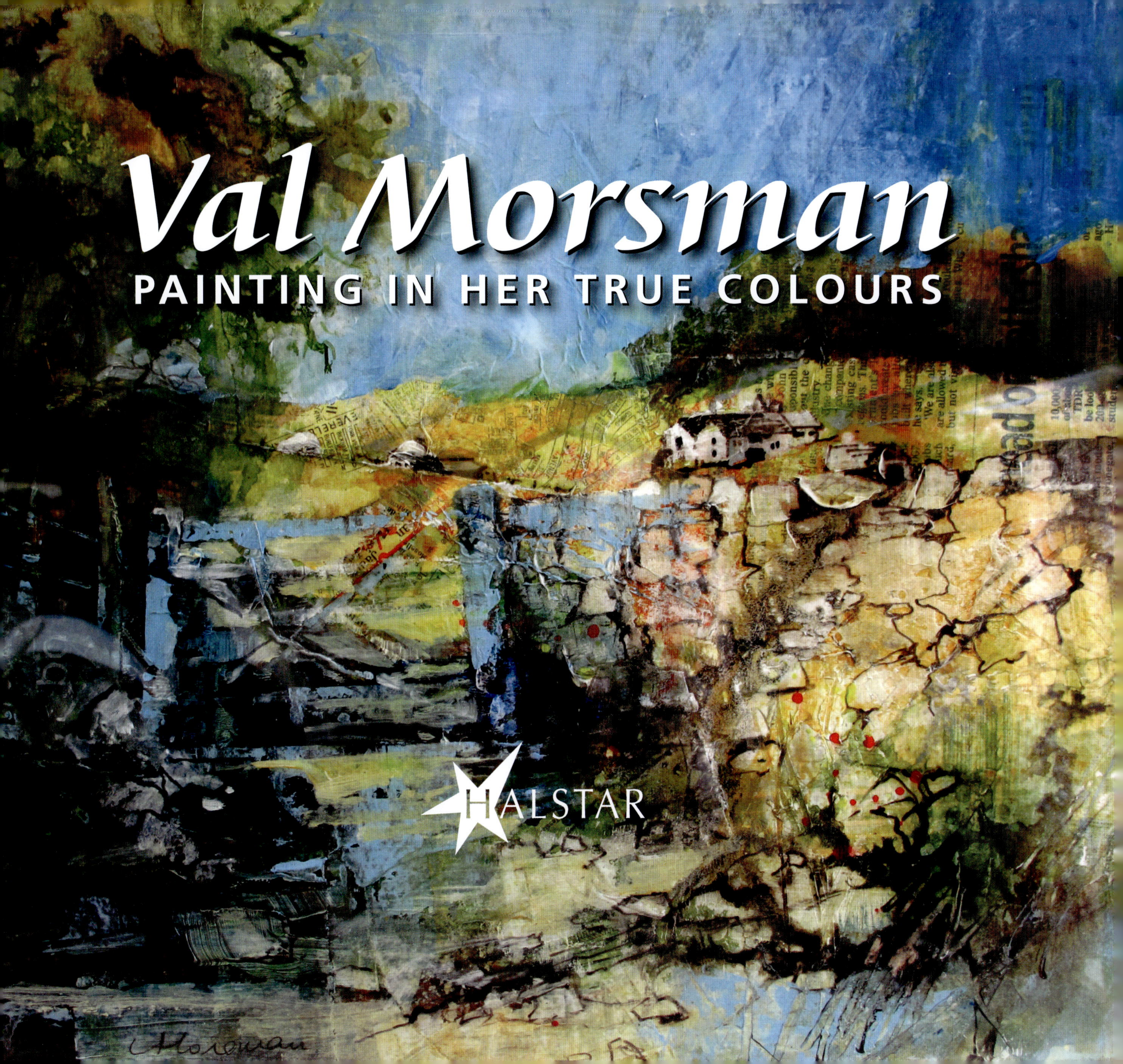

HALSTAR

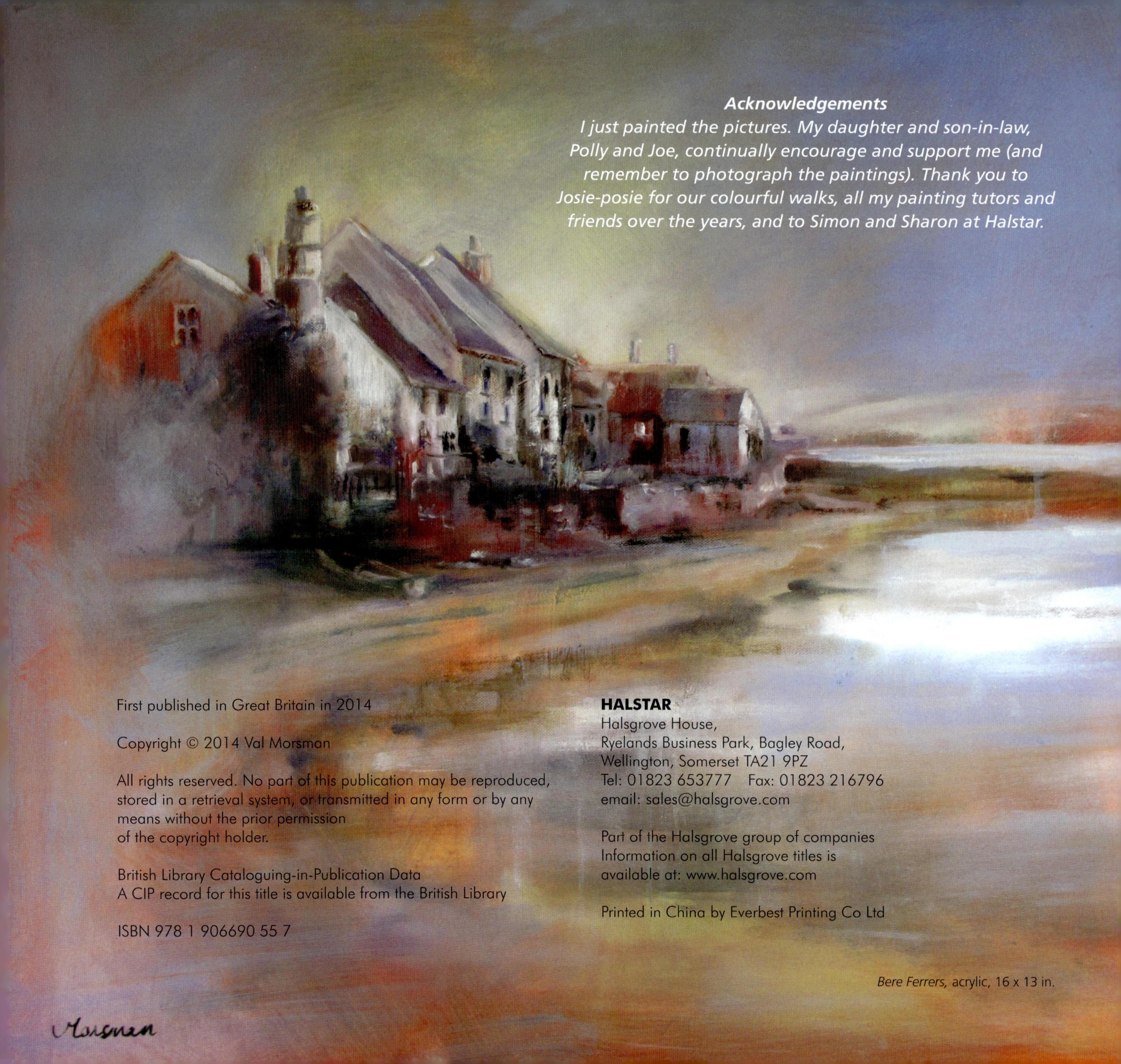

Acknowledgements
I just painted the pictures. My daughter and son-in-law, Polly and Joe, continually encourage and support me (and remember to photograph the paintings). Thank you to Josie-posie for our colourful walks, all my painting tutors and friends over the years, and to Simon and Sharon at Halstar.

First published in Great Britain in 2014

British Library Cataloguing-in-Publication Data
A CIP record for this title is available from the British Library

ISBN 978 1 906690 55 7

HALSTAR
Halsgrove House,
Ryelands Business Park, Bagley Road,
Wellington, Somerset TA21 9PZ
Tel: 01823 653777 Fax: 01823 216796
email: sales@halsgrove.com

Part of the Halsgrove group of companies
Information on all Halsgrove titles is available at: www.halsgrove.com

Printed in China by Everbest Printing Co Ltd

Bere Ferrers, acrylic, 16 x 13 in.

Introduction

I was born in Kent – some distance from the county of Devon where I now live – and both areas influence my visual memory. As a small child my parents sent me out at weekends equipped only with an Ordnance Survey map and a tin of Horlicks tablets and I was not expected to return home until teatime. Inevitably I often got lost; on one memorable occasion aged about seven I had no idea where I was and it had been dark for some time when I was rescued by a troop of Boy Scouts – their good deed for the day. How I finally reached home I don't now remember, but I was scolded and sent to bed with no supper!

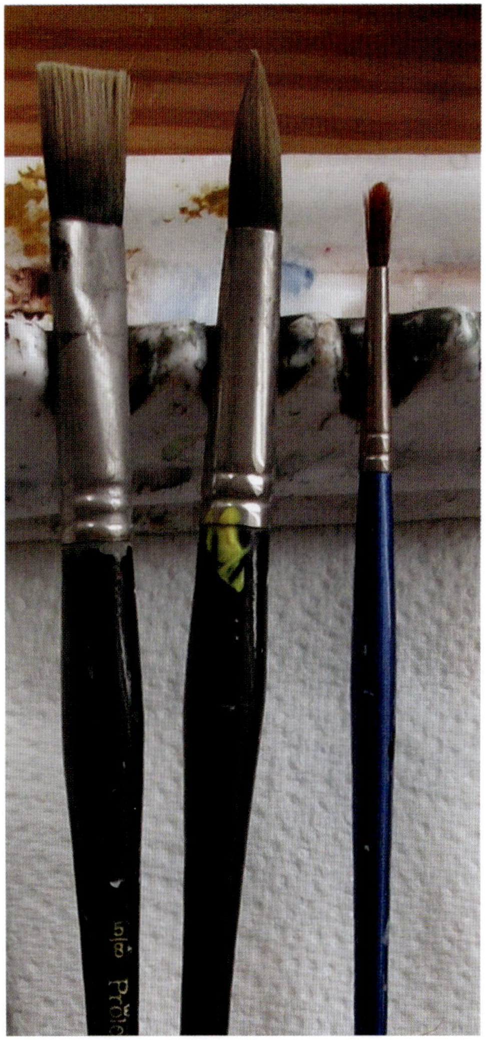

On these expeditions I often tired of walking and would sit and look. The shape and colours of the English countryside, farmland, trees, houses, hills and valleys became very familiar to me and still when I travel through Kentish countryside I am struck by how I can relate to the structure of the area.

My father kept me very busy in the garden for a great deal of my growing up years, but my refuge was always in drawing, and under the bedclothes after bedtime I revisited my rural walks, and often drew peasant-like people inhabiting the countryside. Someone gave me a present of a huge paintbox which was visually exciting and it taught me the names of paints, but the quality of the paints was so poor that using them was not a joy and I stuck with drawing.

Once a week I had to accompany my father to the public library three miles away, down three steep hills, in order to carry his eight books. I was allowed to choose one book to add to the newly chosen eight and had to carry these back home up those three steep hills. Ridiculously, I usually chose one of the big art books from the big-book bottom shelf. More often than not I chose Leonardo da Vinci or Michelangelo and would lose myself in the beautiful drawing and painting. It must have been worth the journey.

So I spent my childhood doodling, drawing, never without a pad and pencil, never showing any real originality but nevertheless gaining a reputation for being good at it. Truth to tell, I was keen but not that good. Both my maternal grandparents were painters, also a great uncle, but closer to home my own parents enjoyed painting so I grew up accepting art as a valid occupation.

I certainly never doubted that a hand-made card or present would be acceptable – my poor grandmother was the main recipient of such things as a cover for The Radio Times (who would want such a thing?), but she gamely used it until it fell to bits.

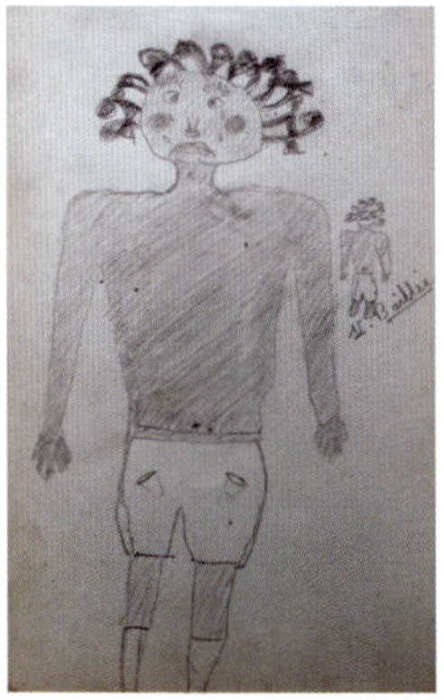

Above: *My grandmother possessed that very Victorian project, an autograph and memory book, beautifully written and painted in by her friends and family in the 1890s. I desecrated it with this picture. She must have agreed to me doing it, but probably regretted it quite soon.*

Right: *My maternal grandmother in her early painting days.*

Below: *One of the inherited pictures. They always hung in my grandparents' house and now hang in mine. Here is a flower study painted on copper – very typical of its time.*

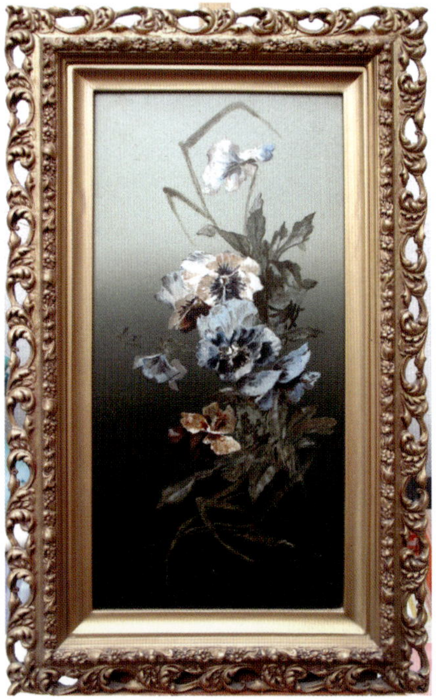

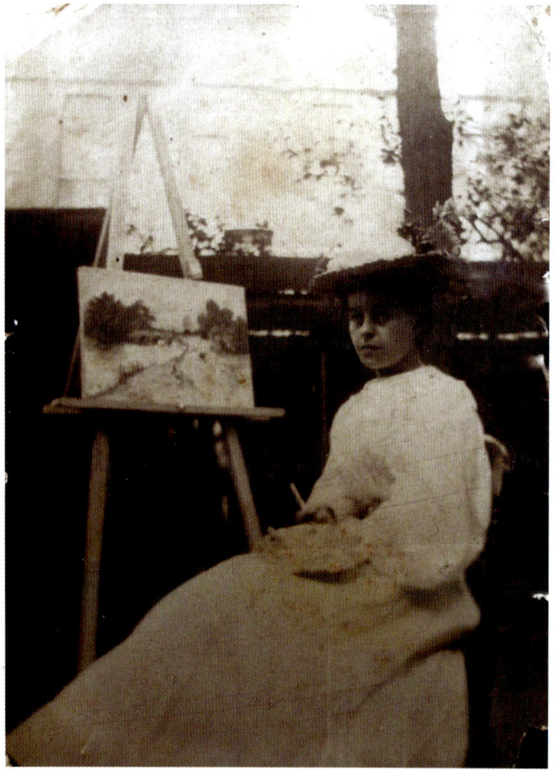

She was a genuine artist, and I still have some of her very accomplished oils, although her painting journey had obviously had its moments. Members of the family would laugh hysterically at the memory of 'landscape with sheep', which unfortunately must have been destroyed before my time. All I can say is the pictures I have inherited are wonderful.

We had two art teachers at grammar school, both very arty and strong characters, but I only pleased one of them. I can see now that her preference was for colour and abstraction and I could do that. I was thrilled when my picture of trees in very unlikely colours went up on the wall. With the other teacher I could do nothing right, as her form of expression was all about design and my best friend would come out of her class glowing with the achievement of repeatedly printing a leaf on linen to form a pattern. I found it all too tight and clean cut for me, but I tried hard to understand. By now I had realised what excited me most – drawing, especially people, and painting with exciting colour and looking for unexpected results with my use of paint.

My parents were beginning to wonder what I would do after my school education. I was just concerned with what A-levels to take and thought that art school would be a great way to go afterwards, but hadn't thought seriously beyond that. My headmistress couldn't encompass the idea of art over university. For her, a university education was what every grammar school girl should aspire to, and that might have happened had we not suddenly moved house.

In the summer of 1958, we moved thirty miles into the country where my father announced that I had to find a job! Nothing had been further from my mind. Deeply miserable, living in a strange place, I knew I had to formulate a plan to earn money. I hit upon the idea of signing up for a secretarial course of shorthand, bookkeeping, typing and economics, a crash course that enabled me to apply for secretarial positions in the City. So, at 17, instead of A-levels, art school or university, I was catching the 8.10 train to London, taking dictation, fighting off lecherous office males and earning £7 a week plus luncheon vouchers. All creative urges had gone.

Working in London I did sometimes manage to get to art galleries and to the theatre but there was always a problem getting a train home late in the evening – I quite often had to cut short an enjoyable evening to catch a train. Also, there were two other problems to contend with. My horticulturist father, while himself still working in London as a senior Civil Servant, had moved us to the country to a house and two acres of a working nursery with fourteen industrial sized greenhouses, coke boilers and soil sterilisers. This was his retirement dream, but it was my mother, my brother and myself who had to make it work in the meantime. My mother, too, at much the same time, began to show signs of illness which would continue over the next ten years until her premature death. What all this meant for me was that, whenever I was not at work, I was helping out at home; usually a very physical task.

After a year working as a secretary I began to think there must be more to life and left home to train as a nurse. In the 1960s, a nurse's life didn't allow for too much time off, but what free time I had, I went home to help.

From 1960 to 1985 there was no painting or drawing, nothing more creative than dressmaking, and for a brief time making teddy bears for extra income. Twenty-five years, all the time knowing subliminally it would happen one day. During that time my father died, ironically the day before he retired and my mother too, eighteen months later. For me there followed several life-changing events including my marriage and the birth of a daughter.

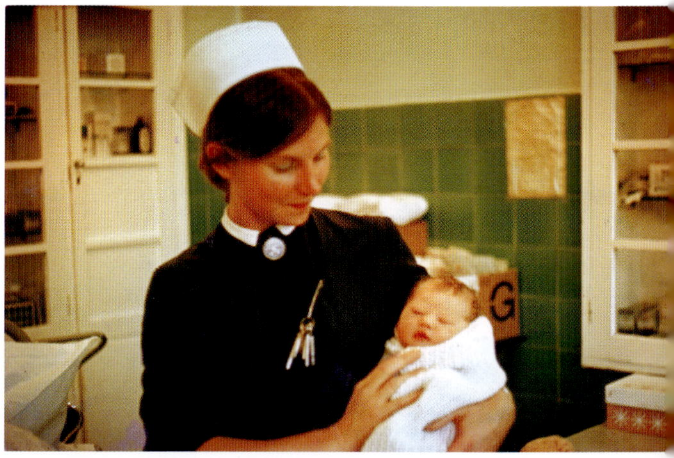

Me as a Labour Ward Sister in 1978, with the last delivery of the night. Anything artistic took a back seat for years while I pursued a career in nursing and midwifery.

I had relatives who farmed in Helston in Cornwall so growing up I had always felt a little bit West Country. Family members used to spend their summer holidays on the farm doing all those archetypal Enid Blyton style activities – collecting eggs, riding on hay carts, taking lemonade and pasties to the men in the fields, helping to make cream and butter, so when I stopped nursing and we moved to Devon in 1984, I felt almost at home. I certainly recognised the countryside, the high stone walls, small fields, stone cottages, crashing seas, craggy moorland and moist air which keeps everything green and mossy. We moved to a lovely south Devon estuarial village called Newton Ferrers, a yachting haven with the sea nearby, the moorland close and Cornwall just over the Tamar, and this was to be my stamping ground for the next thirty years.

A short while prior to moving I had sustained a back injury in a car crash necessitating two bouts of surgery that inevitably left me less than active and considerably weakened. Pain and loss of sleep somehow led to the perusal of art books, mainly Rowland Hilder, during the long nights. For several months that is what I did every night, lying on the living room floor with Rowland Hilder's favourite colours, copying his works of art. He had a list of his preferred colours and they were my first purchase. I don't think it occurred me to copy anybody else's work, I just wanted to achieve a fluidity of wash which I believed I could attain from his 'loose' pictures. Of course, lying on the floor to paint (I now know) couldn't have helped to get a good perspective, but anyway, it certainly got me going and I have never looked back. I cannot recall how Rowland Hilder books came into my possession but I liked his large washes and choice of colour and I thought 'I can do that, it looks easy!' He was mostly famous for his Kentish landscapes and also for illustration and poster art, all of which I still find fascinating.

My inherited paintbox - no longer used but treasured.

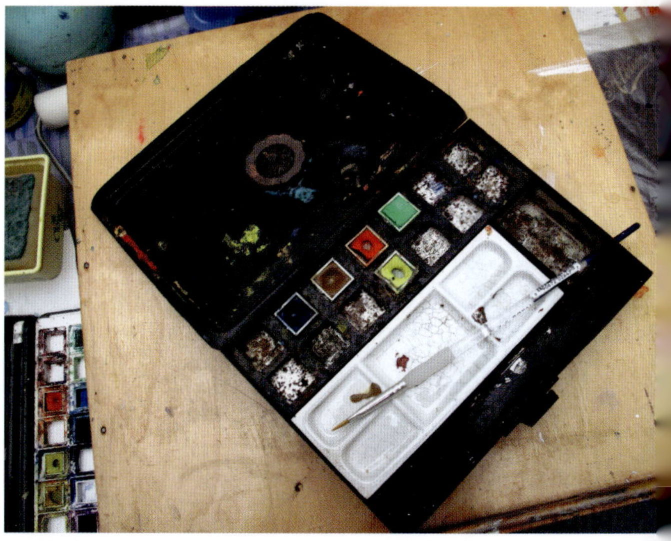

This was when the painting really began in earnest, in my mid forties. After a little while, and realising that it wasn't necessarily as easy as all that, I enrolled in a village class for watercolour. My equipment at first was old 'stuff' I had inherited from my parents painting days – slightly foxed cartridge paper, oil painting brushes, dried up watercolour pans in a metal paint box of great age – I didn't know any better.

The tutor must have blanched. My first purchase was a decent brush for watercolour, a size 20. Why I don't know, but I still use large brushes in preference to small, so that was a fortuitous purchase. From the moment I started this class I was in heaven and I soon sought to find any painting groups in the area.

There were two societies advertising locally both of which I contacted. The Watercolour Society met to paint al fresco once a week; it sounded attractive, but I hesitated. Was I ready for that? The other art group required a portfolio of twenty paintings before admission! I went to view their exhibition which did not fill me with delight and they appeared not to have any young members. I put them on hold. Finally I joined the 'en plein air' group but always managed to hide behind a bush when the resident tutor hove into view, too self conscious to show him what I'd been painting. Bless him, he made no comment on this for a good two years which was the length of time I kept him waiting to see my work.

One class led to another and with rising excitement and a great deal of trepidation I joined a life class. The tutor was a terrifying lady artist whose sometimes scathing comments were enough to concentrate my efforts. These classes took place in a local big house, in the billiard room. The huge table acted as a plinth for the model and we painters were ranged around, free to move if we wanted. It must have been very cold for the model sitting, lying and standing on the slate bed but that didn't occur to me at the time – I had my own problems. We had both male and female models, short poses and long, and at the end of two hours we had to take the scrutiny of the tutor.

Below left: *I attended life classes off and on for about fifteen years and somewhere along the line produced this. I was much better with quick poses of which this was one – I think 10 minutes.*

Below right: *Musical subjects appeal, and my life class one year asked the local Philharmonic to have a practice session so that we could draw them as they played. I have painted from these images several times.* Watercolour 15 x 18 in.

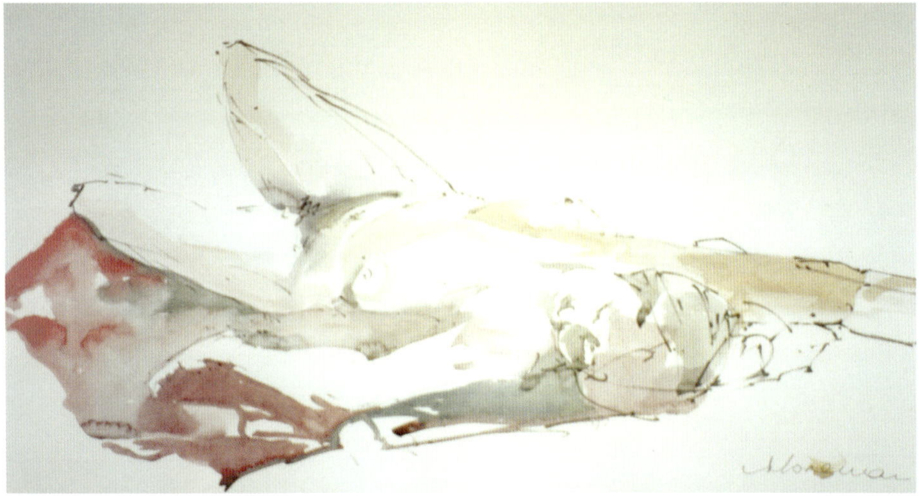

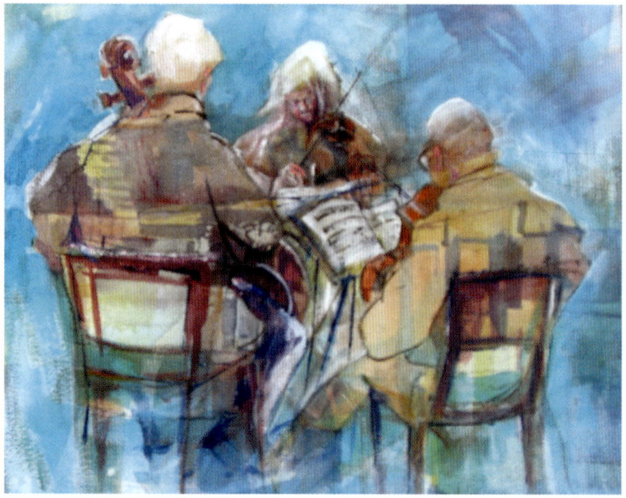

Fortunately for me I was mostly making quite a good job of it, at least it was obviously a person I was drawing even if sometimes the perspective was awry, but it was my first experience of exposing my work to the criticism of others. It is, of course, completely necessary to understand, and be made to see, one's mistakes but harsh criticism can pull me down to the point where I wonder whether trying is at all worthwhile. Improvement will probably follow if one keeps painting enough and looking at other people's work and even at this early stage of my artistic life I could look back in my sketchbook and see a considerable improvement. This was largely due to the fact that I had learned to 'see'.

I was beginning to buy the odd bit of equipment now. Never one to throw my money around I needed to be sure that what I bought was the right thing. Still unsure about what was needed, and especially when faced with a shop full of fascinating equipment I held back a bit with the paints as the life class required only very large cartridge pads, pencils and charcoal, but bit by bit, other things crept in – a putty rubber, three or four artist's quality paints which I thought (quite rightly) would make a lot of difference. I noticed what other people were using but realised that it wasn't necessarily those who had the most impressive equipment who produced the most impressive pictures. Also at this time I was reading a book about a Russian prisoner of war who kept a record of his imprisonment using whatever he could lay his hands on which certainly was not hot pressed watercolour paper, Winsor & Newton paints or soft brushes. The results of his endeavours were brilliant and atmospheric using such things as leaves for brushes, burnt sticks to draw, blood, tea, urine and rain to provide fluid and colour! He not only kept a record of his living conditions and other prisoners' lives, but managed to be an artist in a situation where most might fight only to survive on a very primitive level. When I feel the need to purchase an obscure colour, or try another make of paper, believing that this will be the key to success, I remind myself that if you are good enough you can make do with very little. That, however, doesn't always stop me from having an exciting spending spree in art shops nowadays.

The outside painting group had two exhibitions a year and for one of them there was no selection – a guarantee of a picture up there for public scrutiny. My first ever publicly displayed picture was a badly drawn dinghy in choppy water priced £10.

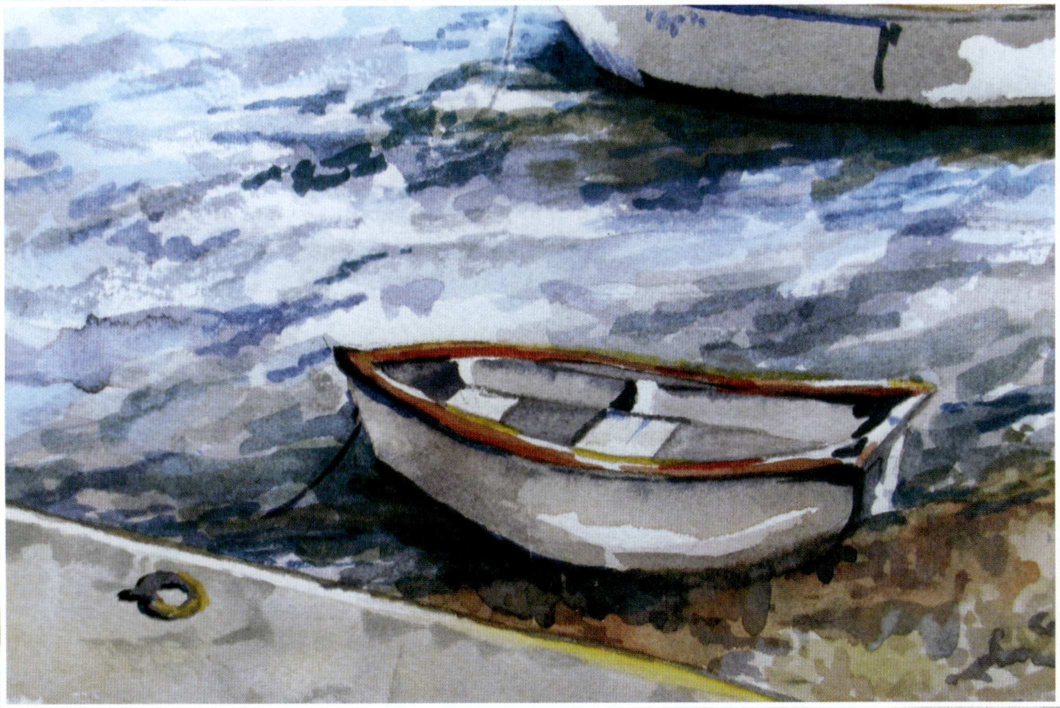

My first hung picture in a local painting society exhibition. A dinghy looking more like a coracle than a boat. Would it float? But at least I had made the transition from the painter hiding behind a bush to one prepared to let a picture be seen in public. Watercolour 10 x 8 in.

At the end of the exhibition I quickly removed it from its position on the wall surrounded by nice work, and rushed out of the building. A handily placed bin in the street seemed the obvious place for it, but a hand suddenly appeared and stopped me and one of the committee tried to make me see that if I kept the picture, whatever I thought of it now, it would provide a comparison for future work and I would be able to see improvement over time. "Anyway" he said, "the frame is worth £10!" He was right, and I still look at it and think about the "beginning". Thereafter I regularly submitted pictures for the exhibition and quite often had mine selected.

I was slowly developing a recognisable style, or so I was told. I was often asked about my "loose" technique. As far as I was concerned large brushes and lots of water and pigment was what made me feel good, and for a long while the only brushes I used were a No.20 round brush and a fine long rigger for detail. Although I have inevitably acquired several other brushes I still feel happiest with a large (2") flat brush and a long rigger for watercolours.

It's much the same for oils too. I constantly think in painting terms; looking at the sky and wondering what colour I would choose to do it, watching water and the light on it, squinting at a scene to condense the shapes into a composition. I came to realise that I had always perceived the colours of life and landscape, that colour had been important all my life. We are all individual in our likes and dislikes, our brains, our eyes, our thought processes, and however we may try to emulate another, it is difficult to fight against our own make up. I still think first of colour before I launch into a picture, sometimes putting colour on the paper before I even know what I am going to paint.

A loose depiction of a canal in Bruges, my second painting holiday where I overcame some of my fear of painting in public. I recall being told to flick my watercolour brush casually behind me if a passer-by became too inquisitive and came too close for comfort.

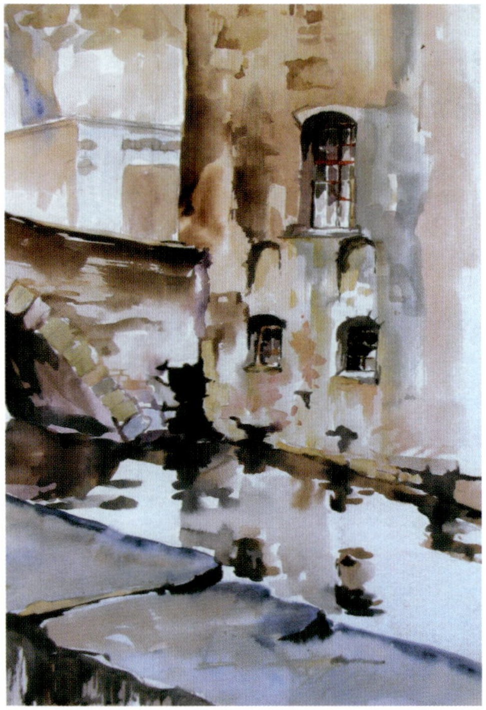

I had been painting for three or four years when I went on my first painting holiday. The holiday was a present so I had no idea who or what it was about and the list of things to take was pretty basic so it had been well chosen for an inexperienced painter. The course lasted a week and by Wednesday I was exhausted from the intense daily concentration. I had never painted all day, every day before. I clearly remember spending at least an hour trying to decide which blue I should choose to finish a painting which needed just a square of blue sky to complete it. I experimented over and over with squares of coeruleum, cobalt and ultramarine and held them in place. Really I had had no idea that such decision making could be involved in a picture. The tutor, whilst sympathising with my predicament, made no move to decide for me which, of course, I found very frustrating at the time but in retrospect was the most helpful thing he could have done. I sold that picture a short time later, but no part of it was more important than that square of blue.

I went away on painting weeks, both in England and abroad, for five or six years and I don't think there were any wasted moments, not only from the painting point of view, but also learning to watch other people's approach to a picture, finding other mediums to work in, using a sketch book to experiment or catch a fleeting moment. The sheer joy of uninterrupted creativity for several days in a row was eye opening and each time I could feel I had made real progress.

Occasionally I would wake up in the morning knowing what it was I needed to paint next. Maybe I should have ignored some of these visions, but the end results were always interesting. On one of my painting holidays I had sheltered under a huge statue of a rearing horse and used my sketchbook to draw it, complete with military rider. Much later I was compelled to use this

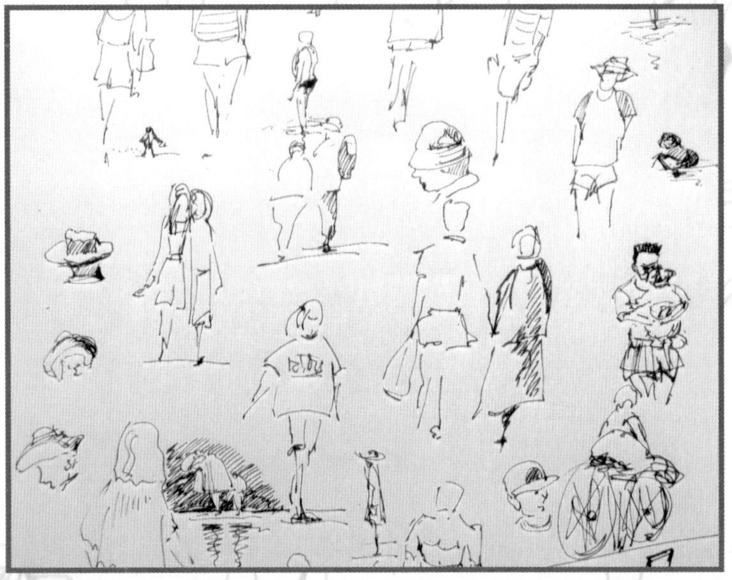

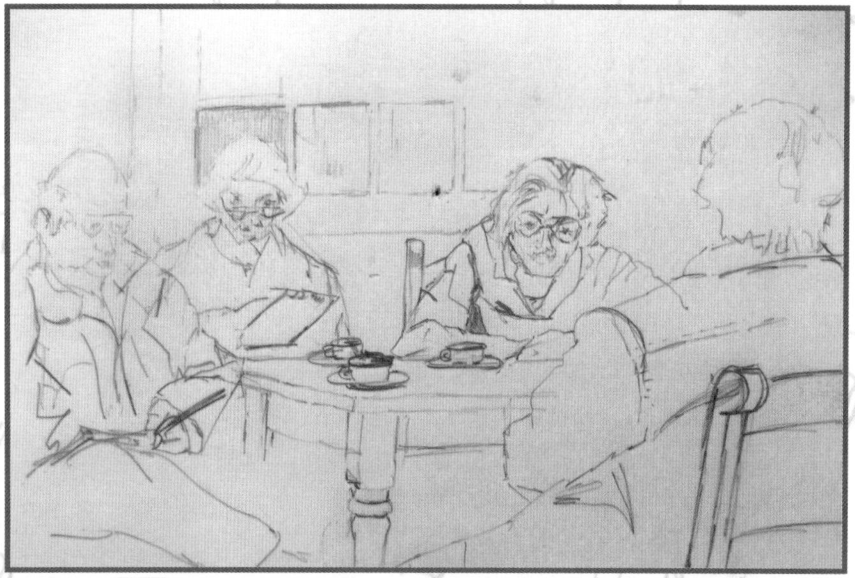

Clockwise from top left: *I do spend time watching people and catching their movement in quick sketches. Sitting in a public place there are so many different shaped people to observe – it is so much more difficult to invent them; these were some of the participants on a course. When you have taken time to watch and draw, you are instantly taken back to the event, years later. More quick sketches, this time in Lyme Regis; Another painting course, this time in Spain; lots of drawing and learning that different colours were needed to get a hint of the heat in Spain; I think this drawing was also on a holiday in Cornwall, and the first time I used a sketch to produce a painting.*

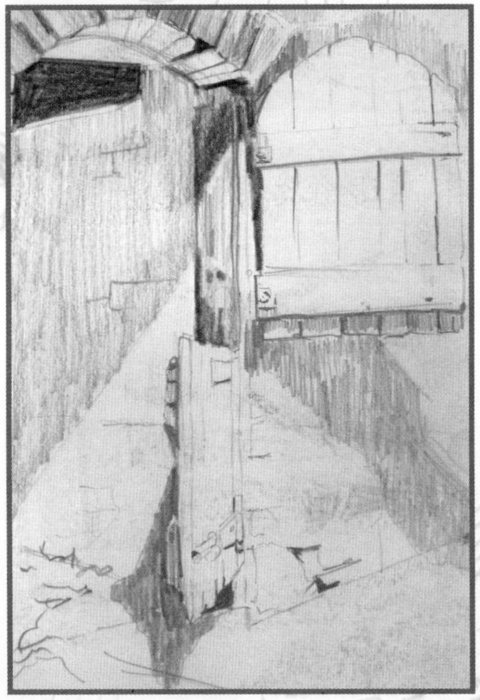

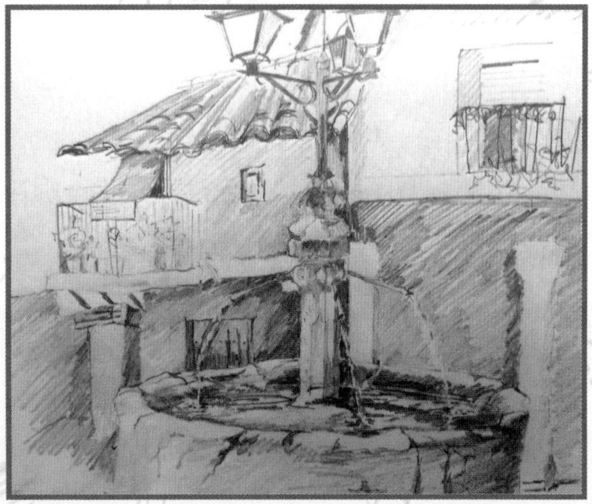

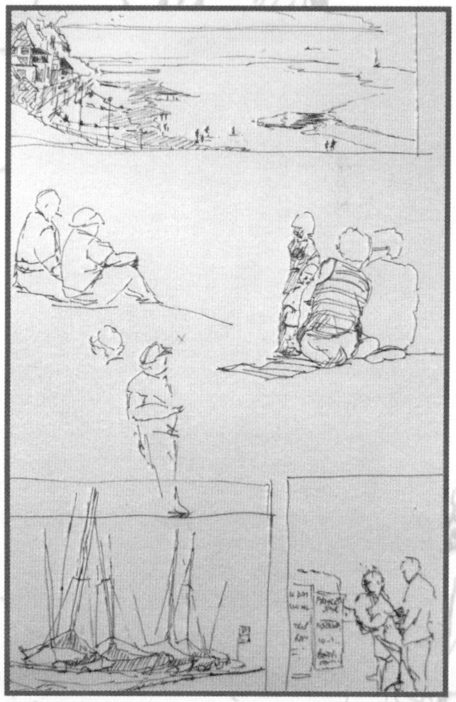

image to fill an entire sheet of paper with rearing horse, rider nearly unseated and, in the background, a fiery battle with chivalrous overtones (flags flying, horses galloping, knights jousting). Even though I say it myself it was an exciting picture and when it was exhibited with my local society, sold for three figures to a couple who were visitors to the town. I had not had the foresight to take a photograph so I have no record of it – only the original sketch, and I deeply regret that now, but when I consider that my marriage was apparently under threat at this time maybe it is no bad thing that I am not reminded of what was obviously a disturbed state of mind!

Who cares, if the results are interesting. The next dream picture, which happened not long after this event, was of three men heaving a log. Why? I have no idea. But it absolutely had to be painted and when I looked at it I knew it was some sort of cathartic event.

In the course of time being on my own has been really helpful. I used painting as a healer and then it became pretty much a full-time hobby, and as I continued to sell quite often I was more than happy to continue. After a while it is difficult to stop, although I have had fallow years, but even then I was reading and looking and thinking paint. Sometimes I wanted to paint in a different way and I was inspired to try collage. I loved the way the paint travelled over stuck-

Below left: *It was raining hard and the statue didn't offer much in the way of shelter. This sketch became the basis of a chivalrous battle picture which I saw in my dream.*

Below right: My second 'dream' picture. *Lifting the Log,* watercolour, 15 x 24 in.

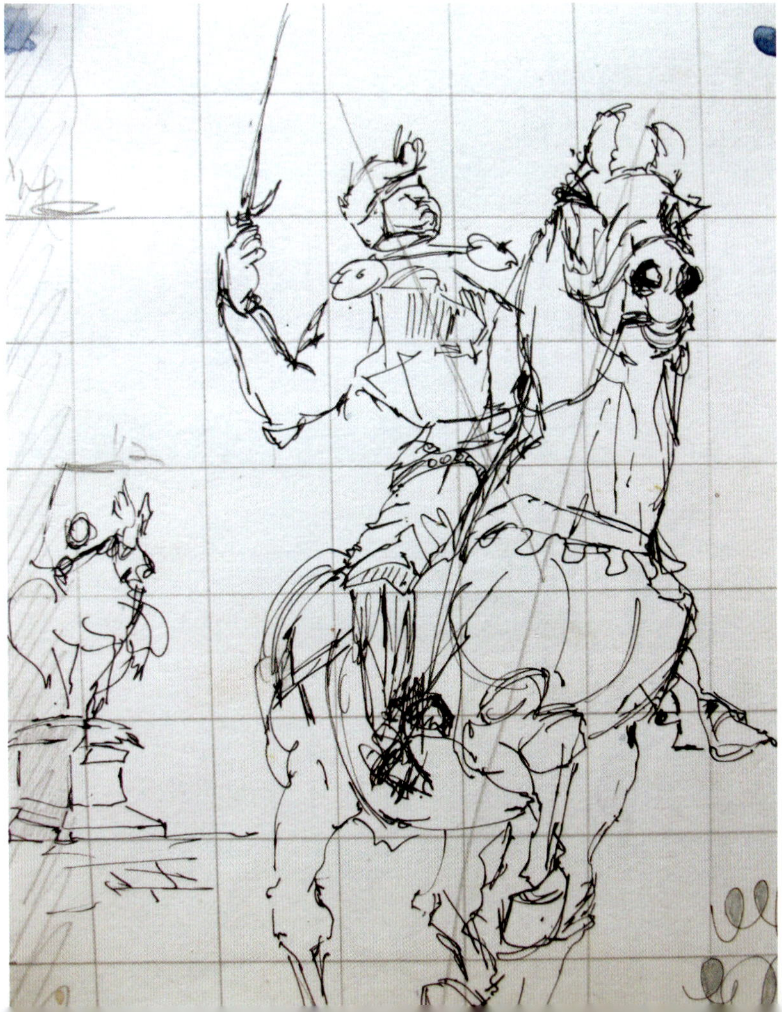

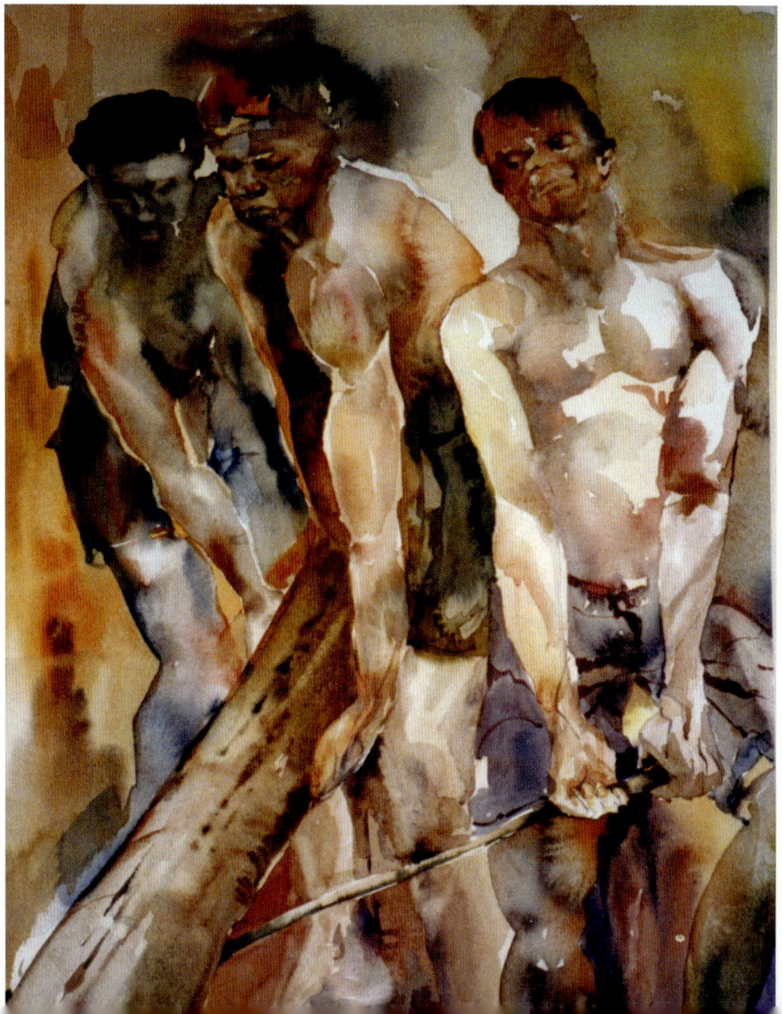

on shapes, creating random runnels. Watercolour didn't work very well for this and I experimented with acrylic inks and paint. So a whole new way of working started.

What I found was that this approach sometimes filled the gap of inspiration which occasionally occurred with watercolours. I would randomly stick on bits of paper, then even more randomly drip on paint, spray with water and wait for the result to inspire a picture. There was usually a

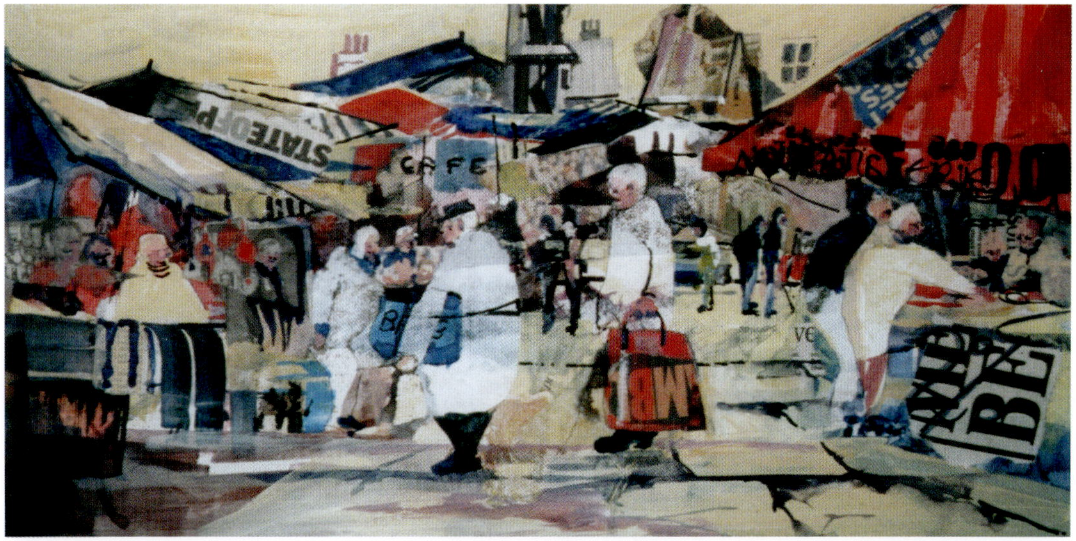

French Market Place, collage, 13 x 16 in

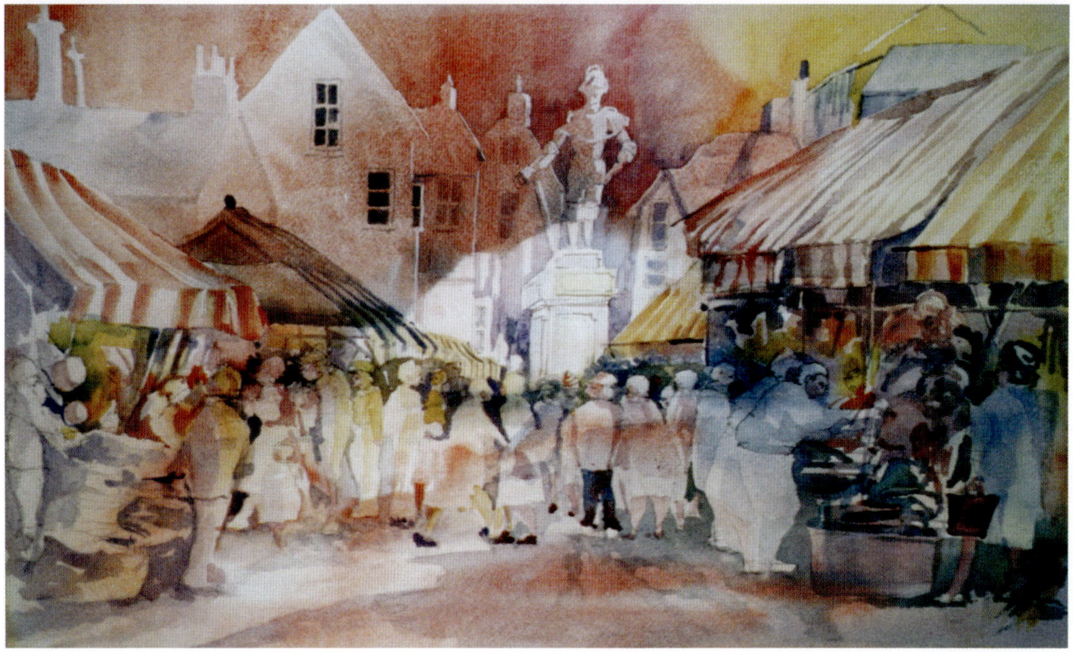

A Knight in the Market Place,
watercolour, 13 x 16 in

The markets I draw are usually imaginary places allowing me to take liberties with the architecture and the people.

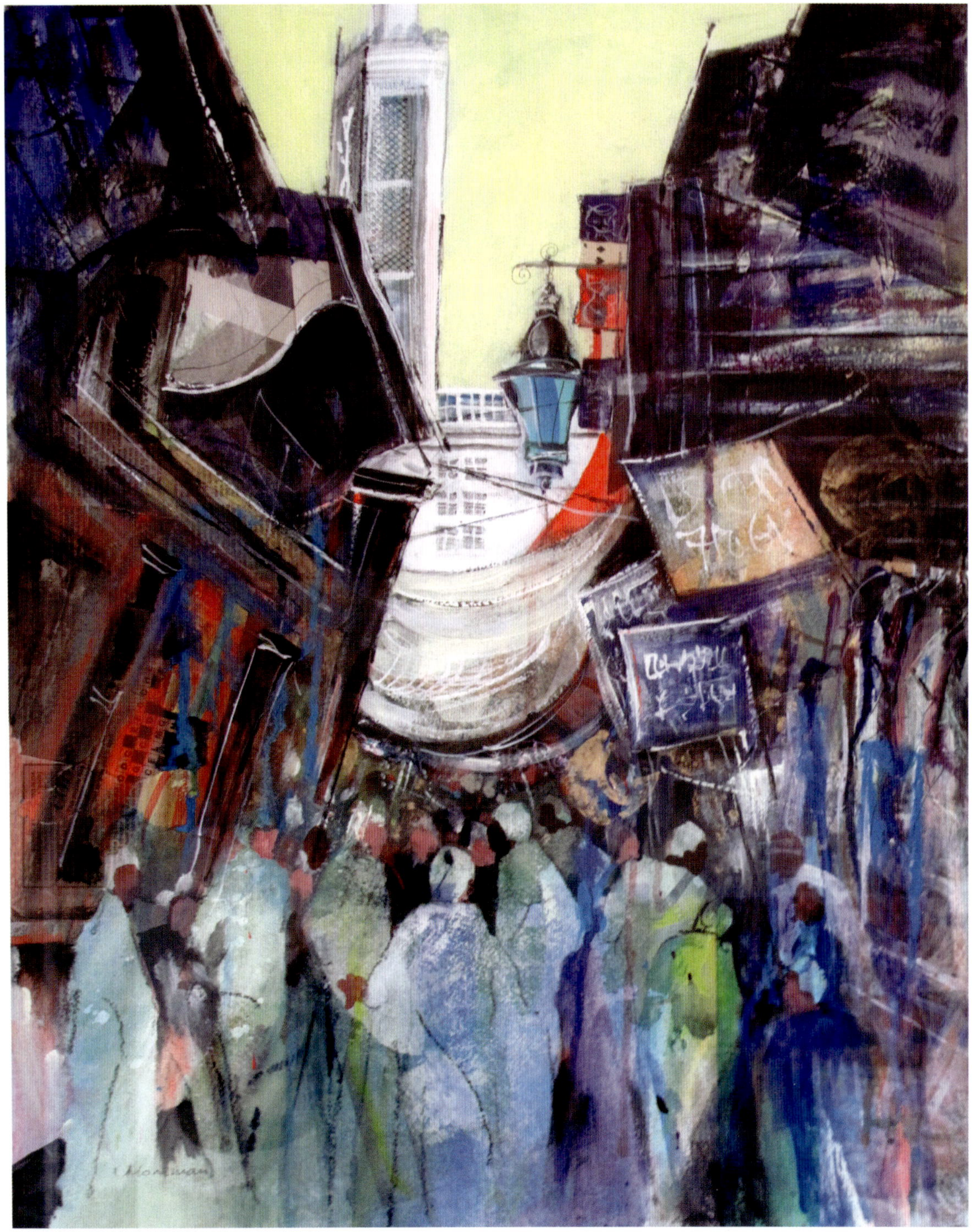

Moroccan Souk,
collage and acrylic inks,
26 x 19 in

Market places I love, especially if I use collage techniques. I have had two holidays in the medina in Fès where the market place atmosphere can be found in plenty.

Basilique du Sacré Couer de Montmartre,
collage and acrylic,
22 x 18 in.

My daughter and I had three days in Paris experiencing the artistic ambience of Montmartre.

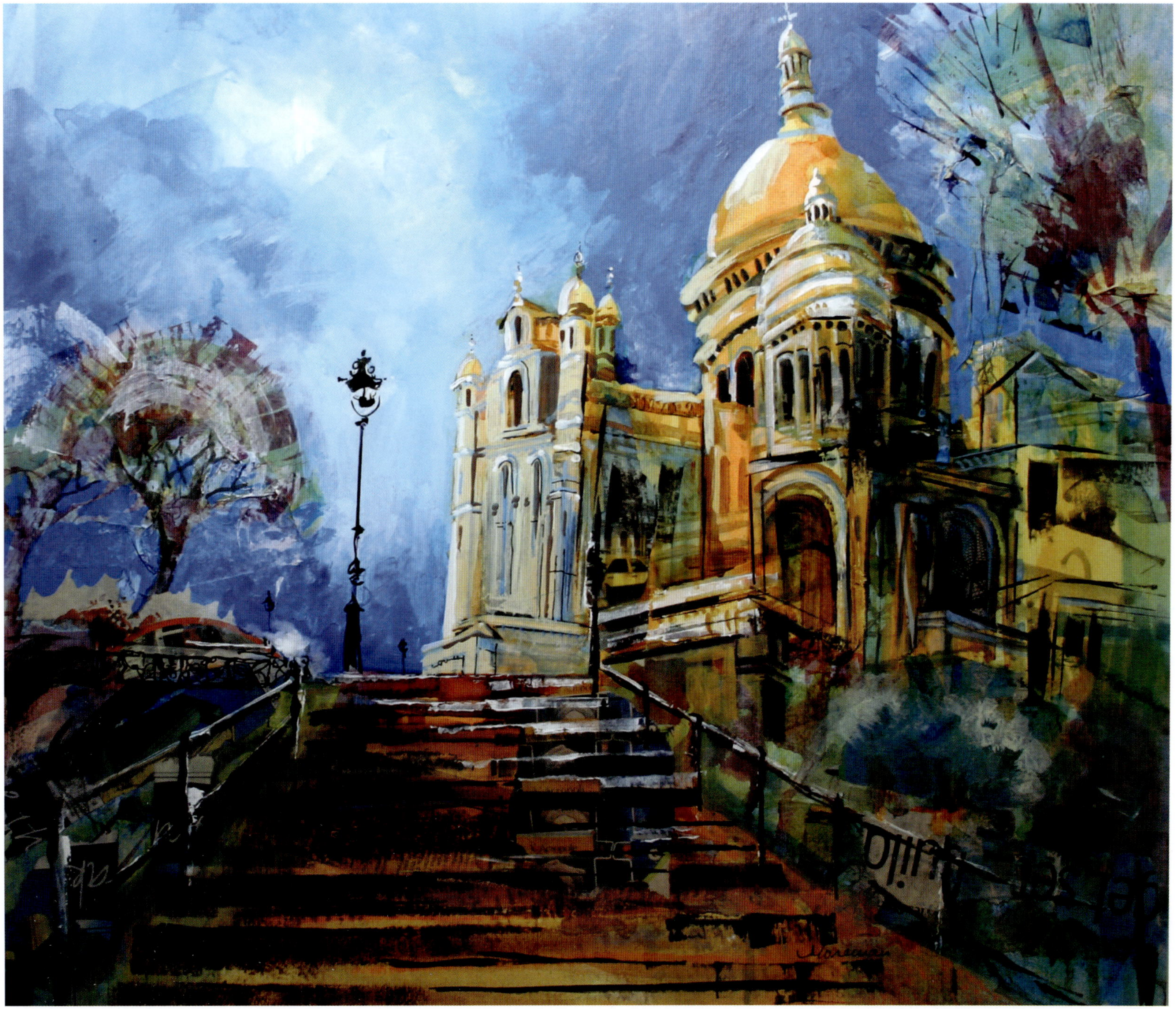

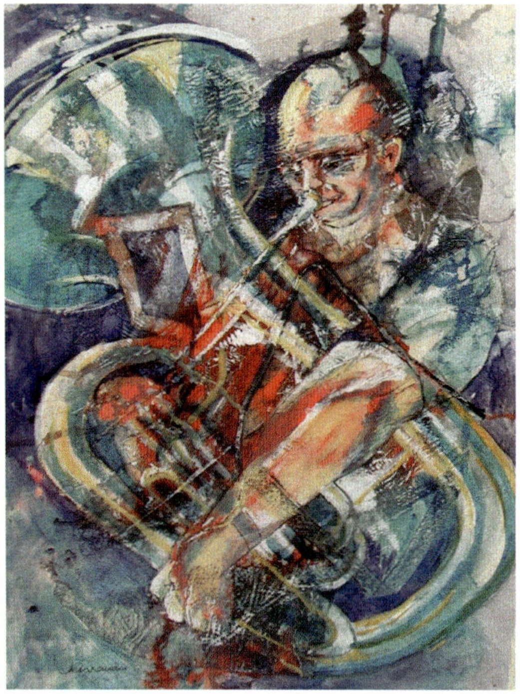

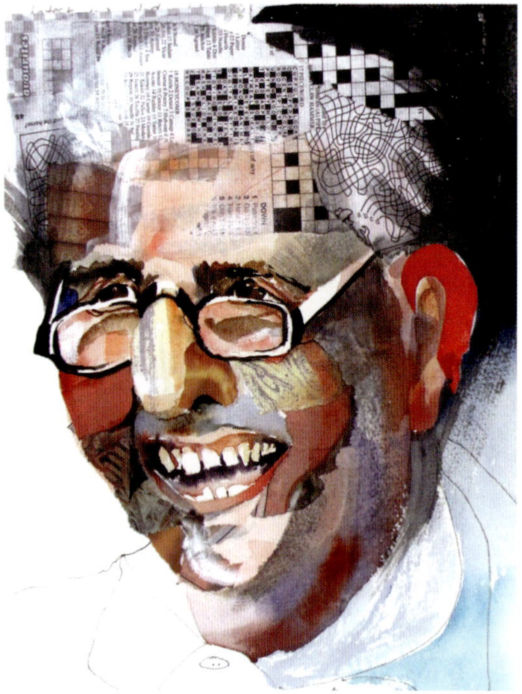

Right: *The Trombone Player,* collage and acrylic, 16 x 24 in.

Musical subjects fascinate me and this one was a collage with acrylic ink done from a drawing at a Royal Marine's Christmas concert. This particular picture has been a drawing, a photograph, a painting, and a stained glass window.

Far right: *Never a Crossword,* collage and acrylic ink, 12 x 14 in.

An exercise in silliness.

shape that started me off in the right direction and, unlike watercolour, I could always add more paper or colour. I became genuinely excited about this process and started to collect likely collage material, tissue paper, newspaper, magazines, fruit nets, doilies, tickets, music score - the list is endless.

It is easy to drown in this sort of stuff and I have to cull things from time to time, after all there is no shortage of paper-based things arriving on our doorsteps every day. I also became aware of the accumulating paraphernalia associated with all image making; paints, papers, collage material, inks, pens and pencils, glues, tape, boards, framing materials, reference books and so many other things that made it all possible. I usually worked on my dining table and, being on my own most of the time, I would surround myself gloriously with ever-increasing amounts of working material to the point where I would panic about visitors when I would have to clear the table in order to eat!

There came a point when not only the top of the table, but also underneath, was full. I decided to invest a small amount of money in making a lean-to shed into a studio. I have had this space now for three or four years and it has been a lifesaver, although I still paint on the dining room table and there is an ever increasing risk of both areas being too full to work in or on. Like so many others my dream is to have a proper studio space (mine is very small) but I have to accept that it may never happen. One of the best painters I know works in a box room about 6 feet by 8 feet on a DIY pasting table and keeps his equipment in a single wardrobe, so I certainly don't think I can blame the lack of it for any shortcomings in my work.

A view of my studio/shed looking as if it's just been tidied!

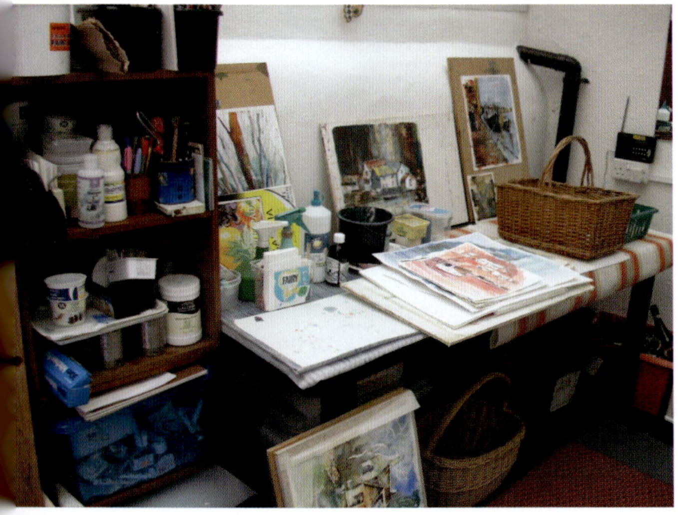

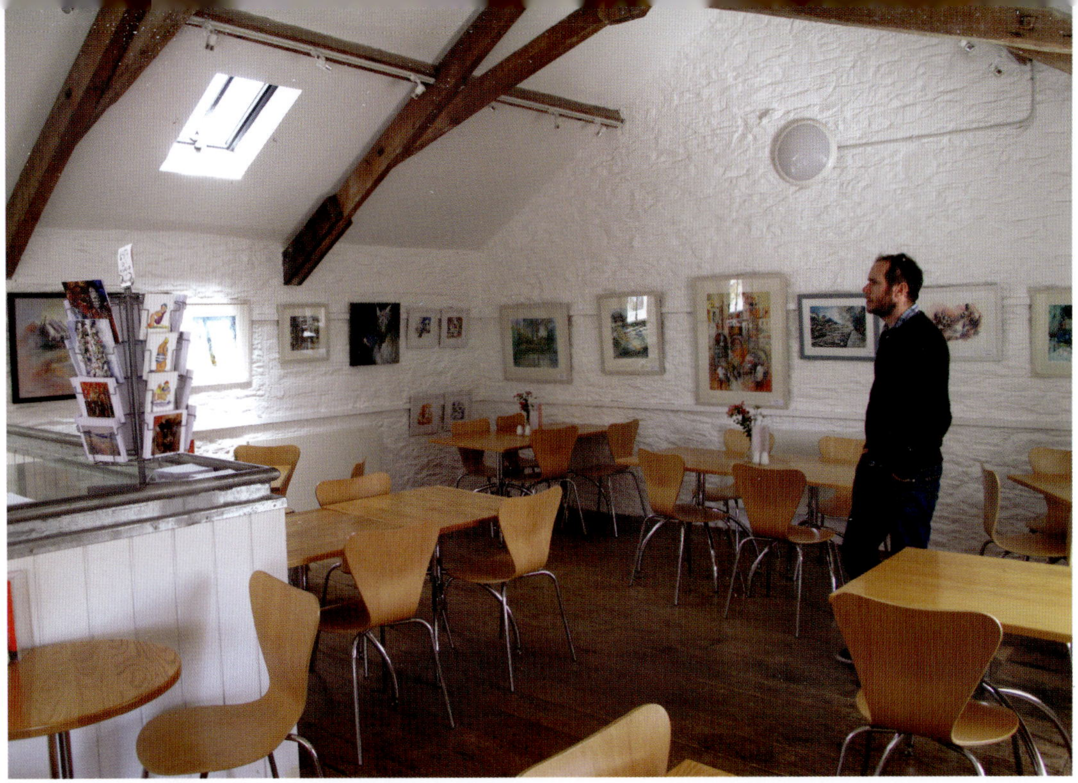

I continue to exhibit with two or three societies and I also run an annual exhibition in my home area where I usually have upwards of twenty pictures on show. I have pictures in galleries all over the South West but prefer to sell by word of mouth.

People visit me at home and riffle through what I have there on the walls or in a browser and often find what they're looking for, which is lovely! I find work difficult to price, however and wish I could just hang something on a wall with a price tag rather than suddenly come up with a price as I usually come up with something ridiculous on the spur of the moment. I have never managed to be businesslike, and if I were ever truly successful the first priority for me would be to employ an agent. That way I wouldn't have to deal with negative comment or rejection.

Talking of negative comment, when my clubs hold their exhibitions members usually have to steward them, so whilst sitting there I often heard some very candid comments from the public who frequently felt free to express their opinions not thinking that they may be overheard, or maybe not caring. A couple of years ago an elderly viewer voiced her feelings rather loudly (presumably her equally elderly companion was hard of hearing) "I don't think something like that should be given exhibition room, I don't even know what it is" I heard her say. Looking up I saw that it was one of MY "loose" pictures she was talking about. Even so, I thought it was pretty obvious that the subject matter was an allotment. There ensued a long, loud and very critical discussion which I had no choice but to eavesdrop on. In retrospect I thought maybe I should have said they ought to think about who may be listening to them, but that would have meant exposing myself as the artist, and I also thought probably one has to take responsibility for one's output if it is hanging in a public exhibition. The memory of it alternately makes me laugh or cringe.

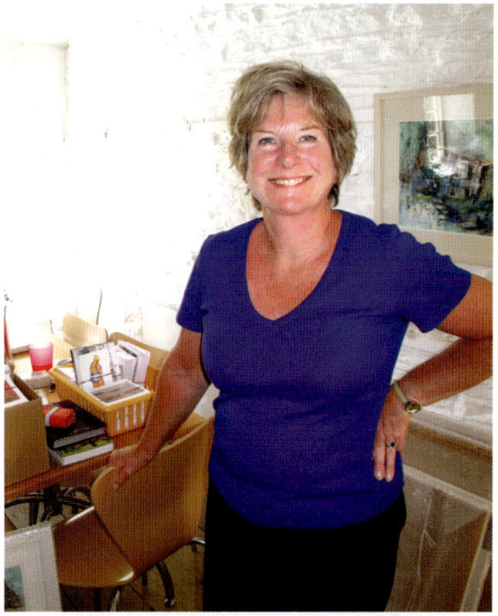

Above: *Happy to be hung – before the exhibition opening.* Left: *A beautifully hung exhibition in a National Trust café and my son-in-law, Joe admiring all our hard work.* Below: *A step forward in being more businesslike.*

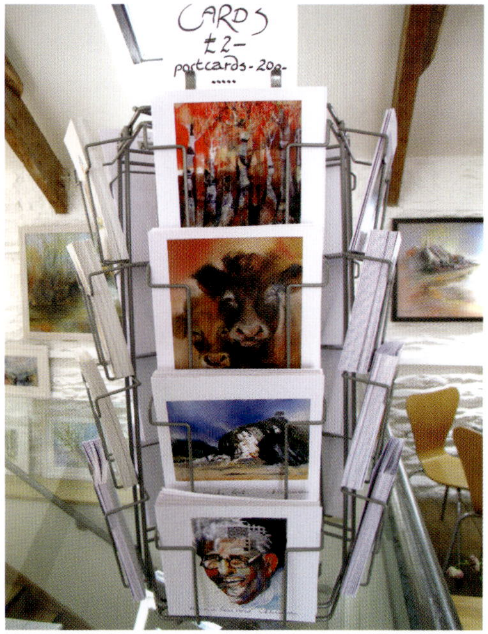

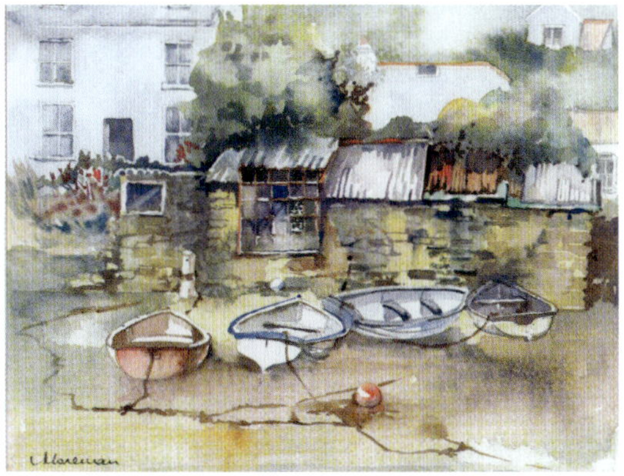

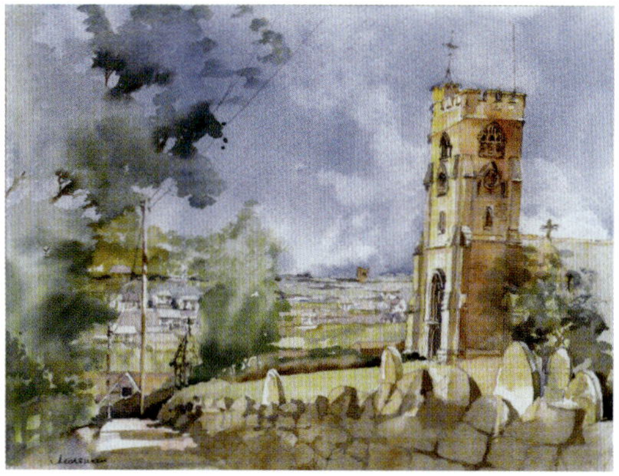

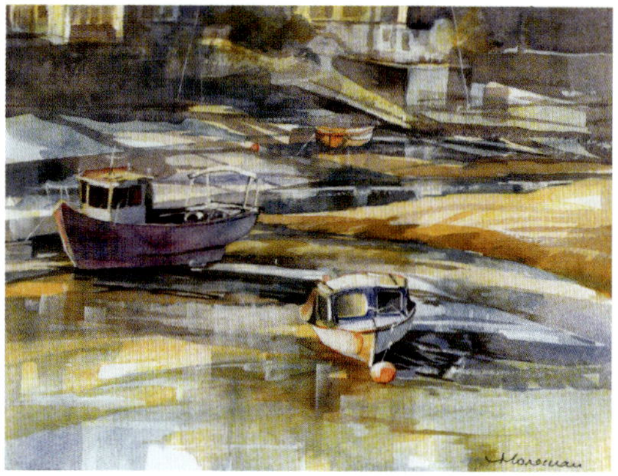

Scenes from a calendar project for Newton Ferrers and Noss Mayo.

I began looking for projects to keep the momentum going and I hit upon the idea of a local calendar for Newton Ferrers and Noss Mayo. I knew nobody would be satisfied with one picture on the front, so I had to produce twelve. I found a local printer and between us we sorted the pictures by month and he printed off 500 copies. I was pretty scared that that was far too many as I was only targeting the two villages depicted, but to print fewer would never work financially. However, they sold like hot cakes and if there was a dip in my local picture sales it was possibly because I know people cut out the calendar pictures and framed them when the year was over!

I produced a second calendar three years later, but found the marketing quite trying and in the end, although it was a successful venture, I hated "selling myself" and decided not to do it a third time.

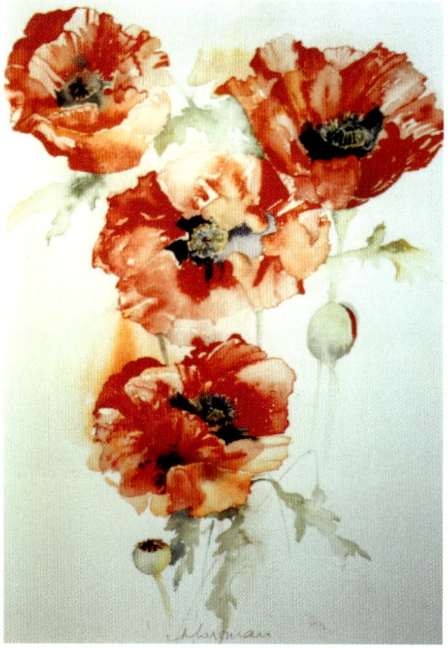

Poppies, watercolour, 16 x 12 in

I was quite proud of this depiction of poppies and still regret it's history. When I started to live on my own after leaving my husband, I moved into an idyllic looking, but very basic, old cottage. I cooked on a camping stove and tried to think of a way to afford to improve matters. A friend recommended a workman who would give me a reasonable work surface and get me started. Noticing that I painted, he asked me if I would paint some poppies for his girlfriend and this was the result. I asked him for £10. He looked very surprised and made a bit of a fuss. He had obviously expected to get a picture for nothing whilst charging me builder's rates for his work. It was an interesting introduction to some people's attitude to 'art' as having little merit or value. It took me several hours, and I thought it was not at all bad. I should have asked for a great deal more, but this was early days in selling pictures for me. All part of the learning process.

From time to time I have a good idea about how to market various images but I always baulk at the effort required to place cards, prints etc. in shops or galleries and absolutely cannot take rejection without assuming that what I am offering is rubbish. I am very happy to hang my picture in exhibitions and take my chances with the buying public, and, indeed, I sell quite a lot of work this way, but I am ridiculously self-effacing in the commercial market place and have to live with my defect in this respect.

Obviously, if I was a younger artist trying to make a living I would pull myself together and have a proper business plan. As it is I can please myself to some degree and hide behind my weakness. Of course, doing it my way I can paint what I fancy and charge what I like and see how it goes. I do enjoy being free of the pressure that goes with keeping up with gallery sales and having to produce only images which sell well. I consider myself fortunate to treat my painting as a paying hobby.

As a painter who sells reasonably well at club shows, I am often asked to demonstrate at workshops and meetings. I managed to say no for a few years hiding behind the excuse that I had no technical answers and am not a natural teacher. Somewhere along the line I weakened and said "yes" and, to date, I have taken many workshops and a good few demonstrations, but I don't relish the experience. I lose sleep, I plan, then lose the plot. I argue with myself about what might/might not work and always decide that everything might not work. I reach a stage where I no longer know what it is I am good at and devise a tutorial that is hopelessly not me. When I finally get to the class I am red in the face, suffering a headache, talk too fast, lose my plan and throw paint carelessly on to paper. What they usually say they want is my "loose" approach and that they certainly get as I lose control completely. I then have to pull something out of the bag and pretend that I know where it is all going. I am always so relieved it's all over that I could cry with relief and swear never to be so silly as to agree to demonstrate again.

Prior to taking a workshop, I usually try to plan my approach and reasoning for working in a certain way. However, I am never sure that any amount of this planning helps on the day. I think I am more of an inspired painter and, in my own time, prefer the gamble of how things might turn out...

It must be obvious by now that I don't deserve to be anything other that what I am – an average painter, well-known within a certain radius of home, sometimes good, sometimes not, unable to be business-like in my dealings with the public or with galleries, but I am after all very happy playing with paint in my small-time bubble.

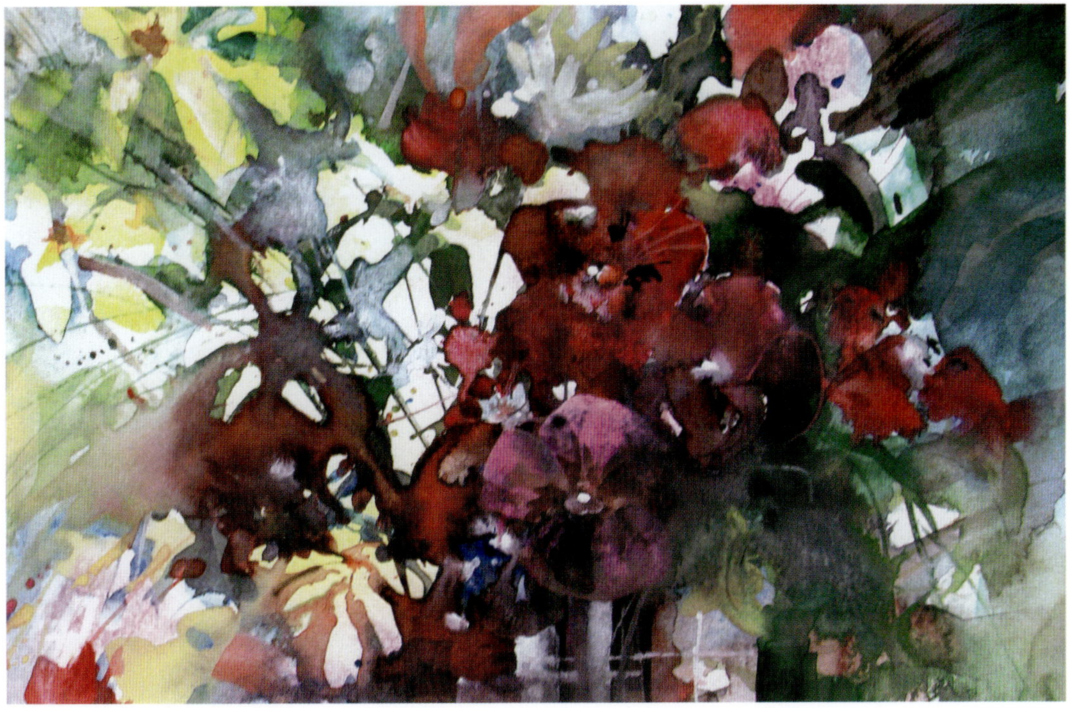

Profusion of Flowers, watercolour, 16 x 12 in

I was asked to take a 'loose' watercolour flower workshop, so had to practise quite a lot, as flowers, so far, hadn't been much of a trait.

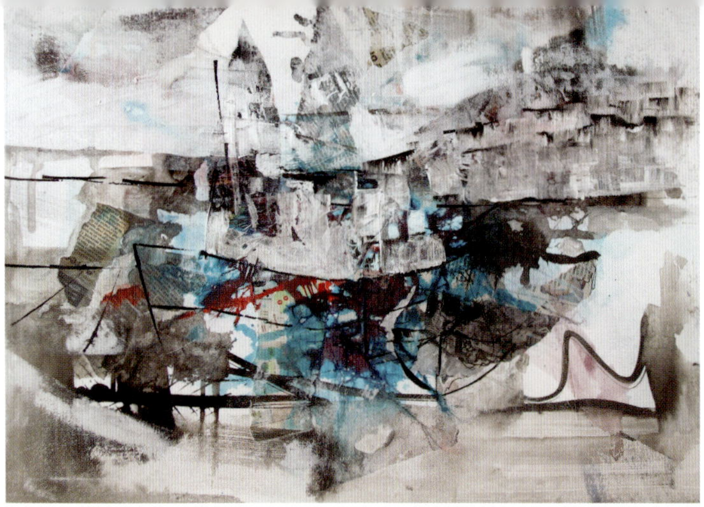

Brixham, collage and acrylic on mountboard, 23 x 18 in.

A progression from rough beginnings to, hopefully, an understandable image – finding inspiration along the way from shapes made by collage and paint.

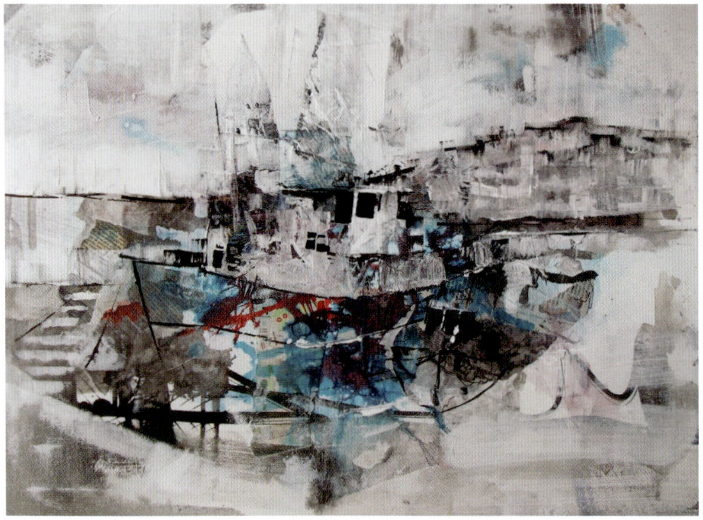

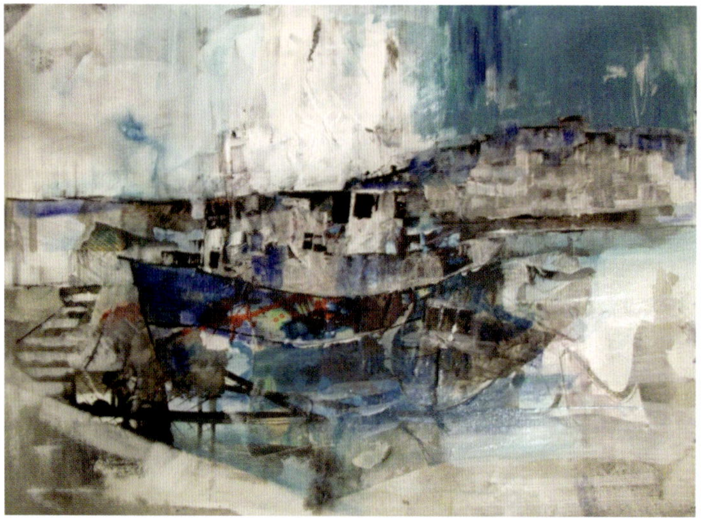

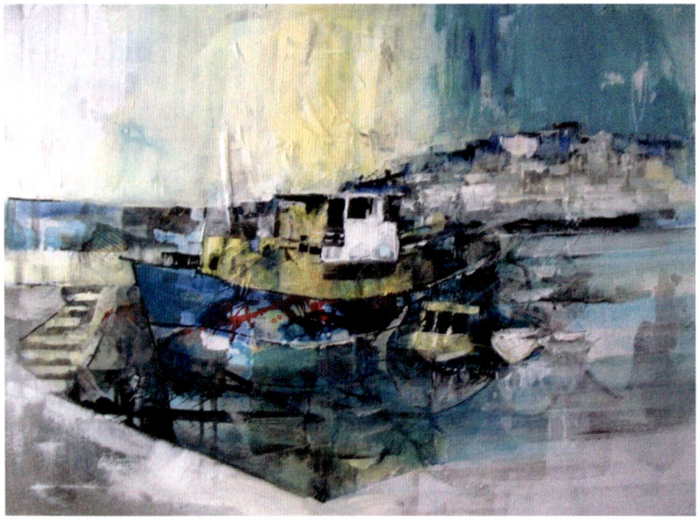

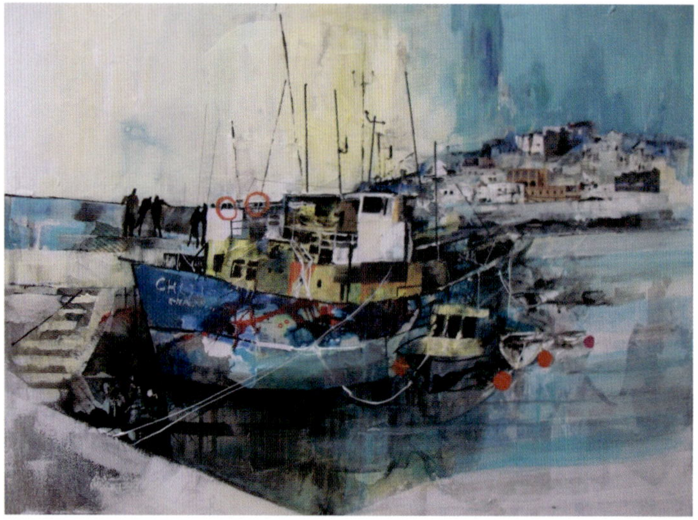

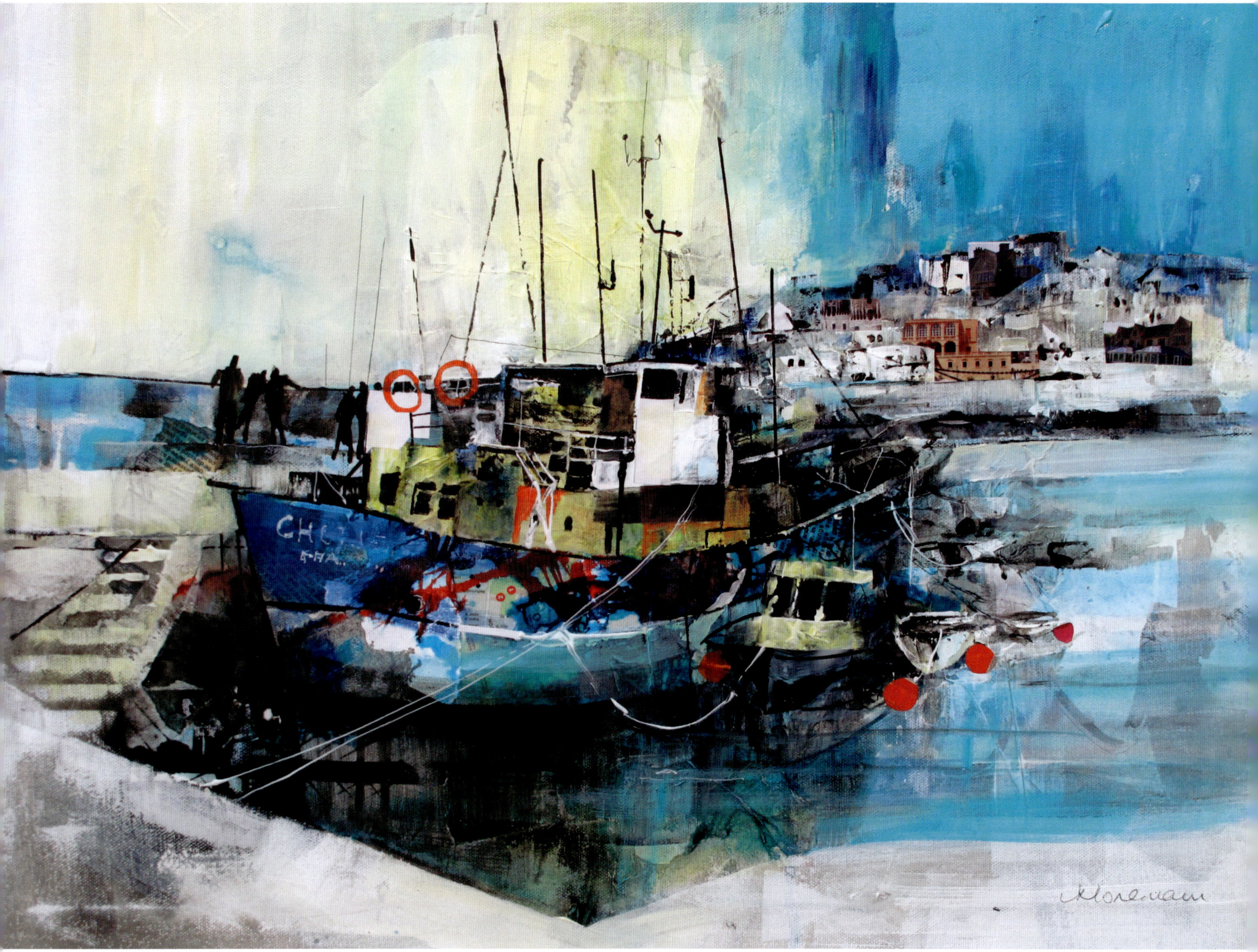

I have painted local theatre scenery several times; big brushes, rollers, emulsion paint and laughter, usually done late at night in a chilly village hall.

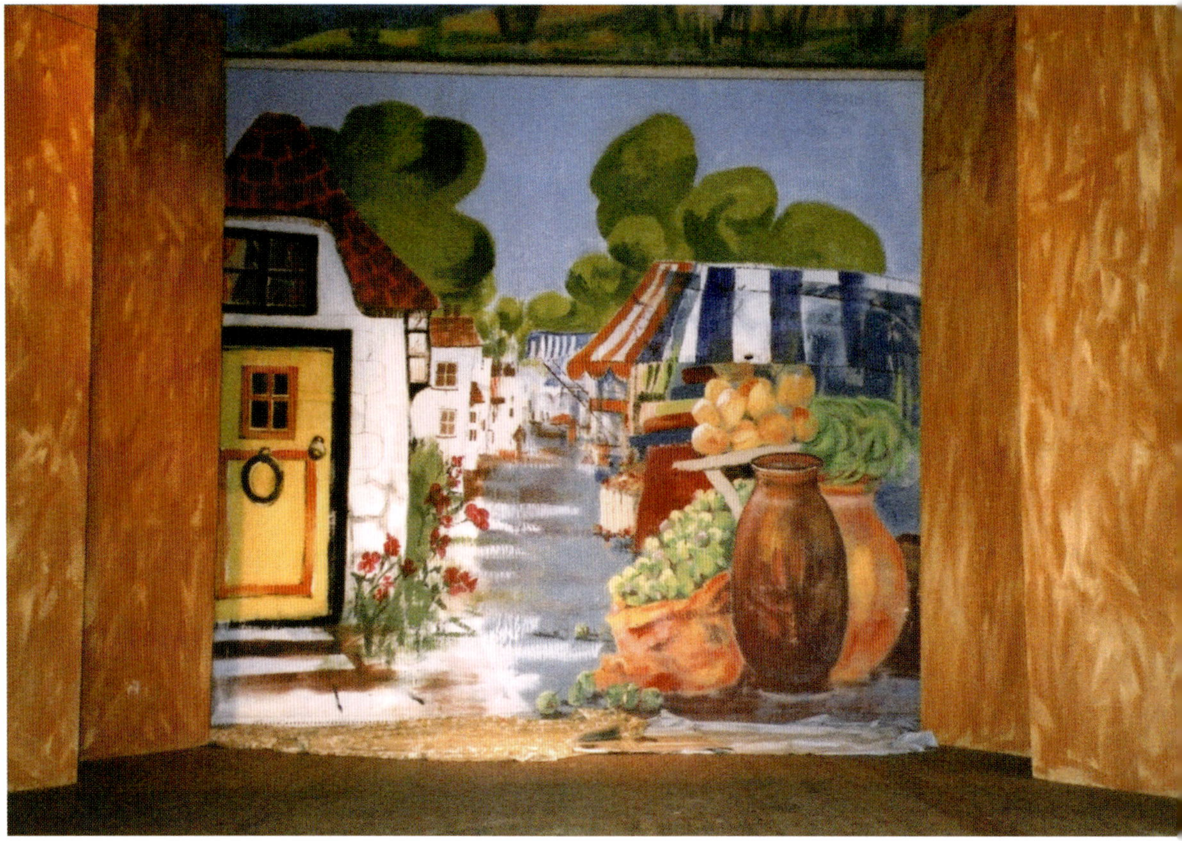

Winston Churchill was for a float in some local event – I forget what. I had to paint him both sides of the board. 6 x 4 ft

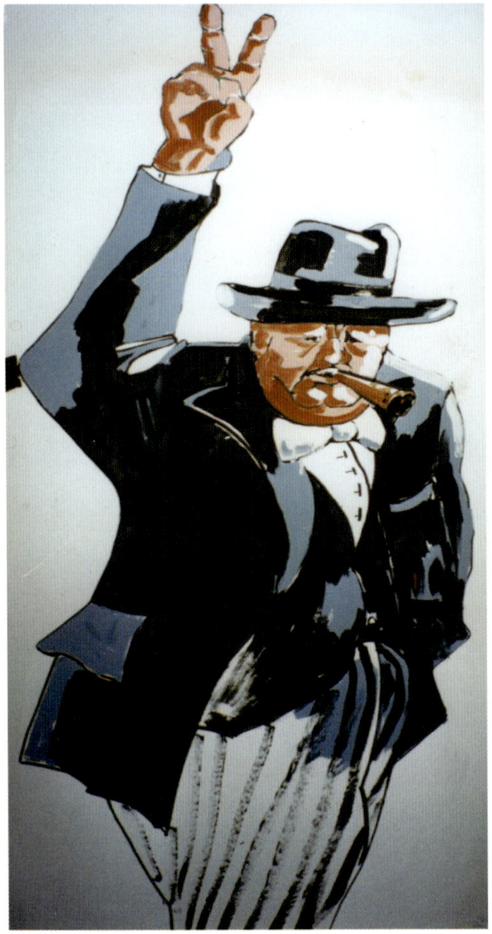

Much of my drawing of people tends towards caricature if I don't keep myself in check, and I was once asked by a local acquaintance for a series of "characters" to decorate some merchandise of his. I sat down and happily produced seaside-type people for him. Unfortunately, it seemed he wanted something a little more risqué than I had imagined, and he rejected them, thank goodness. I am not even sure what his merchandise was – maybe I only just kept my reputation! However, I was the owner of a considerable number of images and wondered if they would make good postcards. I had three of them reproduced and these form part of my ongoing selling strategy, such as it is.

Another year I hit upon an idea which would let me paint outdoors and walk Josie the dog at the same time as enjoying a leisurely commune with nature, especially by choosing good weather. I live close to a beautiful coast path and, coincidentally, it seemed to be The Year of the Coast Path.

So, at regular intervals, I walked my local stretch of path, with Josie (who actually didn't think much of the whole thing as there was no stick-throwing involved), with my camera and paints recording the view every hundred yards or so, making quite a small letter-box shaped watercolour. I had these made up into a small booklet.

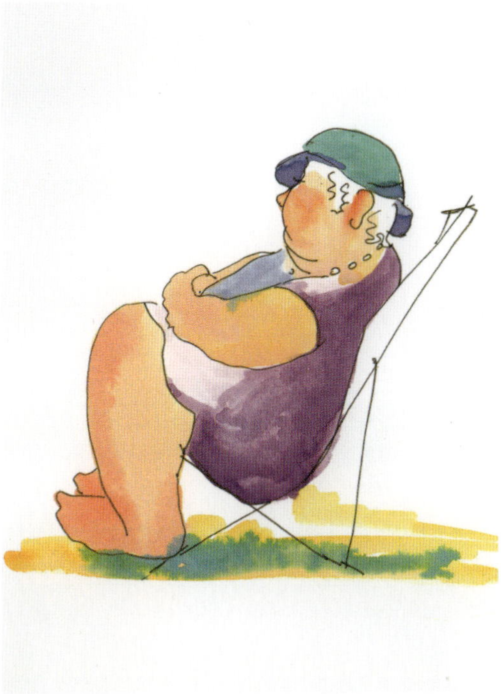

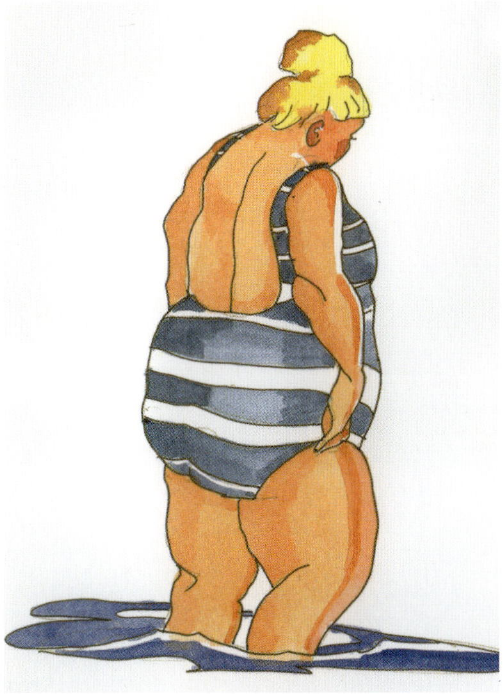

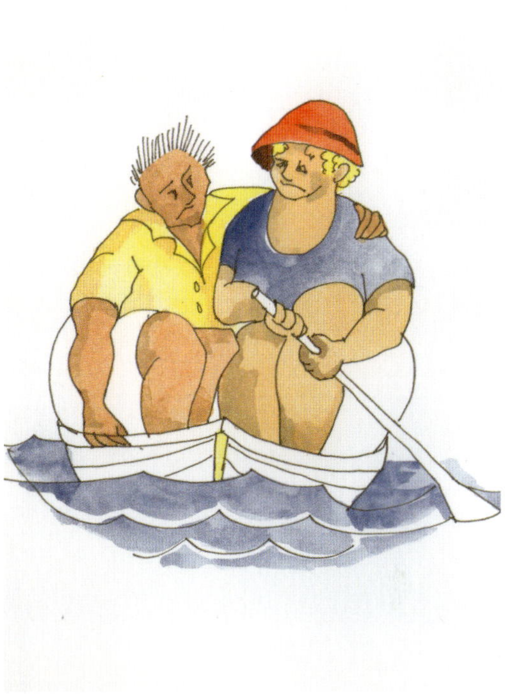

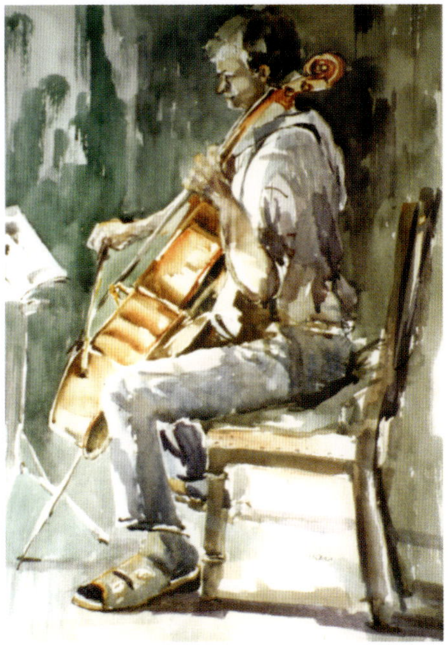

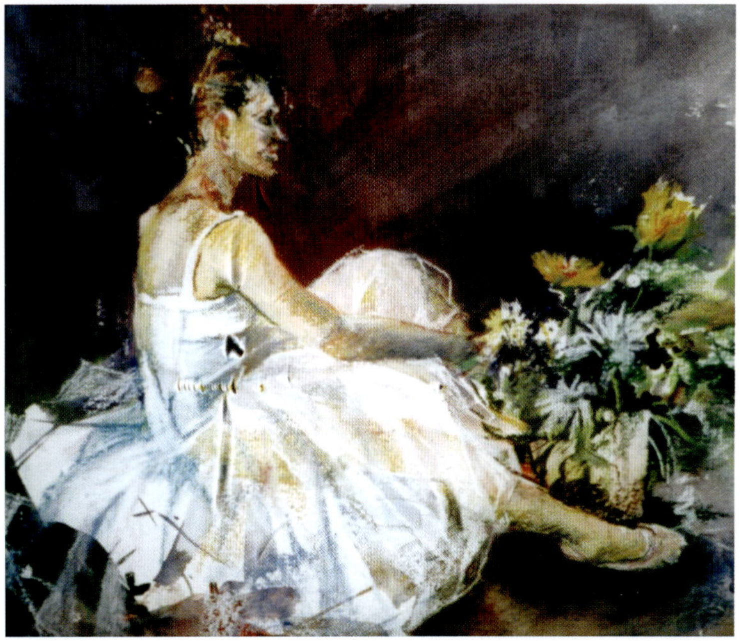

Above: *These are a few images that I chose to make into postcards.*

Far left: *Practise*, watercolour, 14 x 20 in.

Left: *Ballerina,* An early watercolour and pastel, 12 x 14 in.

I like to paint people and these two were painted at workshops locally.

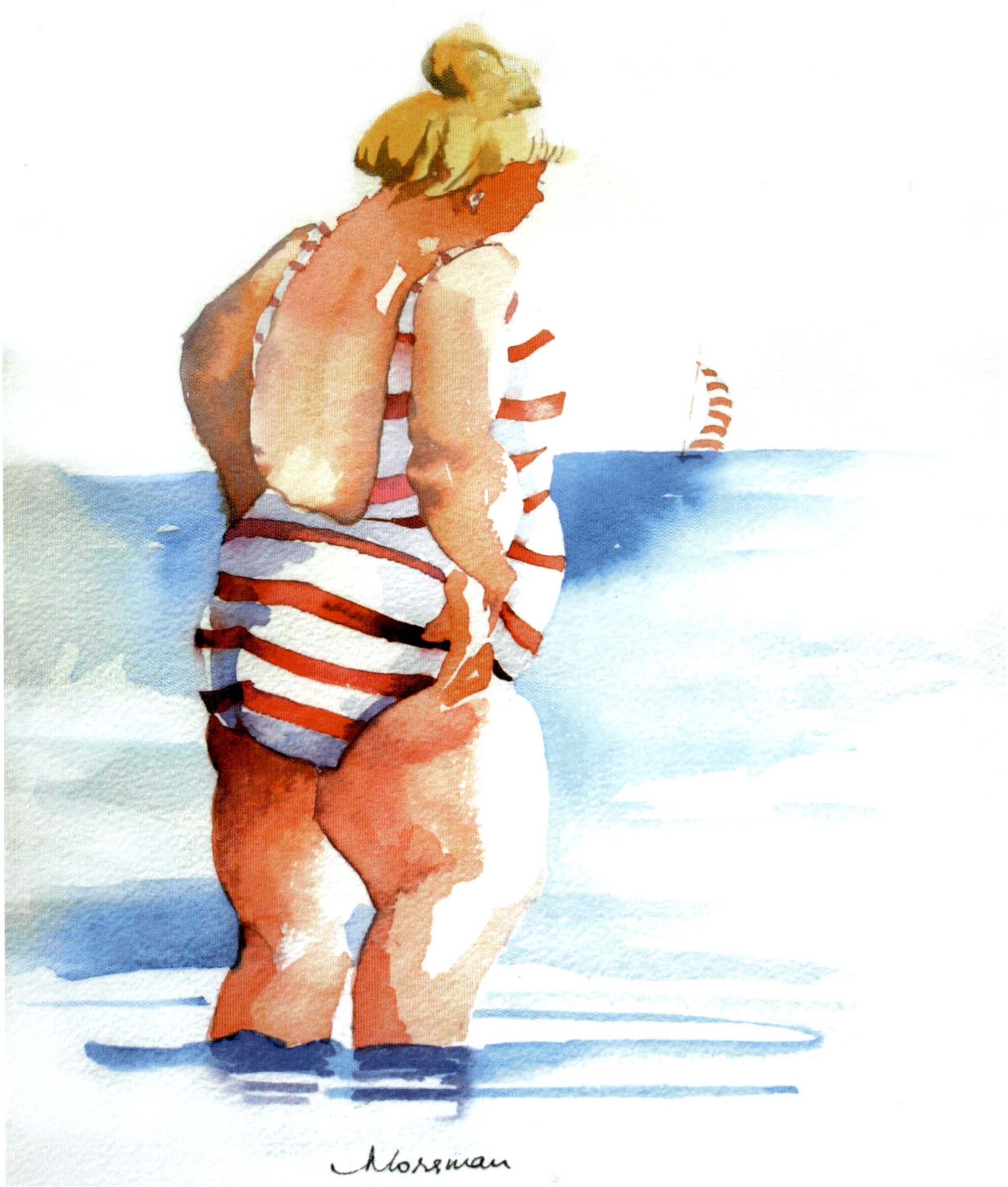

Paddling,
watercolour, 10 x 8 in.

I couldn't believe my eyes when I saw the symmetry of red striped spinnaker and bather.

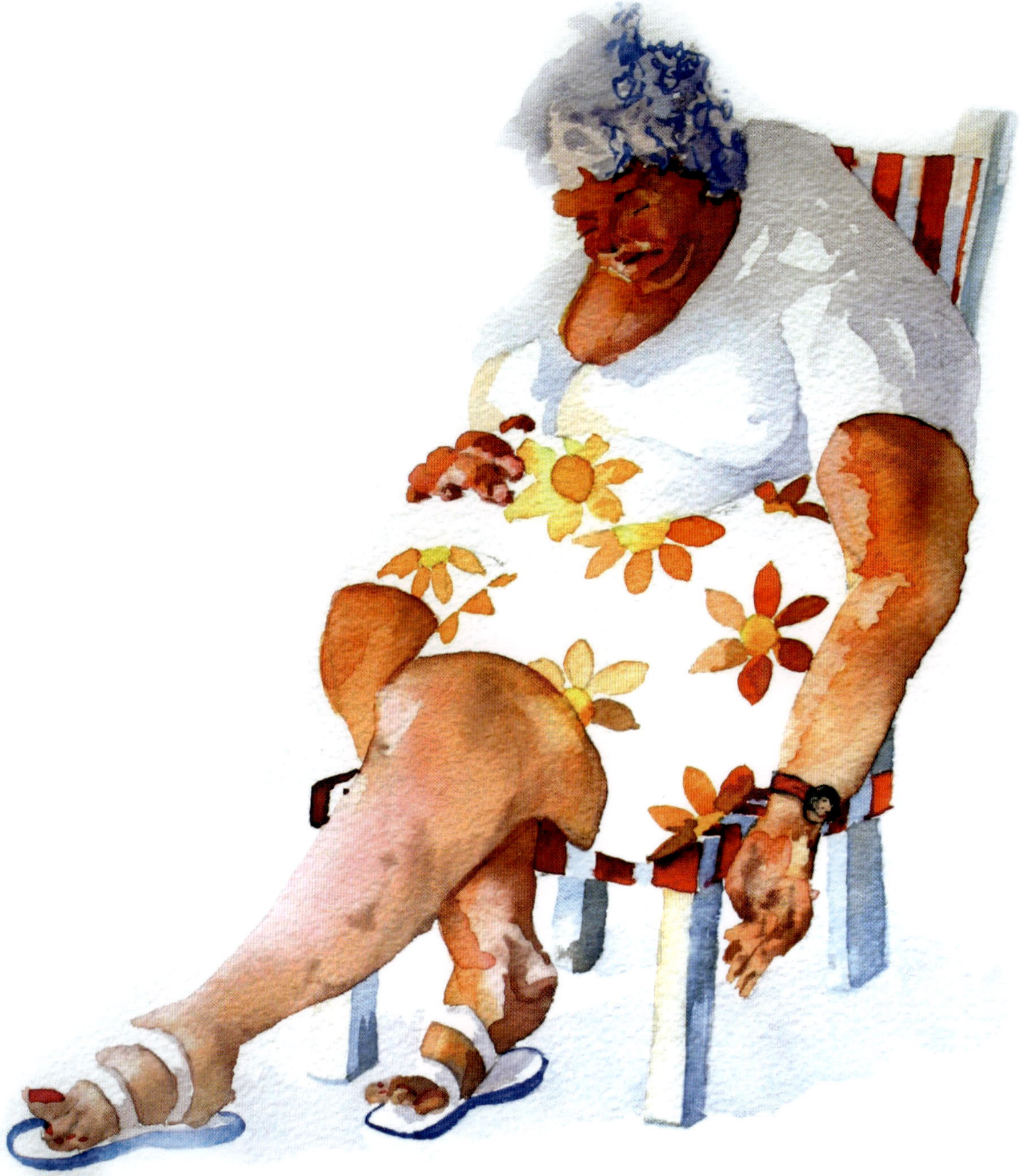

Dozing,
watercolour, 10 x 8 in

I have a tendency to caricaturise and over-exaggerate.

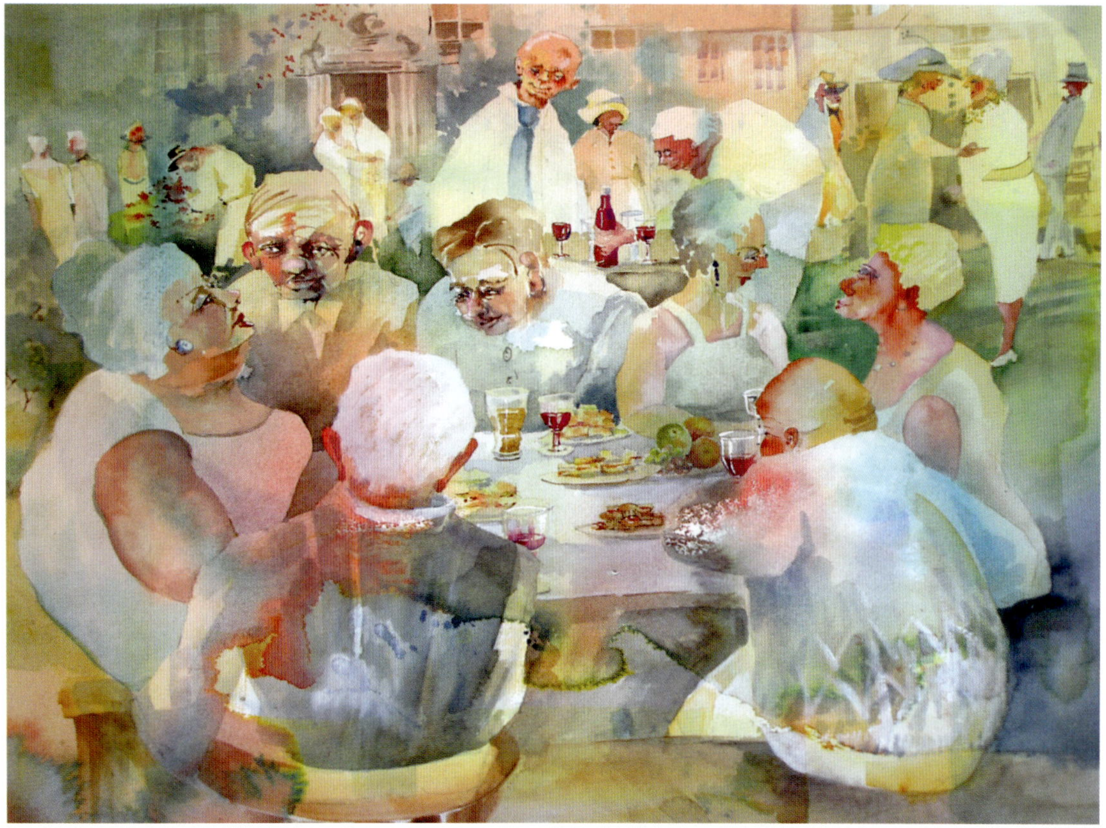

A Garden Party, watercolour, 27 x 20 in.

This picture began by splashing paint all over the paper and gradually 'finding' the people.

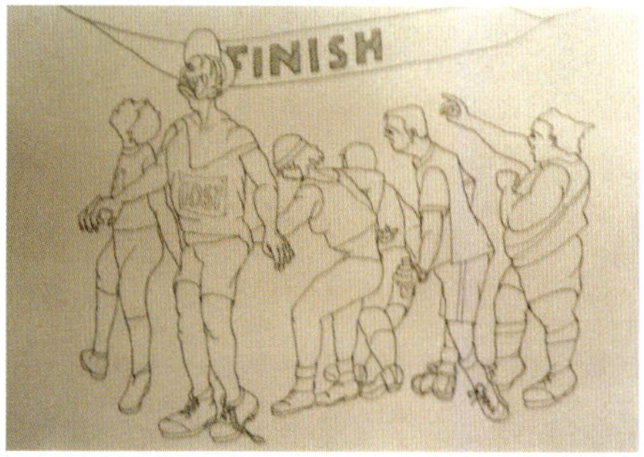

A few characters (after watching a marathon).

Right: *A Blustery Day*, watercolour, 12 x 15 in

More people, created from an initial yellow wash, some other colours dropped in, and the shapes appearing in the wash suggesting these two girls.

Far right: *The Goosebery*, watercolour, 9 x 6 in.

More unfortunately-built people – who I absolutely love to observe and depict!

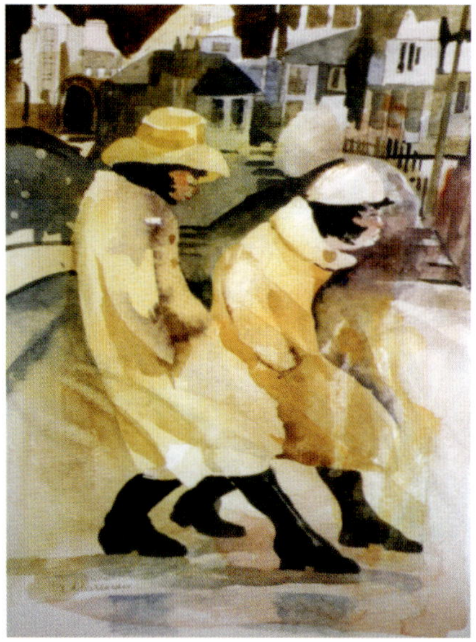

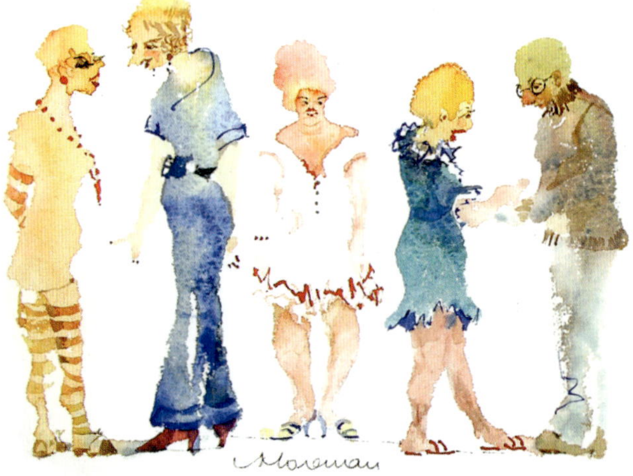

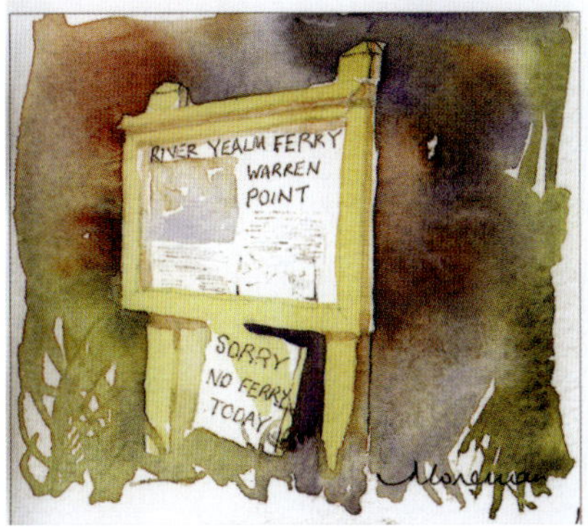

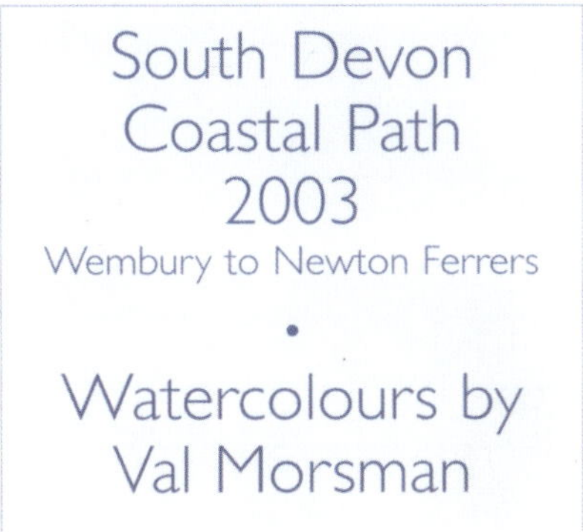
South Devon
Coastal Path
2003
Wembury to Newton Ferrers
•
Watercolours by
Val Morsman

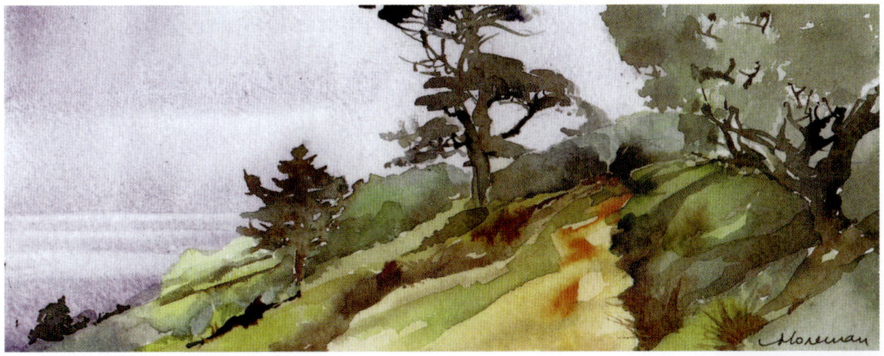

The mistake I made was to print the year prominently on the front cover so, of course, it's life was limited. I could have gone on selling the booklet had I not set it's date in stone; I did, in fact, manage to keep it going for four or five years, but, inevitably it began to look like an old project. I will do a similar thing one day as it was a most enjoyable artistic amble.

Latterly I had prints made of local scenes, mostly the beautiful Yealm river and estuary, always a popular subject, which I am often asked to paint. These were not art prints, but very good ink-jet reproductions on watercolour paper and one would be hard-pressed to tell the print from the original. These were a great success and I should repeat the exercise but I have painted these scenes so often I really have to be in the right mood to do them well. This, obviously, marks me down as a rank amateur, but actually I like it that way and I will get on with it when I am ready!

I have become quite well known locally and I do get asked to paint special commissions. I am, of course, flattered to be asked and nearly always accept them, but I am thrown into a spin at the constraints of a commission and the expectations of the client. I usually end up producing three examples to choose from and I always ask for as much time

A sociable enterprise – many walkers stopped to watch me paint – and to comment!

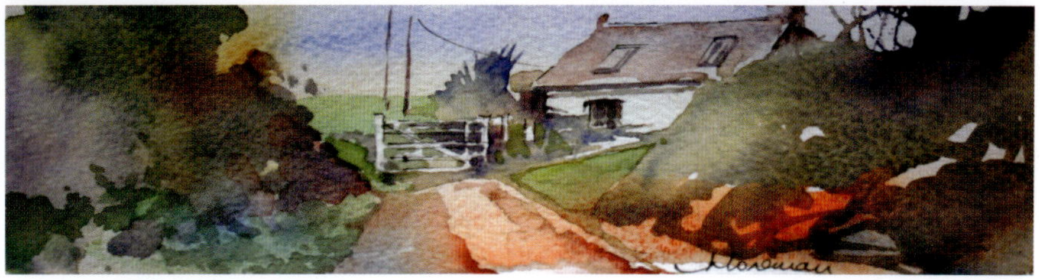

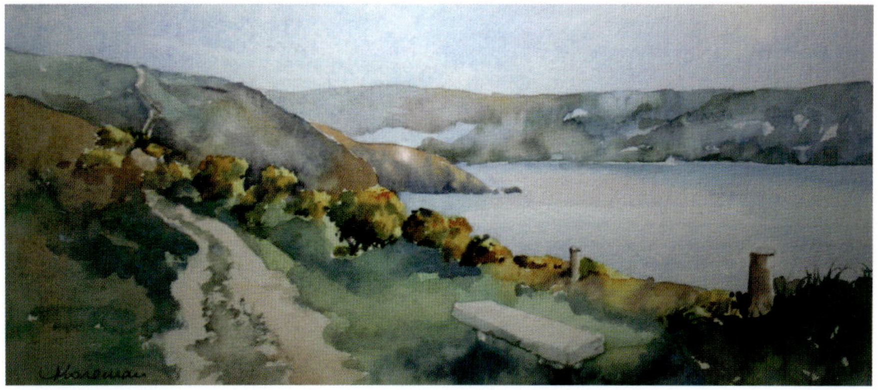

as possible – even months – so that I don't have to panic. Is it worth it? It usually works and people usually express pleasure at the end result. Only one lady was reduced to tears! She was someone I knew well and she had many grandchildren who persistently reached the age of 21. At each important birthday she asked me to paint the view from her house of the river which they had all swum in and sailed on as they were growing up. For several years I painted the same view, varying the colour, season, state of the tide as much as she would allow. One year, I don't know what got into me and I really should have known better, I decided to paint a slightly different view from her window. This was what reduced her to tears and I had to take it away and paint what the customer really wanted.

Another commission was for two girls who were starting up a picnic-hamper business and needed a postcard for distribution showing the contents of their hampers. I really enjoyed this one as it was a different challenge.

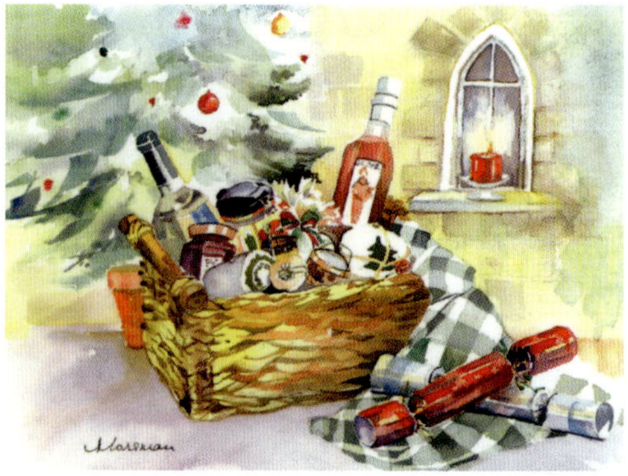

A card for advertising a local hamper company.

A very good friend recently celebrated her 60th birthday and asked me if I would paint her rather lovely cottage and garden as her birthday present from me. She provided me with photos and left me to it. I felt some pressure over this picture, as her house and plants were all important to her, but I have to say that the end result was quite good and, as it hangs in a prominent place in their cottage, even I get pleasure from it when I am there. On that subject, I often see my pictures hanging in local houses and rarely enjoy the experience, feel slightly embarrassed actually, and don't like to confront them full on.

Below left: *I was asked to paint a white horse, but never managed to get it right for the customer.*

Below right: *Richmond Quay, Plymouth,* watercolour, 12 x 14 in.

An evening out with the watercolour society.

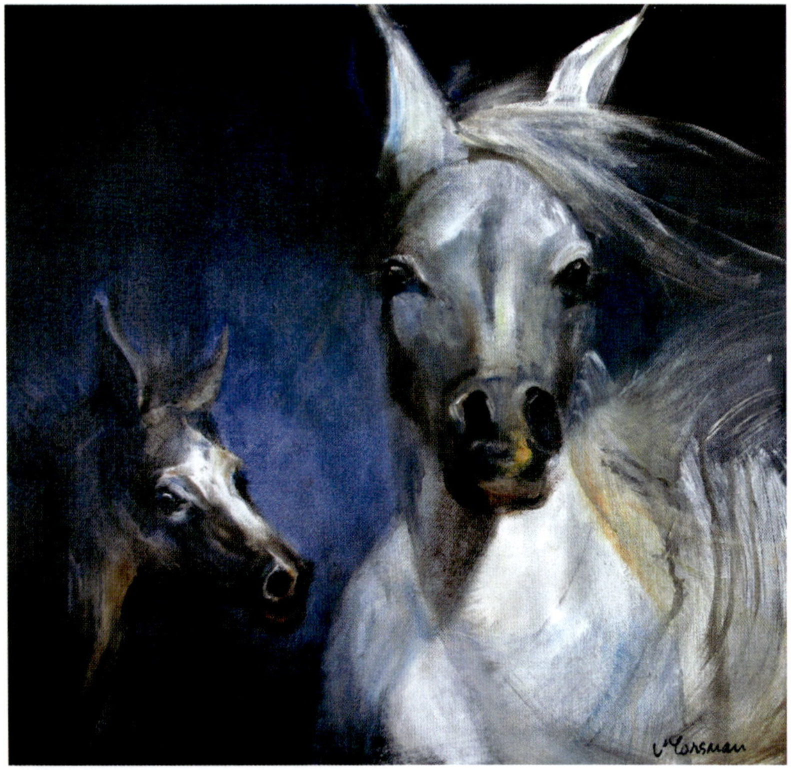

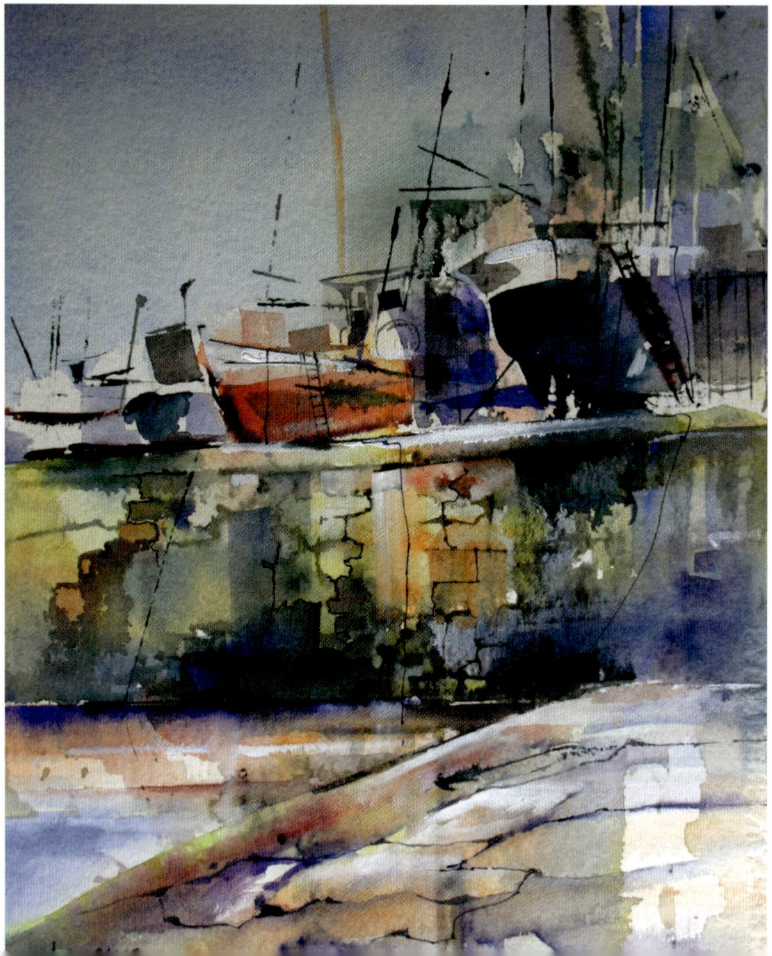

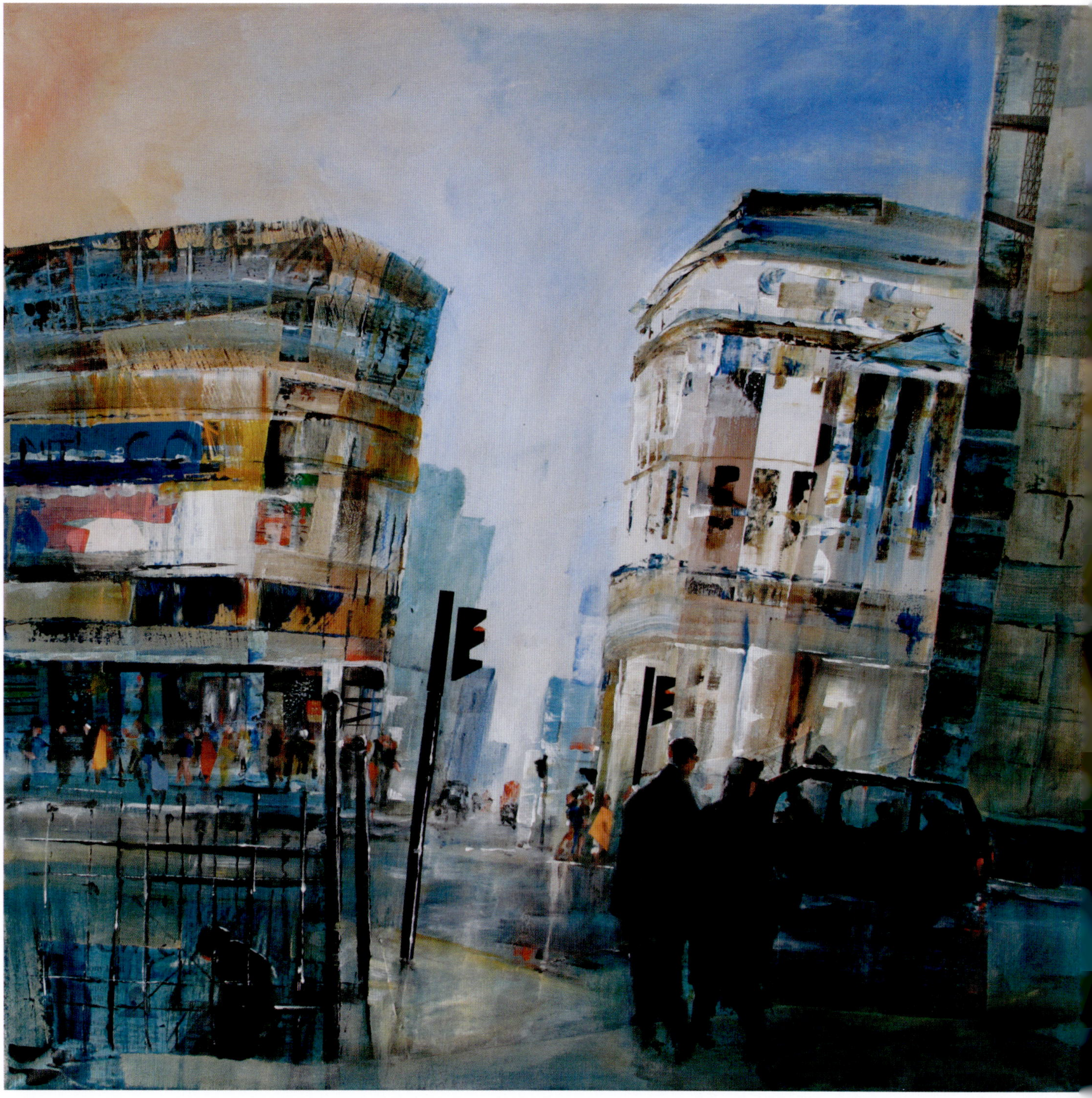

London Street,
mixed media, 22 x 19 in

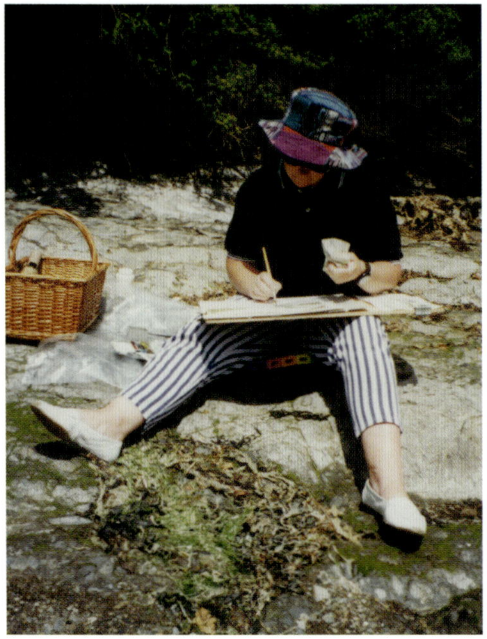

Me working on the river bank.

Opposite: *I'm not a precision sketcher – just a few lines will usually do to remind me of a scene. Sometimes my sketches are more about doodling and making abstract marks. These are sketches spanning a number of books and years.*

I have already mentioned that I started with old and minimal equipment and only slowly introduced variety into my collection. It helped that there is a paucity of local art shops in my locality to tempt and I hadn't found art catalogues early on. Watercolour paper was an early education and, because I use a lot of water, I had to have thicker paper which wouldn't cockle, or use paper blocks glued down on all sides. I also found painting large made me more comfortable, and when I discovered art catalogues I began to order paper to be delivered, and the big brown cardboard package arriving still thrills me. I now mainly use 200 or 300lb not, Bockingford, Arches or Royal Watercolour Society paper, but occasionally try something else which catches my eye. I prefer really white paper which allows watercolour to sing. Apart from framing, the cost of the paper is the largest expense in my work; I find paints and brushes last me a long time and I only rarely buy any other aid to watercolour painting. The same goes for collage and mixed media – acrylic paints and ink last a good while and I usually paint on good quality watercolour paper or on mountboard. Oil painting, which is relatively new to me, seems to be going the same way, although one canvas costs a great deal more than one sheet of paper. I have a fairly standard collection of oil paints and I use ready-made canvases at present, being still a beginner. Watching the pennies, I often use a deep, box canvas so that I do not feel the need to frame it.

As mentioned, I have quite a crowded area in terms of brushes, bottles, tubes, etc., but actually use a very limited amount of equipment, a good deal of which has been acquired, not bought, and you never know when it might come in useful. I might suddenly adopt a whole new approach to painting and want to throw everything at it. Recently, an old painter friend died and his widow gave me all his brushes, pens, pencils and many tubes of watercolour. How could I not incorporate these into my own work?

I have many sketchbooks; different qualities, different sizes, some bought because the cover was alluring, some given to me as presents, some big, some small. In hindsight, I wish I had used all the same size books and labelled them chronologically for ease of reference and storage. Some have been with me on painting holidays and show a record of a great week in Bruges or France or Lyme Regis, for example.

I don't do beautiful sketches. They are mostly quick line drawings in ink, occasionally quick paintings and I love to sketch people walking by, particularly in a busy concourse as at an airport or a bus station or just by the riverside. At one time I asked my local theatre if I could sit in the stalls to sketch as a ballet company performed their warm up class on stage. I loved this! The dancers wear layers of clothing interesting to the eye and, of course, perform feats of movement not seen elsewhere. I had a lovely time just watching them and had to remember to put something down in my sketchbook as well.

My local painting group used to paint outside once a week, sometimes by the sea or the river or Dartmoor and sometimes at a venue such as a farm with chickens and horses

I also use my sketchbooks as a diary from time to time. Certainly there are lots of notes and reminders scattered around, such as weather, noises, people's names and colours and ideas that come to me for a possible picture, not necessarily associated with the sketches I've been drawing. I frequently use a small scale square to plan an approach to a subject, often getting more pleasure from these miniscule pictures than the finished article.

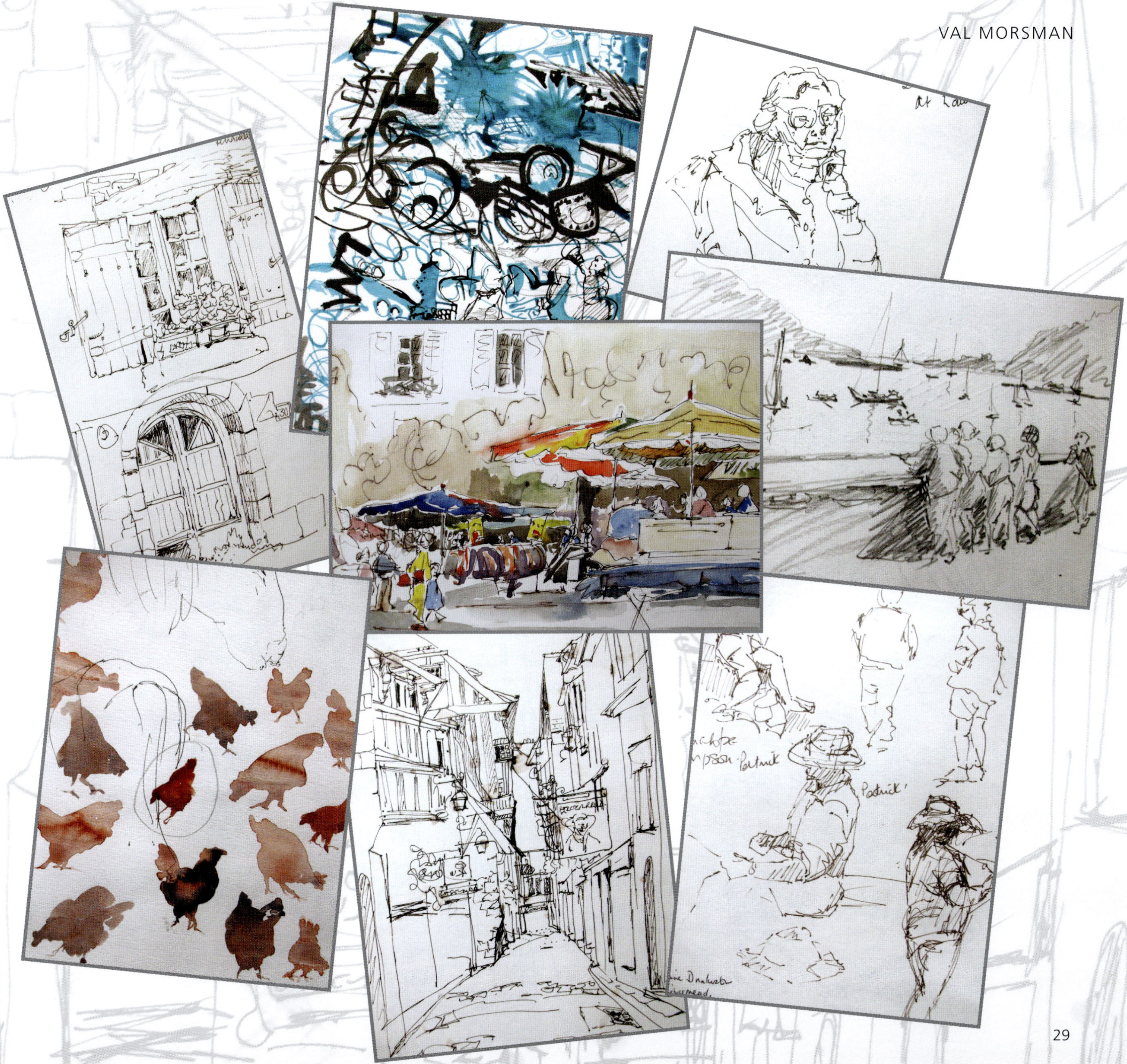

The other use of a sketchbook for me is pure and simple 'playing'. Playing with colour, shapes, pens and paint. Just getting to know how some things work (or not) without the pressure of a finished product. I love to play with watercolour, watching unexpected mixing on the paper, adding drops of this and that to see the effect.

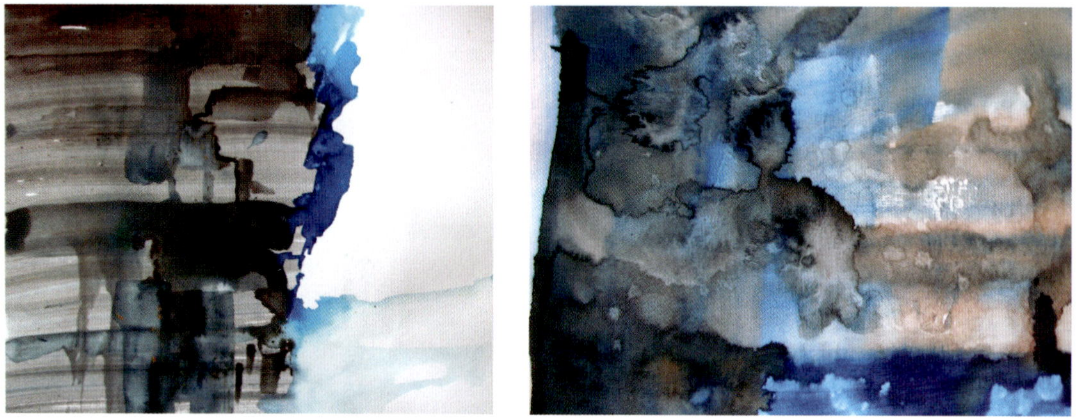

Right: *Playing with watercolour.*

Below: *I often use a small square format in my sketchbooks to judge the composition of an idea.*

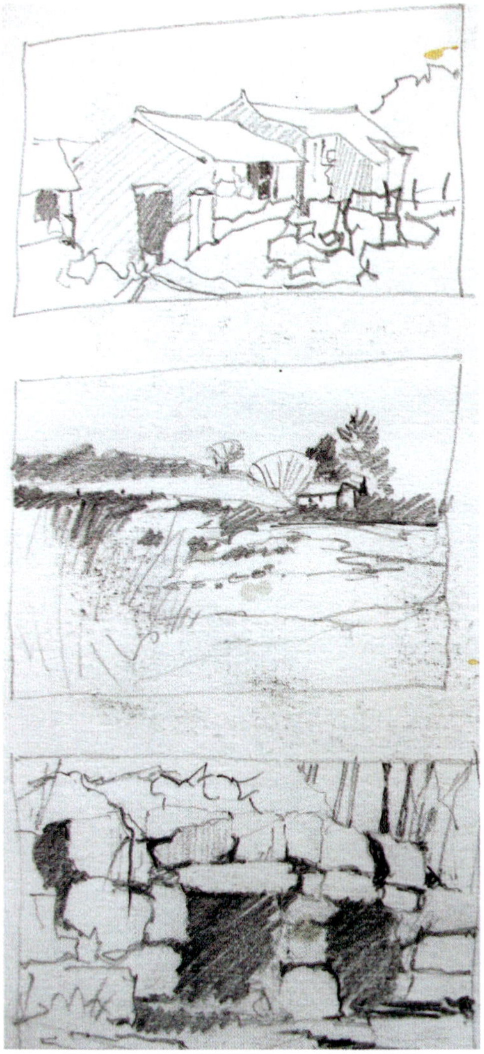

I have two easels; one collapsible, tubular steel, useful for outdoor work, with slightly bent legs from being squeezed into the car too fast, and one huge, wooden easel I made many years ago predating the need for large canvases but now really coming into its own. This one makes me feel like a real artist even to the point of encouraging the typical oil painter's stance, back on one foot and well away from the work. I remember making this easel in the garage and being flummoxed by the need to make some holes to take the dowelling rods needed to vary the height of the canvas. I was working with just a saw and a screwdriver. As I stood in the garage contemplating a way round the dilemma, the fish man in his van drew up and, having purchased some fish cakes and haddock, it turned out he actually had the necessary tools on his van and within fifteen minutes he had drilled the requisite number of holes and went on his fishy way.

I constantly change the way I work, sometimes sitting, often standing to ease my back. Presently I have cleared everything to the edges of my studio and really like the sense of space in the middle, where stands my easel, and about three-quarters of my work can happen in the upright. The dining room table is where wet watercolour happens on the flat, and detail is easier in that position too. I feel nervous about spreading myself too far on this table, big as it is as I sometimes feel there will be a point of no return. My table is actually a bit like the Mad Hatter's Tea Party where I just keep moving round to the next activity; there is the sewing machine corner, the computer corner, the correspondence corner and even an eating corner which is, in truth, in a lot of danger of disappearing. I do also have friends who come to stay, and then there is a great clear out. I think I know where everything has gone (sometimes only under the table) but inevitably getting back to "normal" is tricky. I do dream of having a purpose built studio with lots of room to splash about and have several things on the go at the same time, but it will have to remain a dream for now, and I expect that however big a studio is it will never be big enough, so I will just get on with what I have got and be grateful!

A few years back I did my own framing and mounting and this, of course, required its own equipment. I went to a framing class and then had to purchase corner clamps, saws, wood, mountboard, tape, mount cutters, backing board and staple gun. I had the glazing done elsewhere, and there were often comments about my angles! Eventually I realised I was spending too much time sawing and swearing in my shed, and, after all, I was selling enough pictures to justify paying a framer. Fortunately I had a friend who set up a framing business in his garage so it was much easier to get him to do it and the end result was so much more appealing. Better still, I could get rid of a great deal of gear and concentrate on painting. I still mainly use the same framer business which is slightly more affordable than a gallery. Nevertheless, framing is a considerable expense especially if one paints large as I often do, and in the current economic climate I am having to think about this quite a lot. There is nothing worse than skimped framing and I am trying not to go down that route. If only I painted miniatures!

I have almost everything framed in the same way – a neutral gallery type framing, lime-washed tulip wood and off-white mountboard. It makes for a cohesive display in an exhibition and reduces the cost of materials. I am still having to think about how to frame oil paintings as that is newer to me, and I am still experimenting with that.

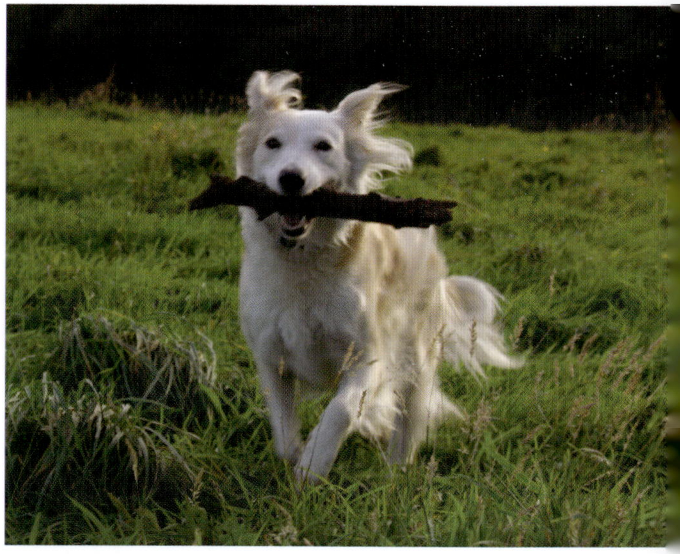

This is Josie who never wanted me to stay still to paint! She never quite grasped the artistic concept of patience…

I do use photos for reference and for ideas, and I have a vast number roughly filed under subject matter. At any one time there will also be small piles of photos around the house and in the studio, perhaps ready for the next picture, perhaps abandoned for the moment. I more often paint from my imagination, usually inspired by colour first, and random applications of paint or collage until something emerges.

I would like to paint outside a great deal more and always thought my dog and I would roam the countryside and moors, and choose a lovely spot to work and sit.

Unfortunately she is no art lover, has no sensitivity to the elements and I have sketch books full of unfinished drawings trailing off the page in a linear scrawl where she has dragged me off the scene having been there and done that in less than ten minutes. She is incapable of staying still for long, and I am reluctant to go out on my own painting for long periods without her, so, for now, I find compromises. She is an elderly lady as I write and I am sure some time I will get out there with my easel, but it will be lonelier.

I try to work at something every day, whether it is only thinking or sketching an idea, but more often it is actually painting. I stick my paper to a board and will then work one of three ways - a rough drawing, adventitious collage, or random splashes of paint. Any of these three approaches can be used in any order and it depends entirely how I feel as to how I start a picture. I love the freedom of throwing paint at paper and manipulating it hoping an idea comes from it. I may work on several pictures at the same time, sometimes waiting for inspiration, but more often just having to wait for paint to dry before I can move on.

My area of Devon had ten days of organised Open Studio events in which I became involved for the first time in 2013. I opened up my cottage and studio/shed to display pictures, cards, sketch-books and prints to visitors. People came from quite a distance to view and most were drawn to

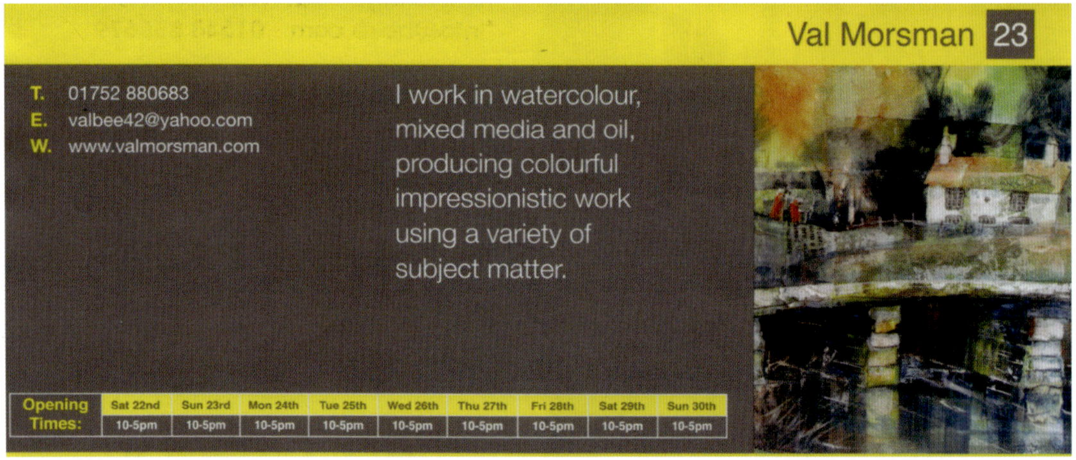

Open Studio brochure for the South Hams 2013.

particular venues which caught their attention in the well produced colour brochure. There were people I knew and also complete strangers, but the general feeling was one of positivity and of sharing an artistic experience.

Ever on the lookout for new inspiration I have tried to see if my painting is affected by my choice of music. It seems that whether I listen to classical, jazz, musicals or pop, there is no appreciable difference in colour or subject in the end result – actually my concentration on a painting is so absolute that the music has often stopped unnoticed!

Over the course of the last year or two I have entered a few competitions mostly as a fillip to the imagination and as a discipline regarding the timeline involved. The most recent was a portrait that had to be of someone familiar to me. Portraiture has never been my forte but it certainly made me think in a different way and I was quite pleased with the overall concept of my picture even if the likeness itself was less than perfect. Ultimately, the picture wasn't displayed but I felt a certain achievement in even submitting it, so I will do more of this in future.

Recently, as a present, my daughter gave me a week's oil painting course with a well-known London artist called James Hart Dyke. At first I was horrified as I had no oil painting experience or skill. Then resignation and a certain amount of optimism crept in as I thought I could only improve my ability under his guidance. Up to this point I had enjoyed watercolour and collage so much that I hadn't found room for much else. I had tried once or twice with oils, but didn't really appreciate the chemistry of the various oils, spirits, varnishes involved. There was a list of specific equipment to take which I dutifully bought and packed. This included ten small canvas boards which I thought sounded reasonable for a beginner; painting in a small format would allow for lots of experiment. Nobody else on this course took any notice of the list. Some had huge canvases, some had every known colour of paint – none except me had ten small canvas boards and I felt as if I had been a bit unimaginative. In the end, of course, none of that mattered and I learned so much in the course of the week about oil paint and its application that I now paint as much in oils as in any other medium.

Mothecombe Rock, oil 10 x 8 in.

This was my first oil painting after a week's introductory course.

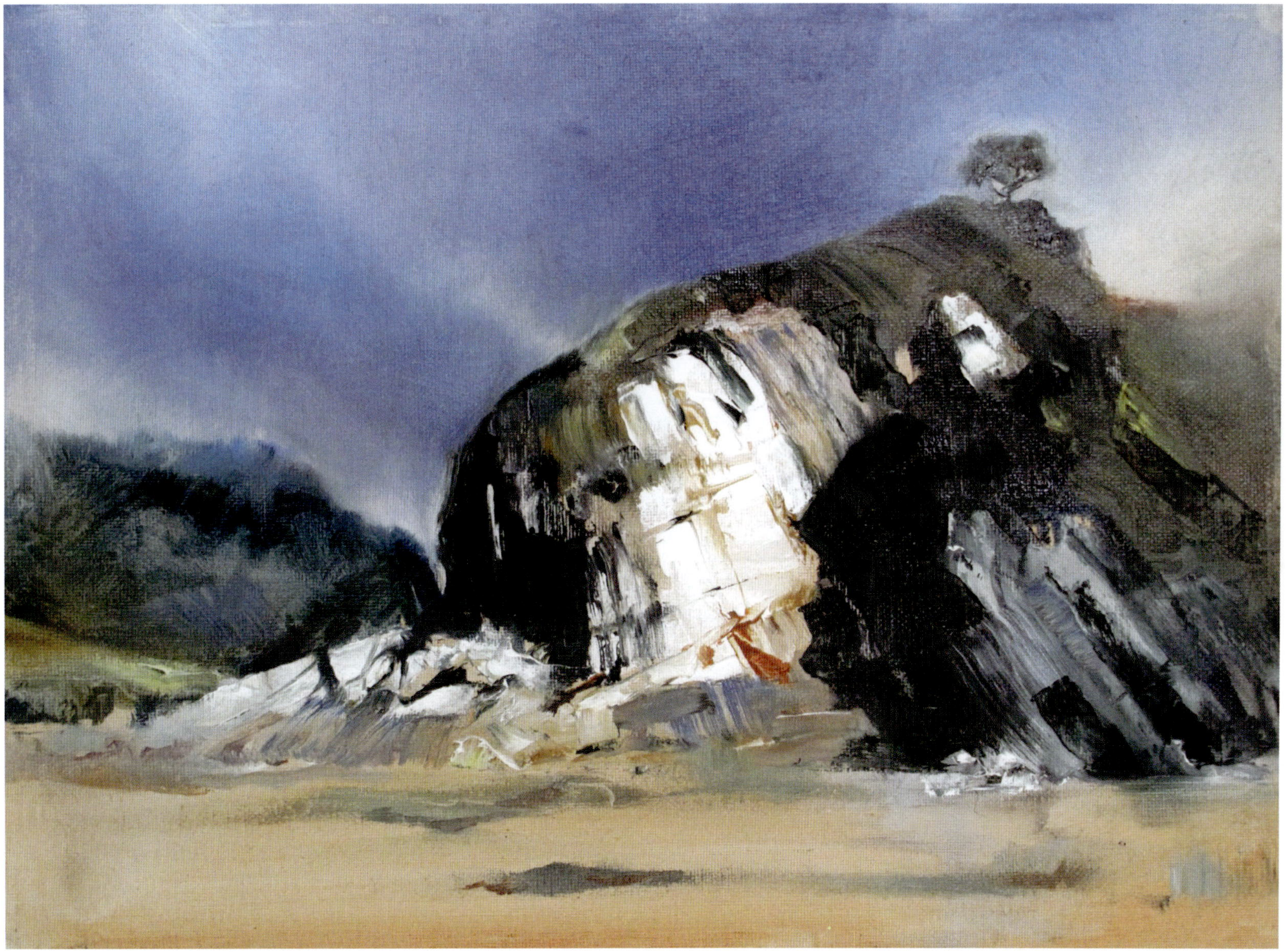

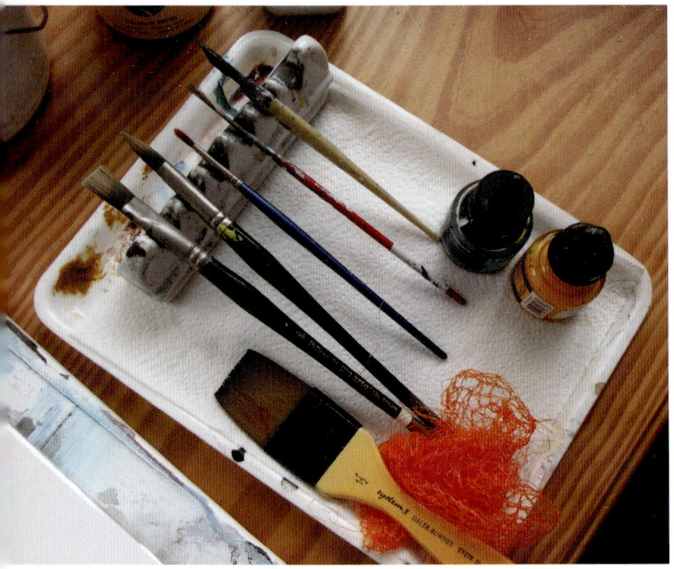

My mainstay brushes – big and small, and not much in between.

Another aspect of a painter's life James imparted was the dedication to promoting his work which he claimed took him out most weeks to events or openings in order to keep his name in the minds of the public. It had, of course, worked sublimely for him, he is a well-known young man, having his own exhibitions in prestigious situations and he has worked alongside Prince Charles more than once. He also has a great deal of talent.

Several years ago I submitted two pictures to the Royal Academy's Summer Exhibition which I thought would be an interesting venture. Having got through the paperwork and the payment I then had to present my work at the prescribed time. In my case that meant travelling on the tube with two really quite large heavy watercolours (why didn't I paint smaller?). I felt an achievement just in submitting them and went home to wait for the postal verdict. Some time later I was thrilled to receive notification that one picture had been selected to hang. Having seen how work is selected I was amazed that someone had noticed my work as submissions are moved past the selection panel quite rapidly, so I suppose an unusual subject, colour or approach may stand out. Anyway, I had to go back to collect the pictures at the end of the Show and joined the queue at the back door ready to resume my uncomfortable journey on the tube, when I noticed several artists just throwing their (framed) works into a strategically placed skip by the door. Maybe they were one-off, try-the-Summer-Show artists, or were they so disillusioned that they couldn't face keeping their failures? It made me recall my badly drawn dinghy all those years ago that I so nearly put in the bin. Perhaps I should have stepped in and urged them to keep their pictures or at least have pointed out that even the frames were worth saving, as someone did for me all those years ago.

I have been painting seriously for about twenty-five years and can now be realistic about amateur art and my place in it. I have reached a point at which I recognise that I am not in competition with anyone else, I can paint and just enjoy the process, I can play and not worry that there is no end result. I know I am never going to hit the high notes in the art world, but I can get pleasure myself from what I produce (more often than not). I still love the feeling when even a tiny area of a picture has worked beautifully; it almost doesn't matter about the remainder of the image.

I shall continue painting, whether it be watercolours, oils, acrylics, printing, collage, until I am no longer able and the happiness I have from these occupations cannot be measured. I am very grateful to be even an average painter. Picasso would not have encouraged talent which fell short of genius, but I am not seeking to change the world's view of art, only to enjoy myself during the process, which counts for everything.

My choice of materials

Paper: Bockingford 200lbs - RWS paper 2-300lbs - Saunders Waterford

Colour: tube watercolours, tube acrylics, acrylic inks

Brushes: Round, size 20 - A Rigger – a Flat brush 1.5 inches.

Found Materials: Lace, netting, tickets, tissue paper, newspaper, maps, etc.

Other equipment: flat boards, masking tape, dip pens

The Gallery

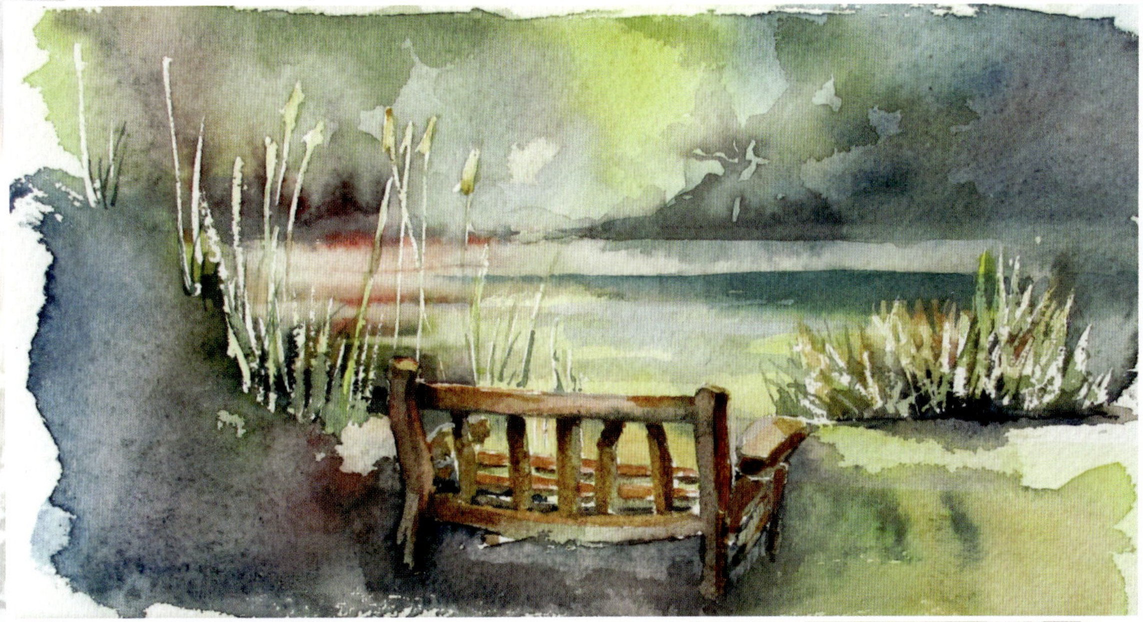

Contemplation, watercolour, 12 x 7 in

This quiet seat was in a friend's riverside garden and had become part of nature – covered in lichen.

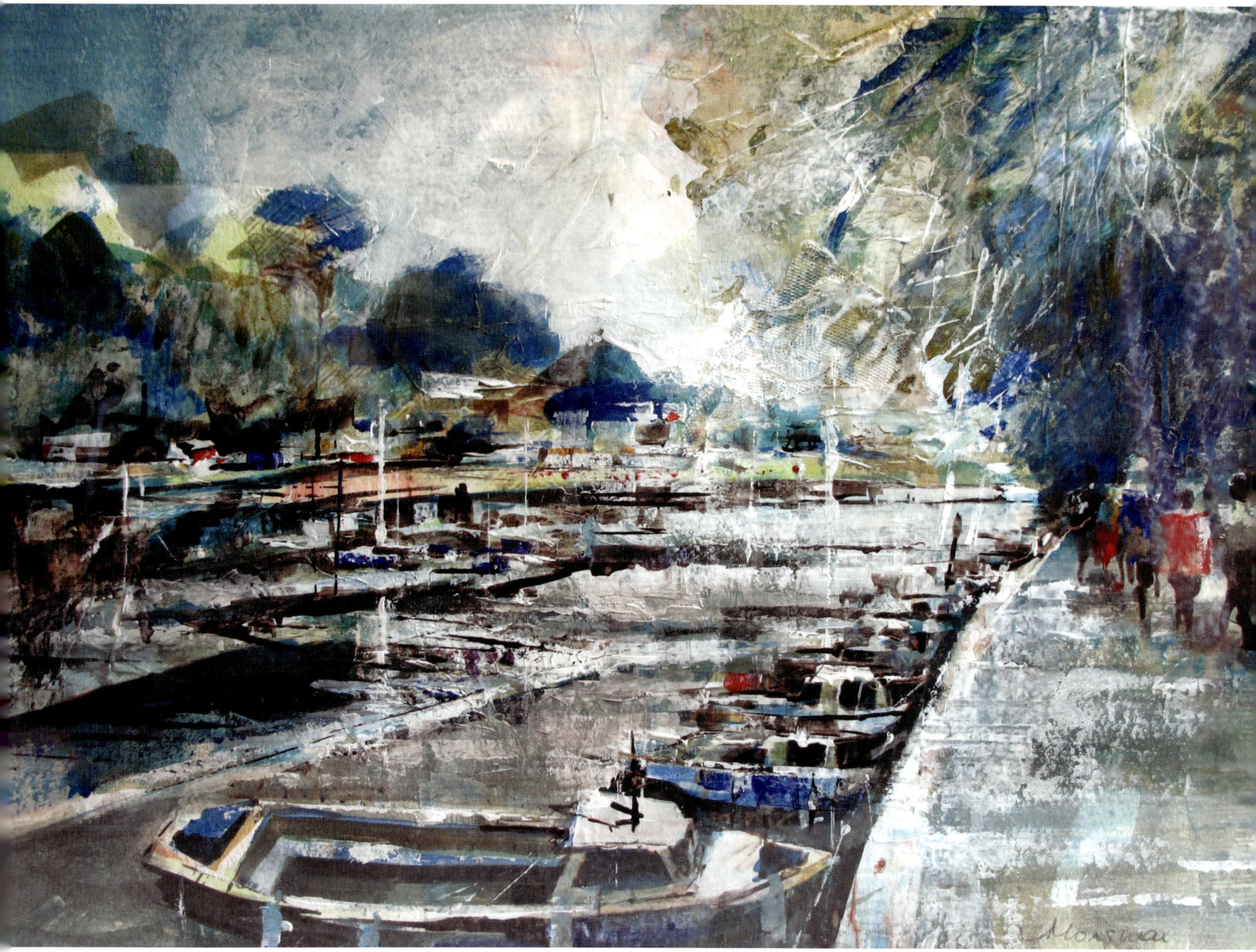

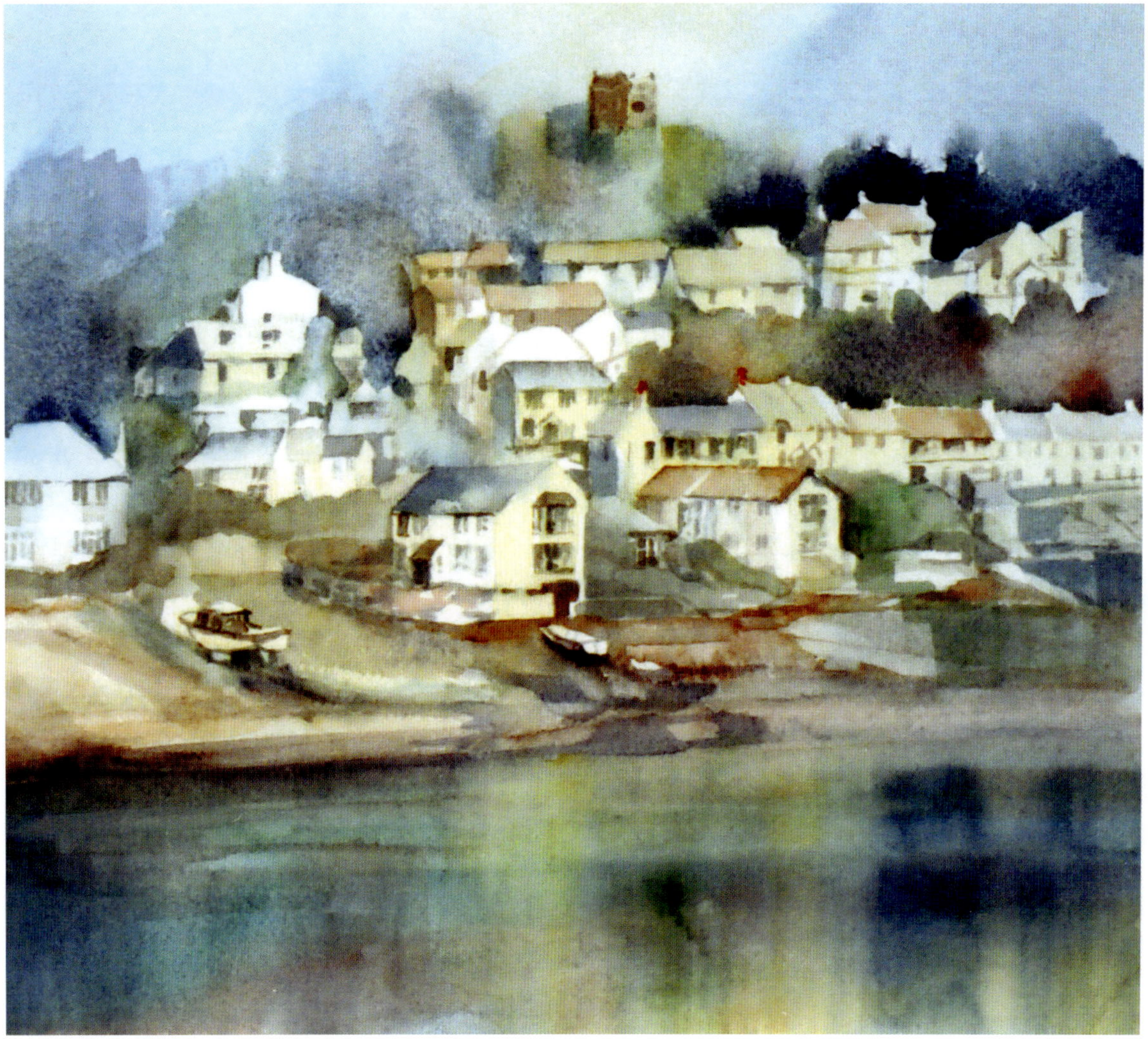

The Brook, Newton Ferrers, watercolour, 12 x 11 in

Kingsbridge, mixed media, 14 x 12 in

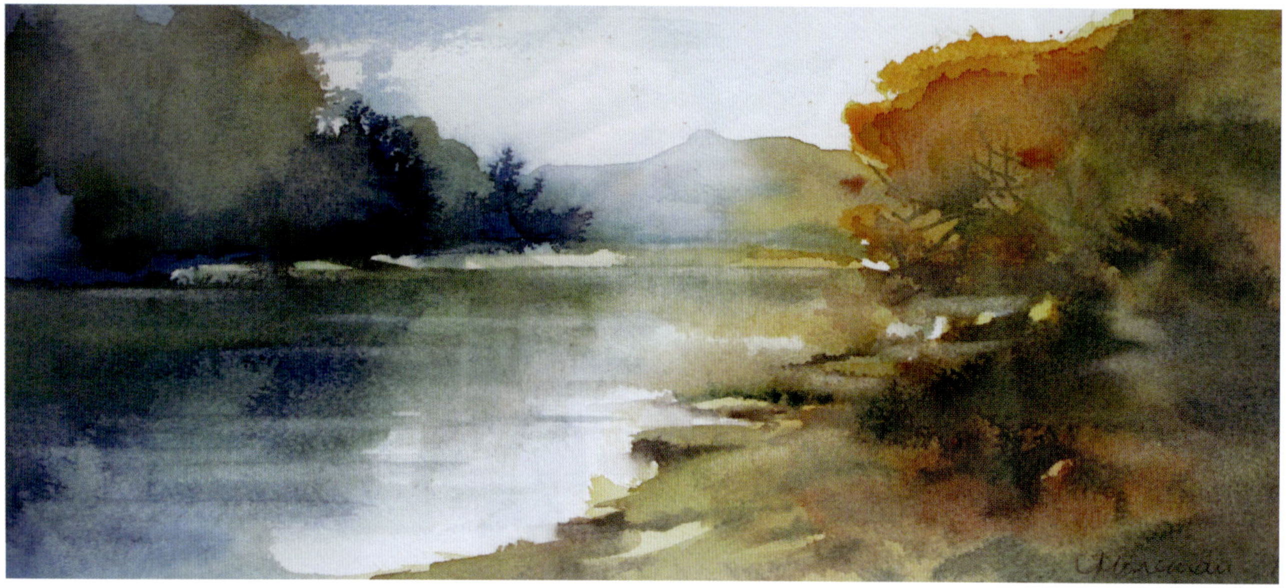

High Tide I,
watercolour, 10 x 6 in

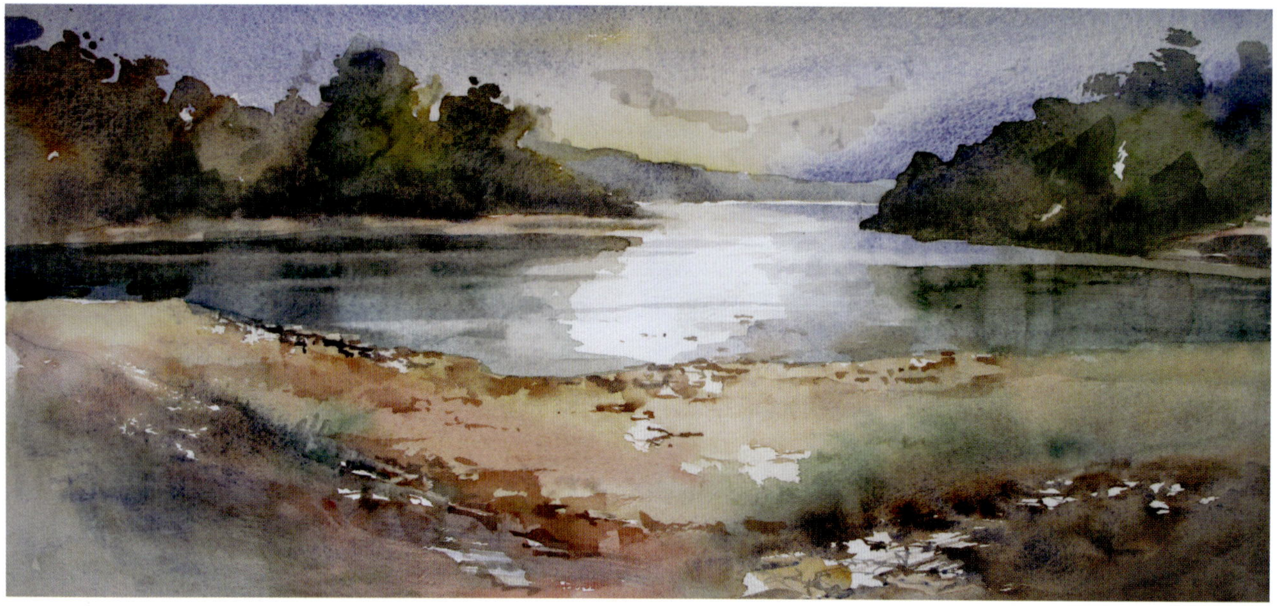

High Tide II,
watercolour, 10 x 6 in

Tide in at the end of my road – always beautiful.

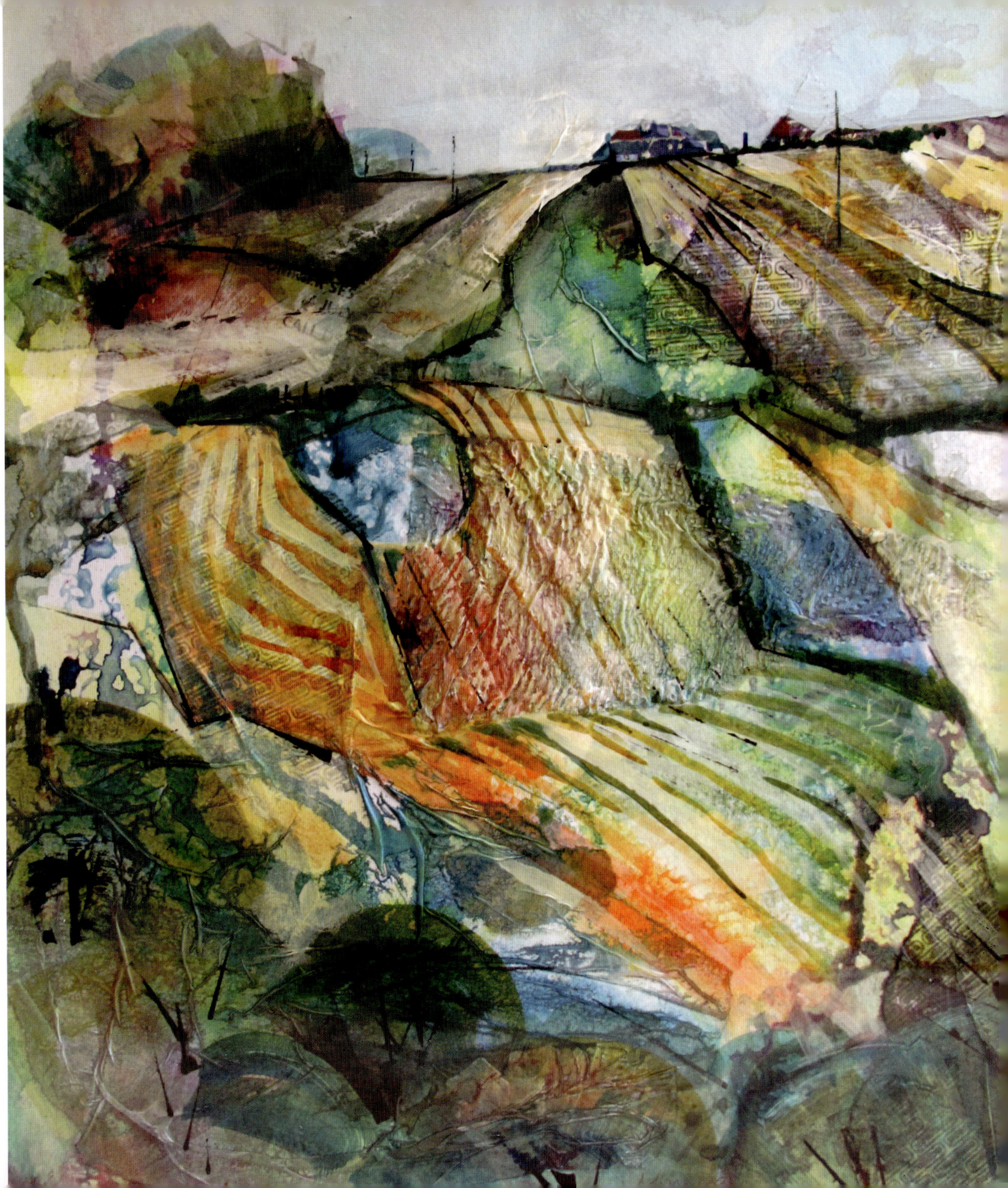

Harvest Festival,
mixed media, 16 x 14 in

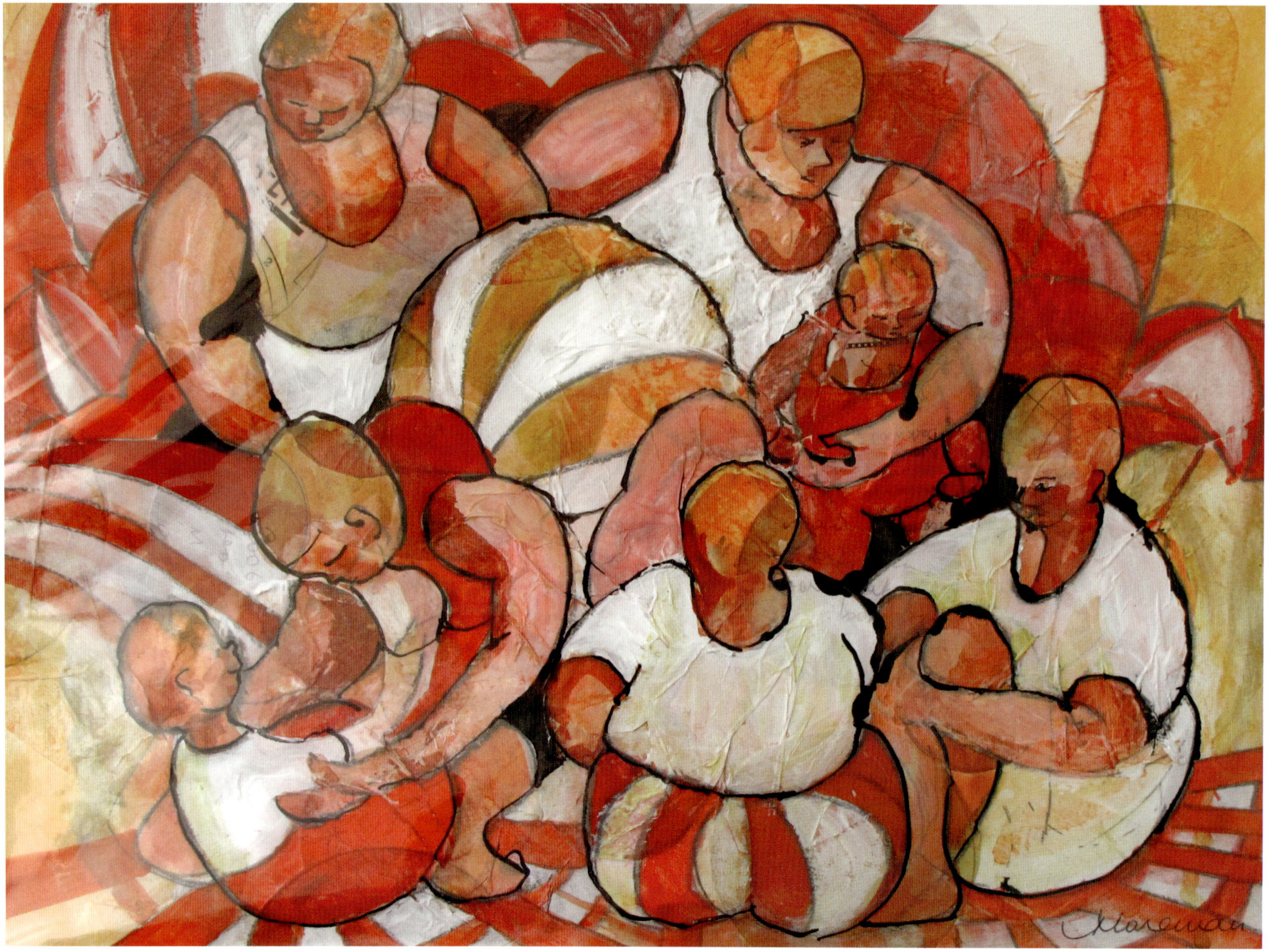

Beach Babes, mixed media, 13 x 10 in

Inspired by a group of mothers and children on the beach.

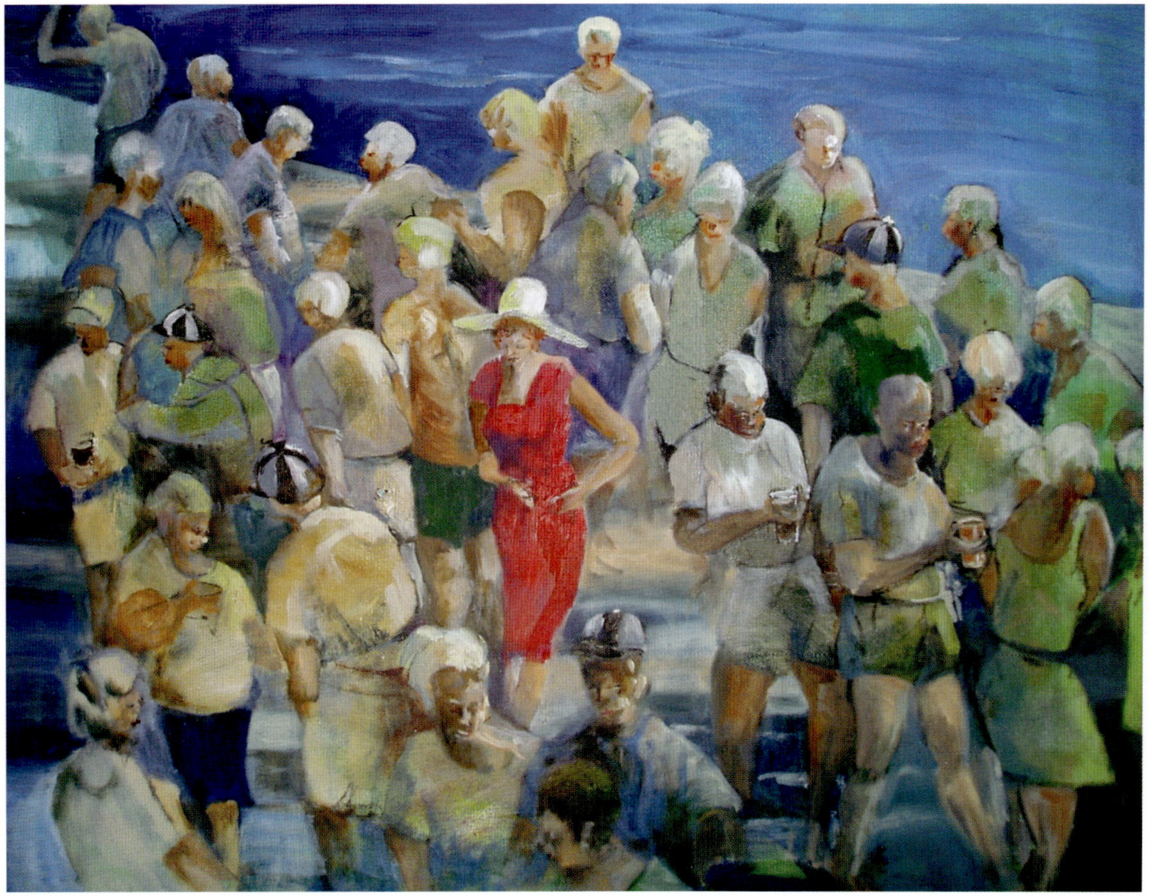

The Boat Race, acrylic, 22 x 16 in

I was intrigued by what was obviously someone's mother in the midst of sweaty student rowers.

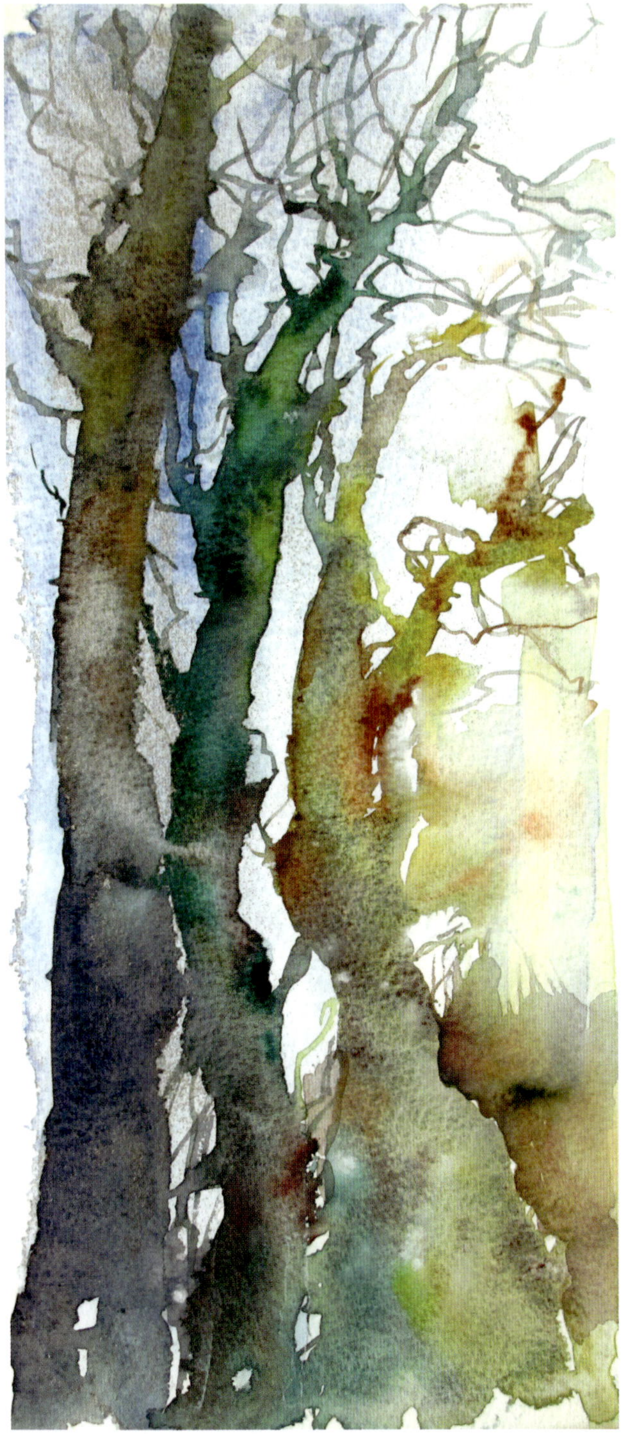

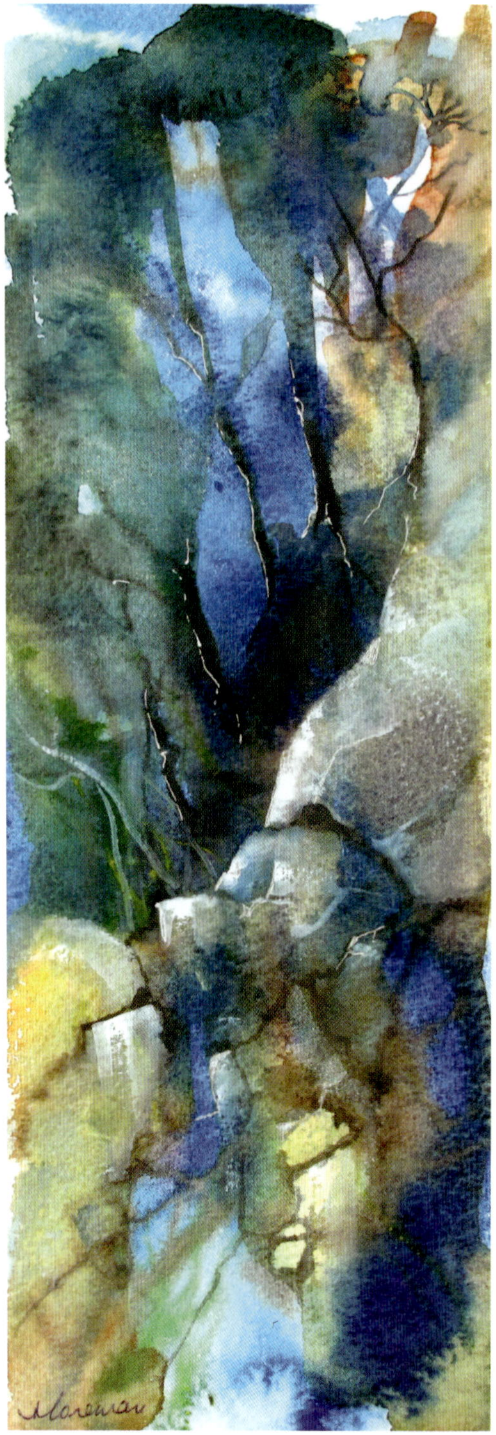

Far left: *The Woods,* watercolour, 11 x 6 in

Left: *The Crag,* watercolour, 11 x 6 in

Opposite: *Blurred Boundaries,* watercolour 22 x 18 in

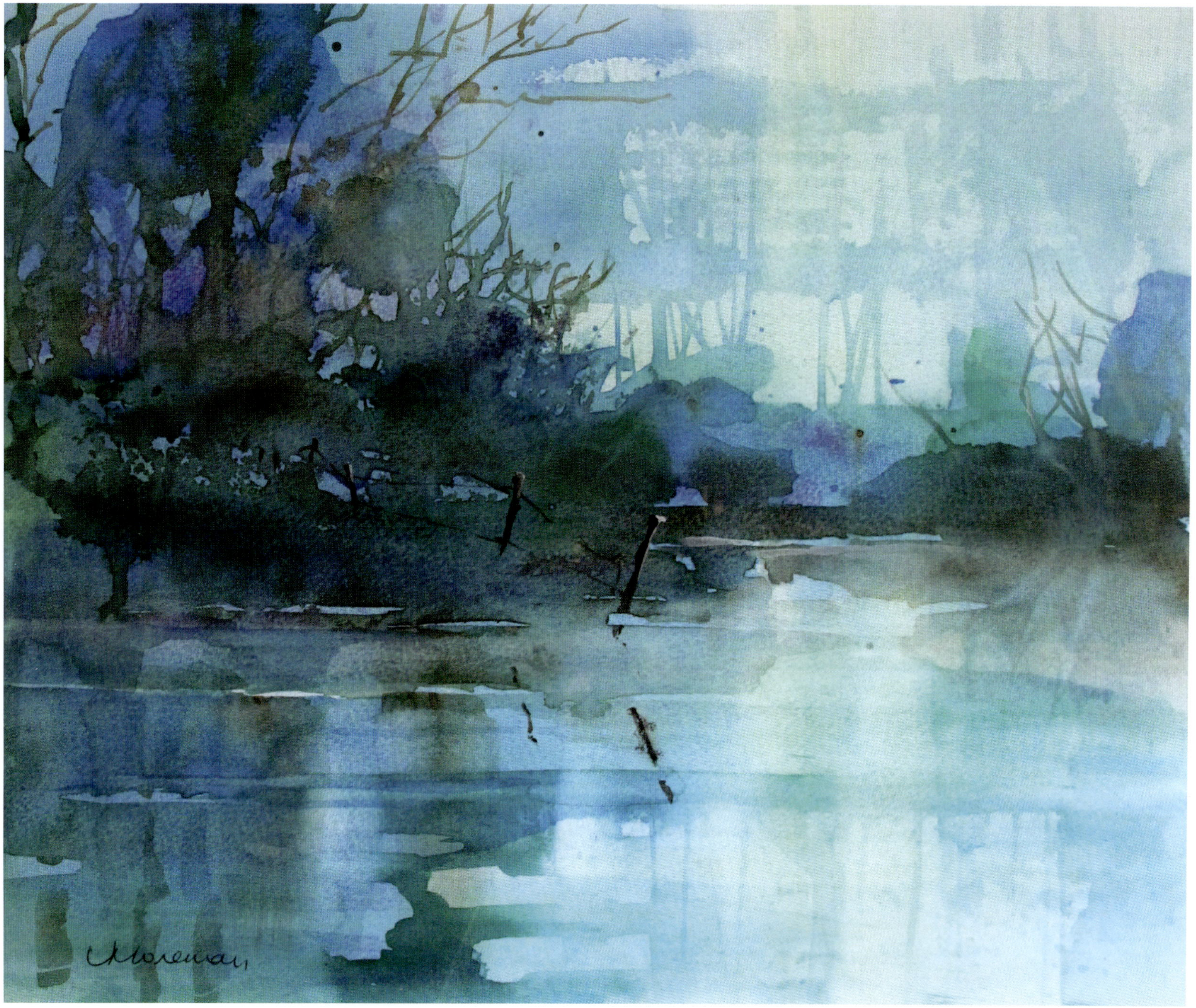

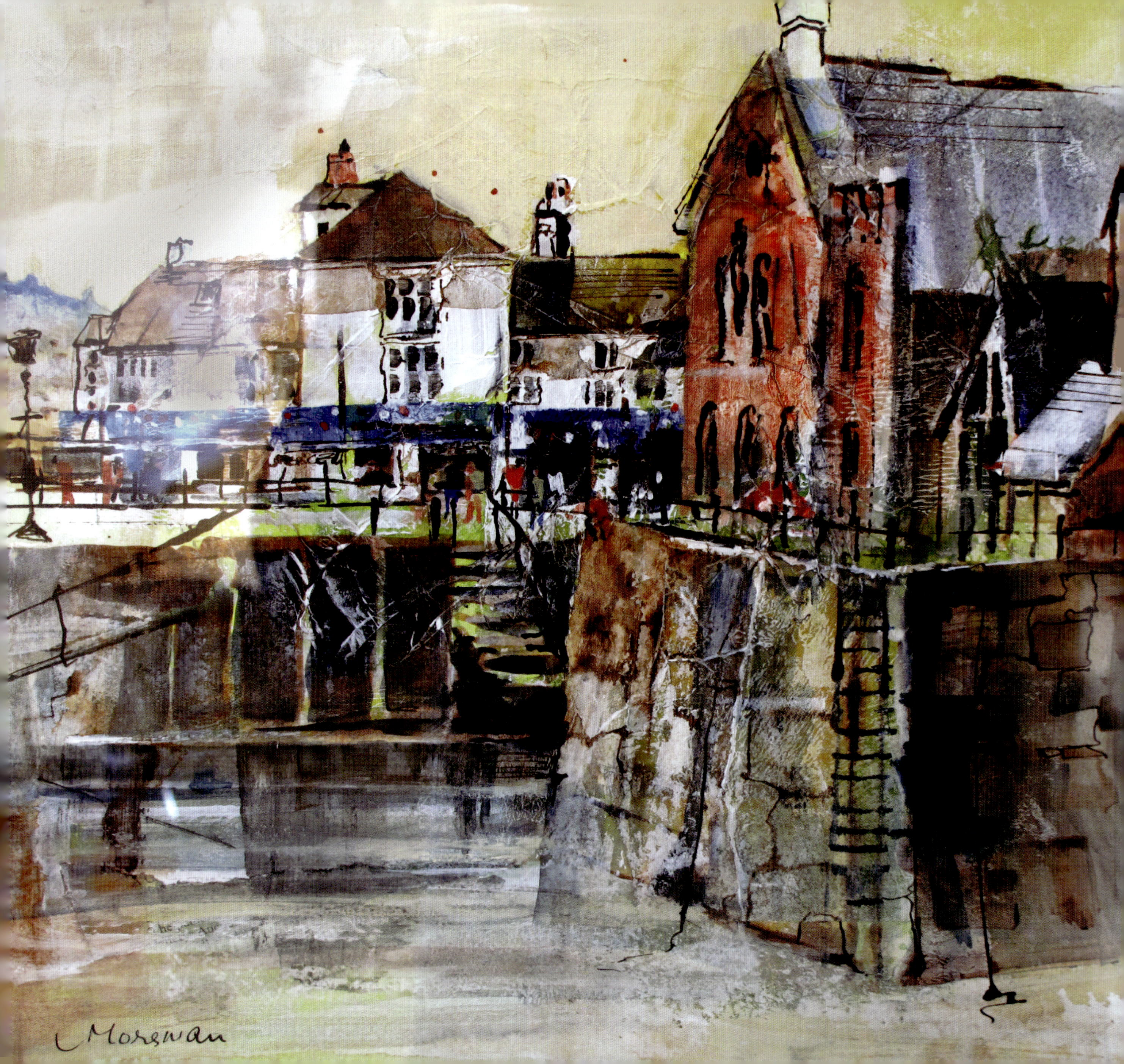
Moreman

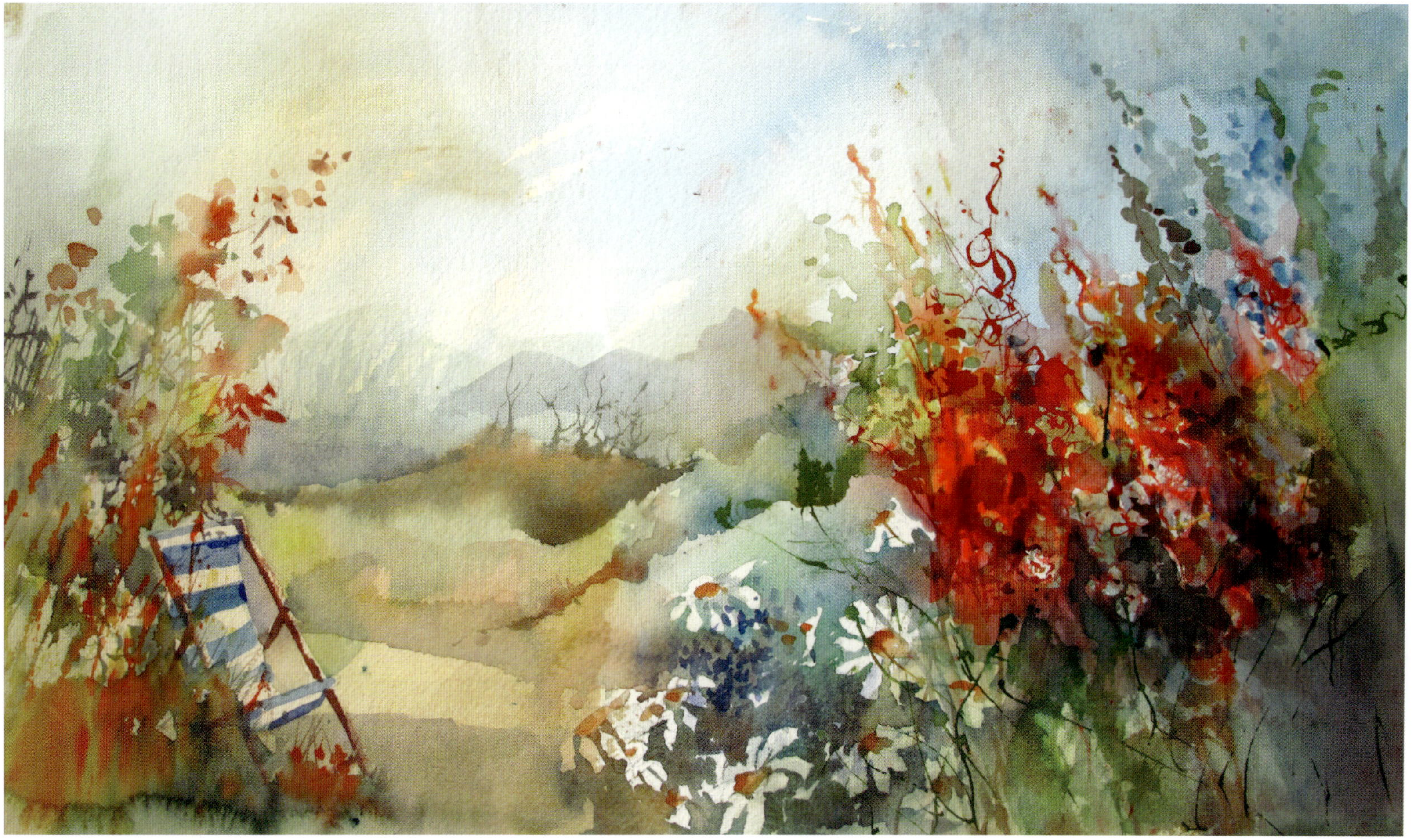

Lazy Daisies, watercolour, 14 x 10 in

Cornish Harbour, mixed media, 18 x 14 in

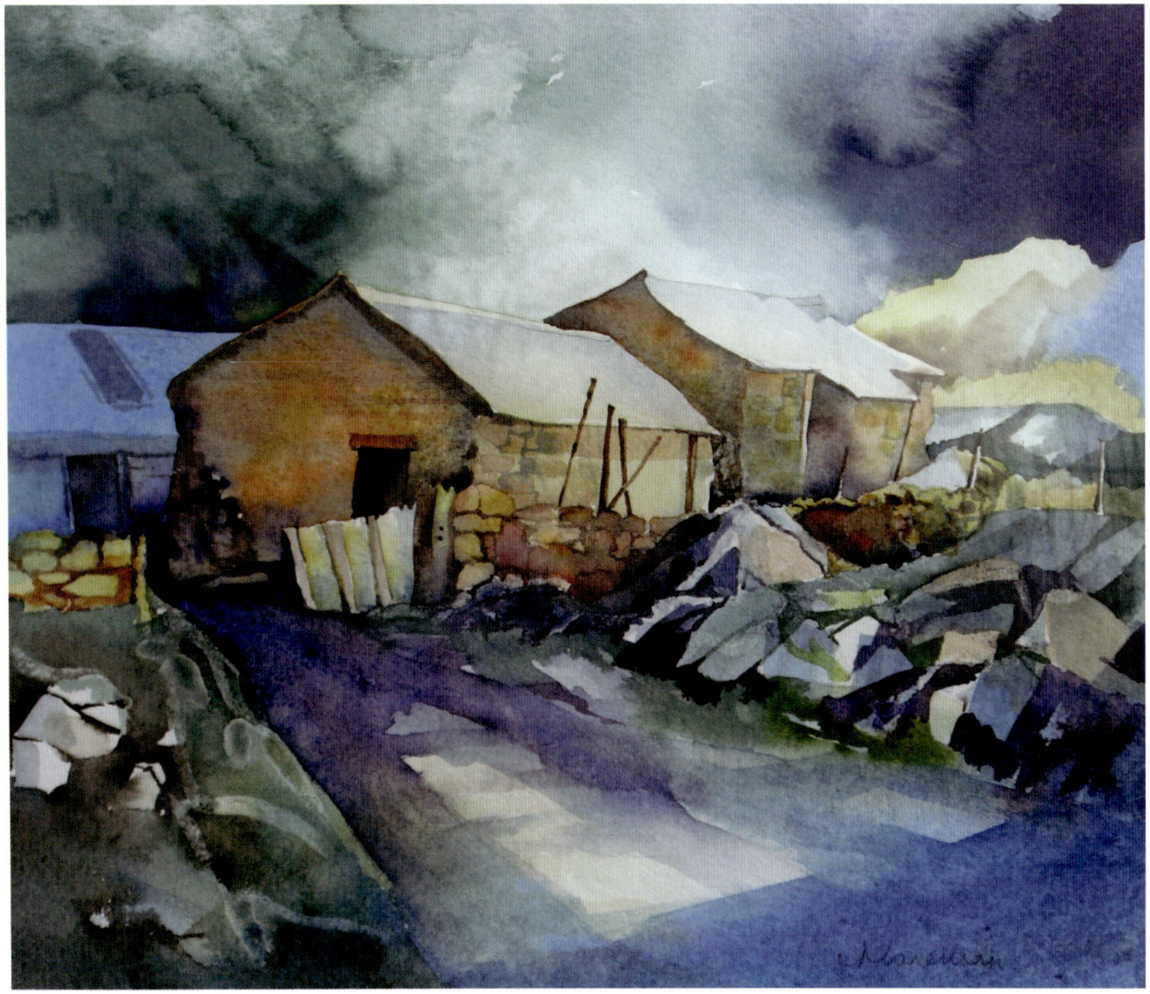

Refuge from the Storm, watercolour, 14 x 11 in

Village Square, collage, 14 x 15 in

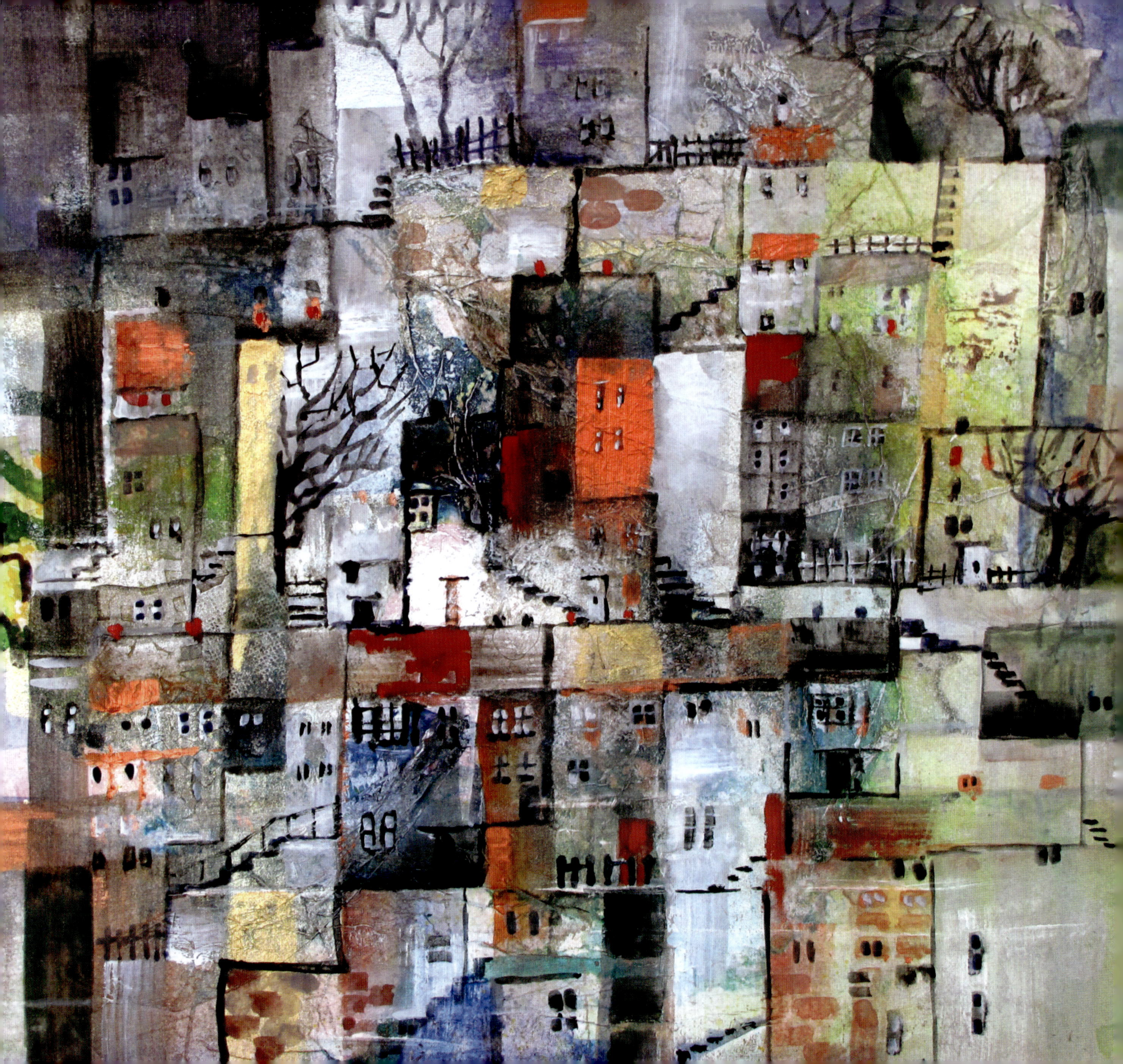

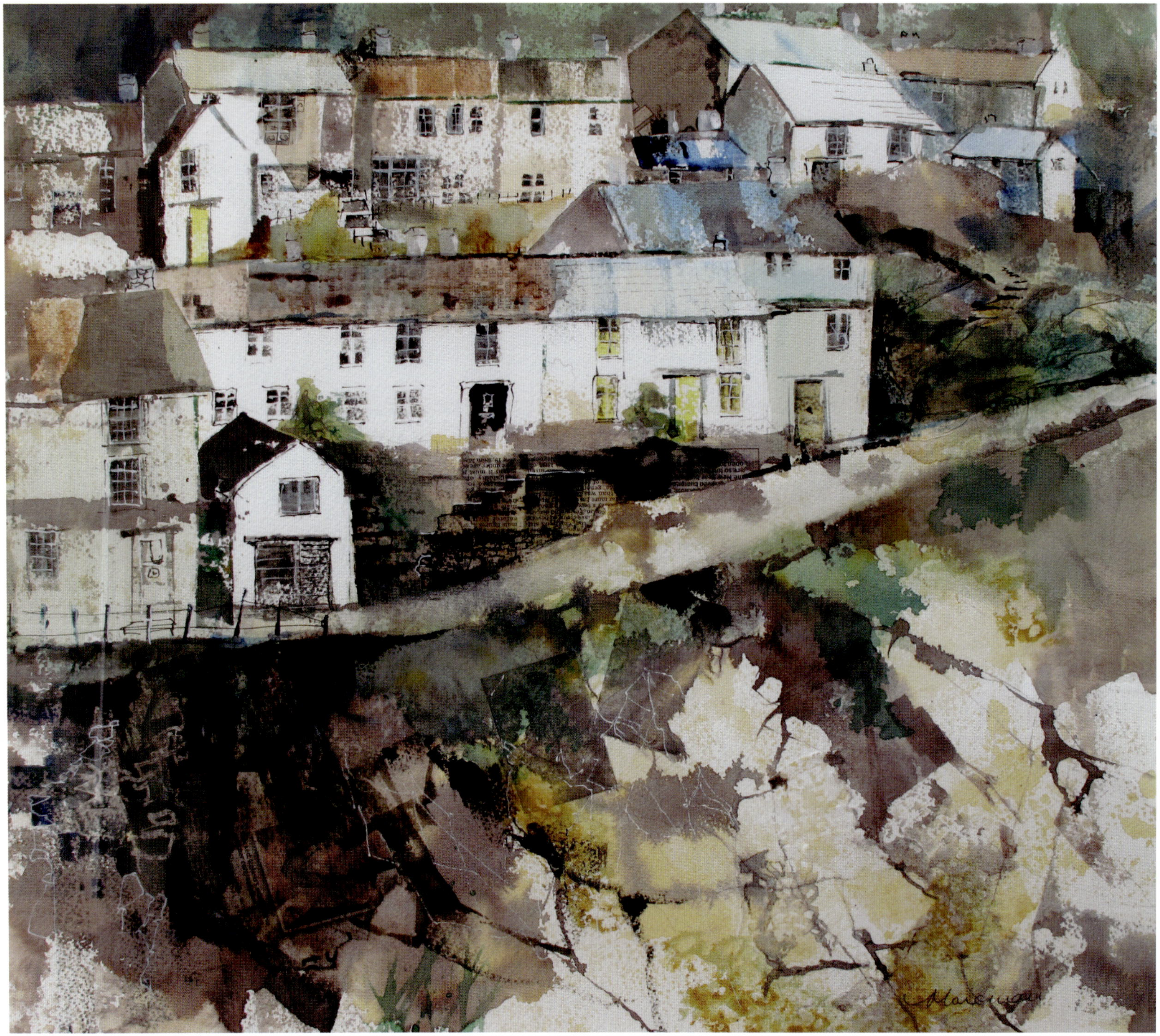

Portloe, mixed media, 22 x 18 in

Bruges, watercolour, 12 x 14 in

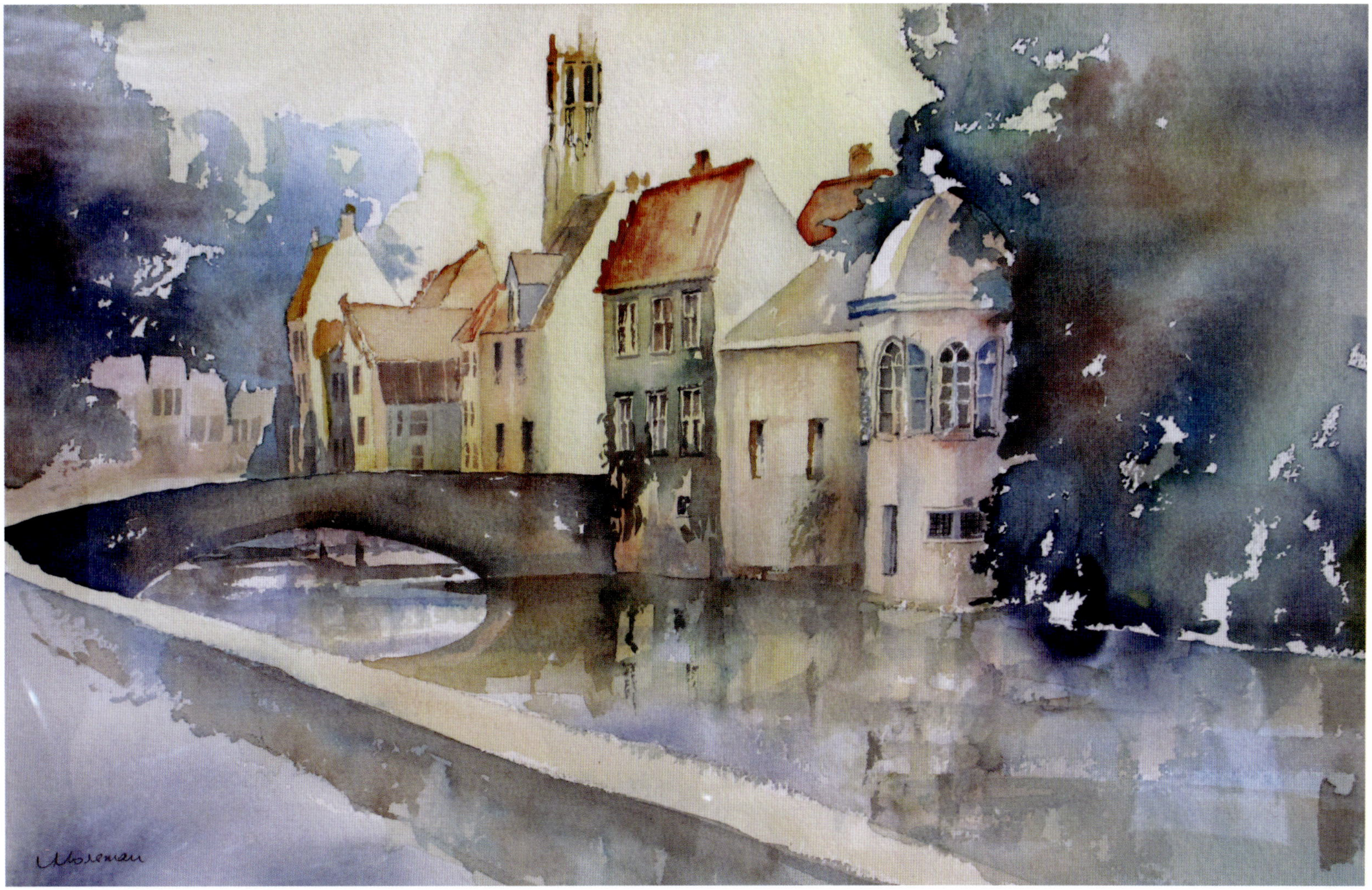

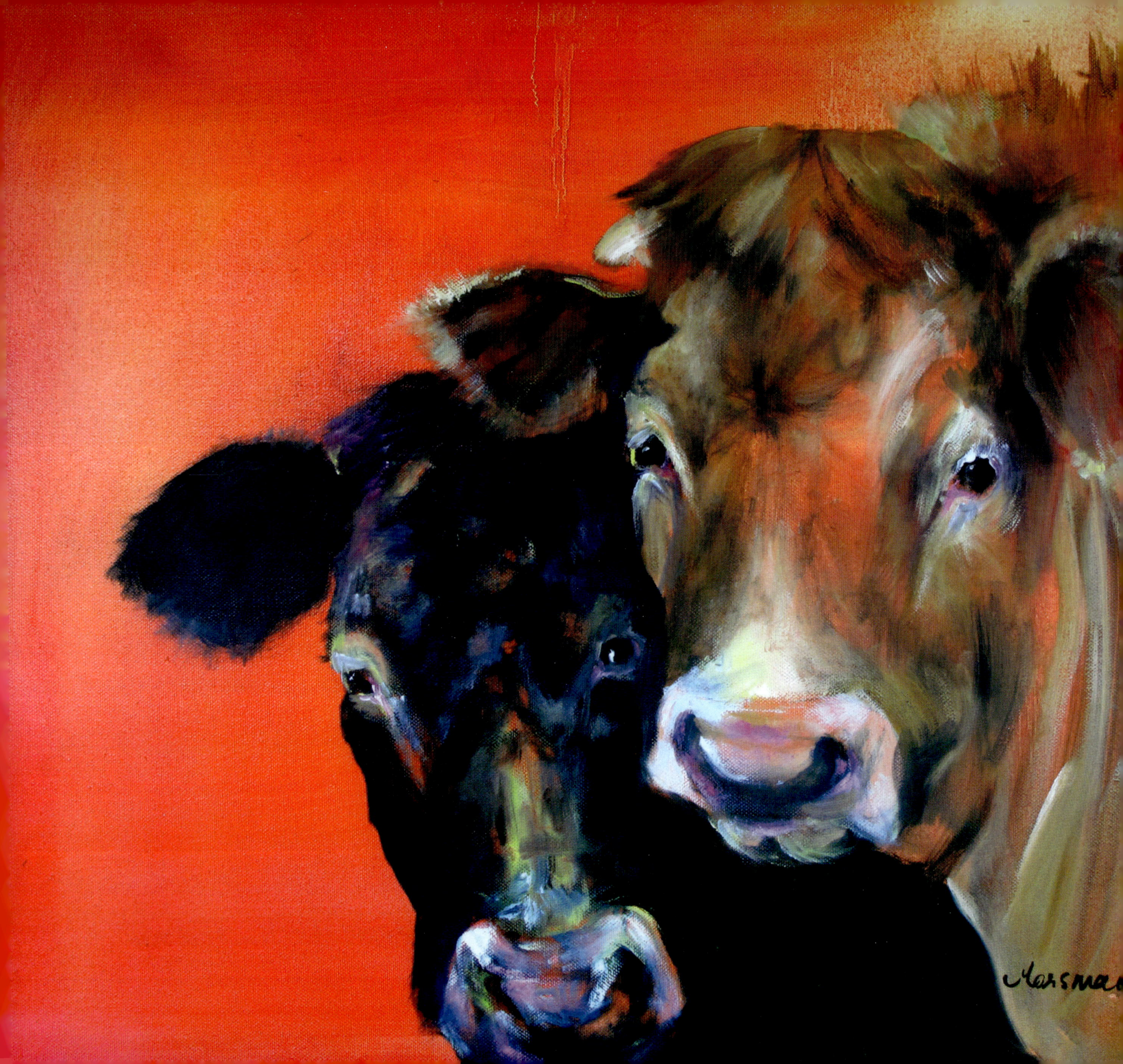

Ruminants in Red, oil, 23 x 19 in

Cows offer endless opportunities for my amusement in painting!

Cow Lick, collage, 14 x 13 in

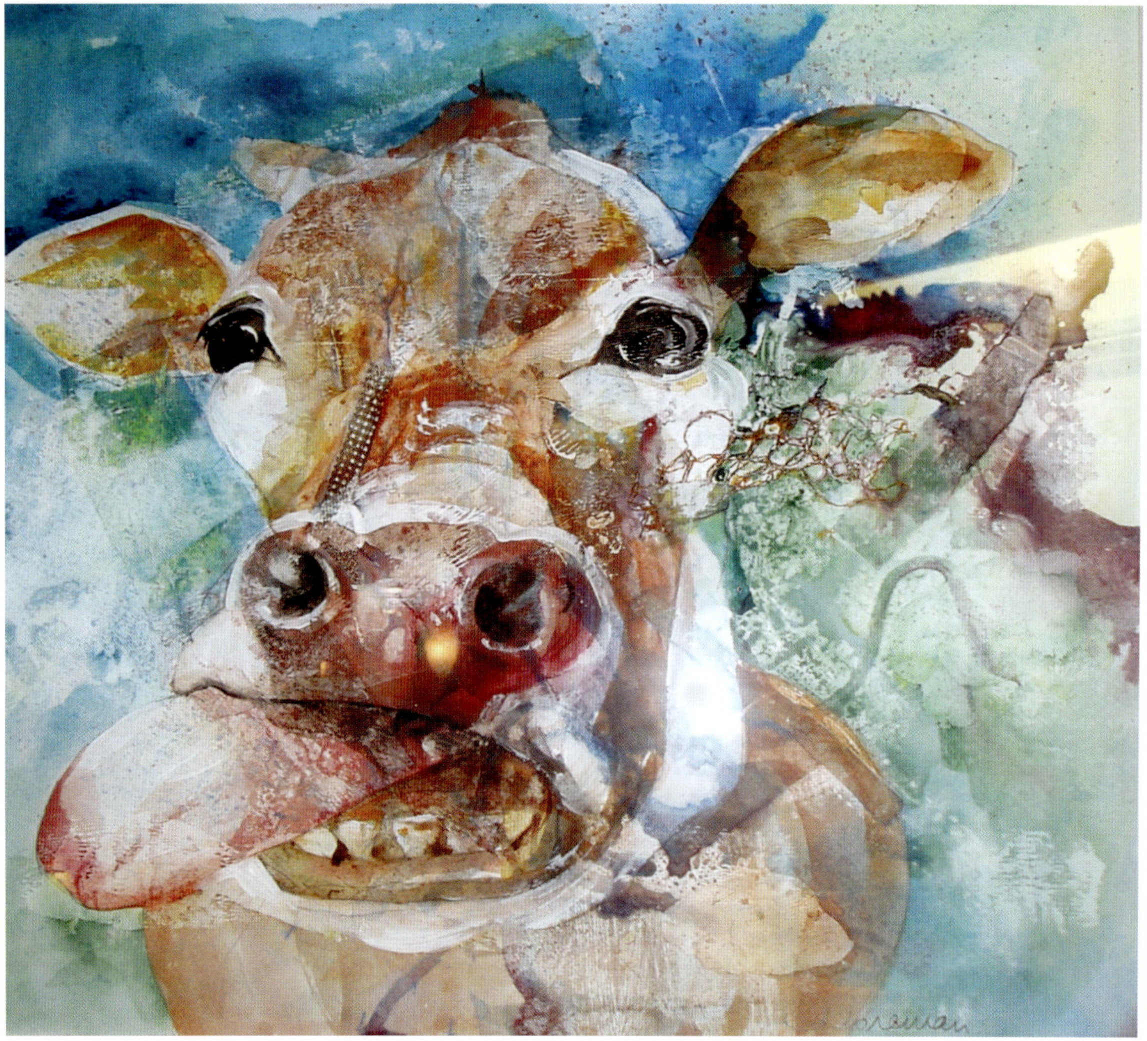

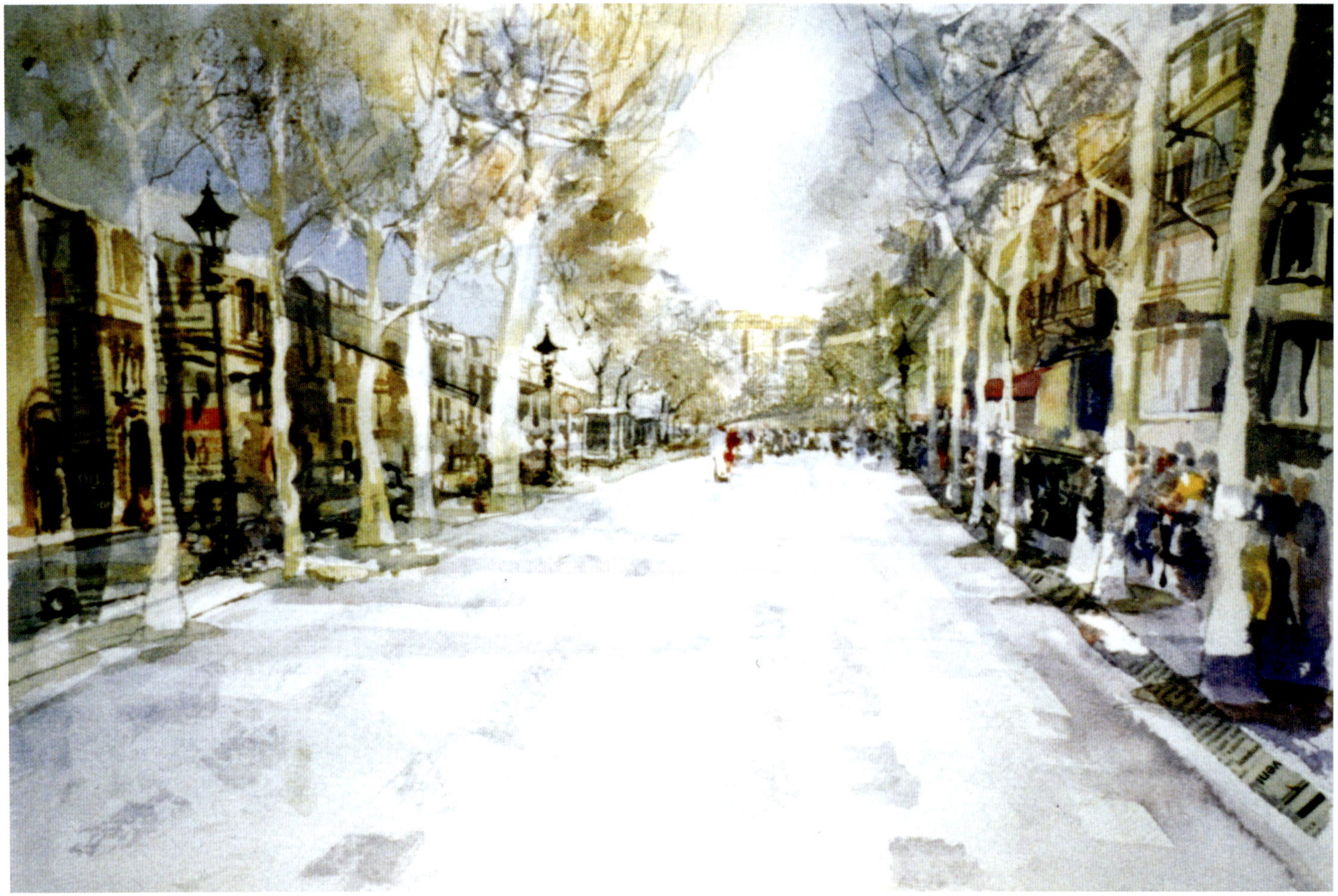

Paris, watercolour, 17 x 14 in

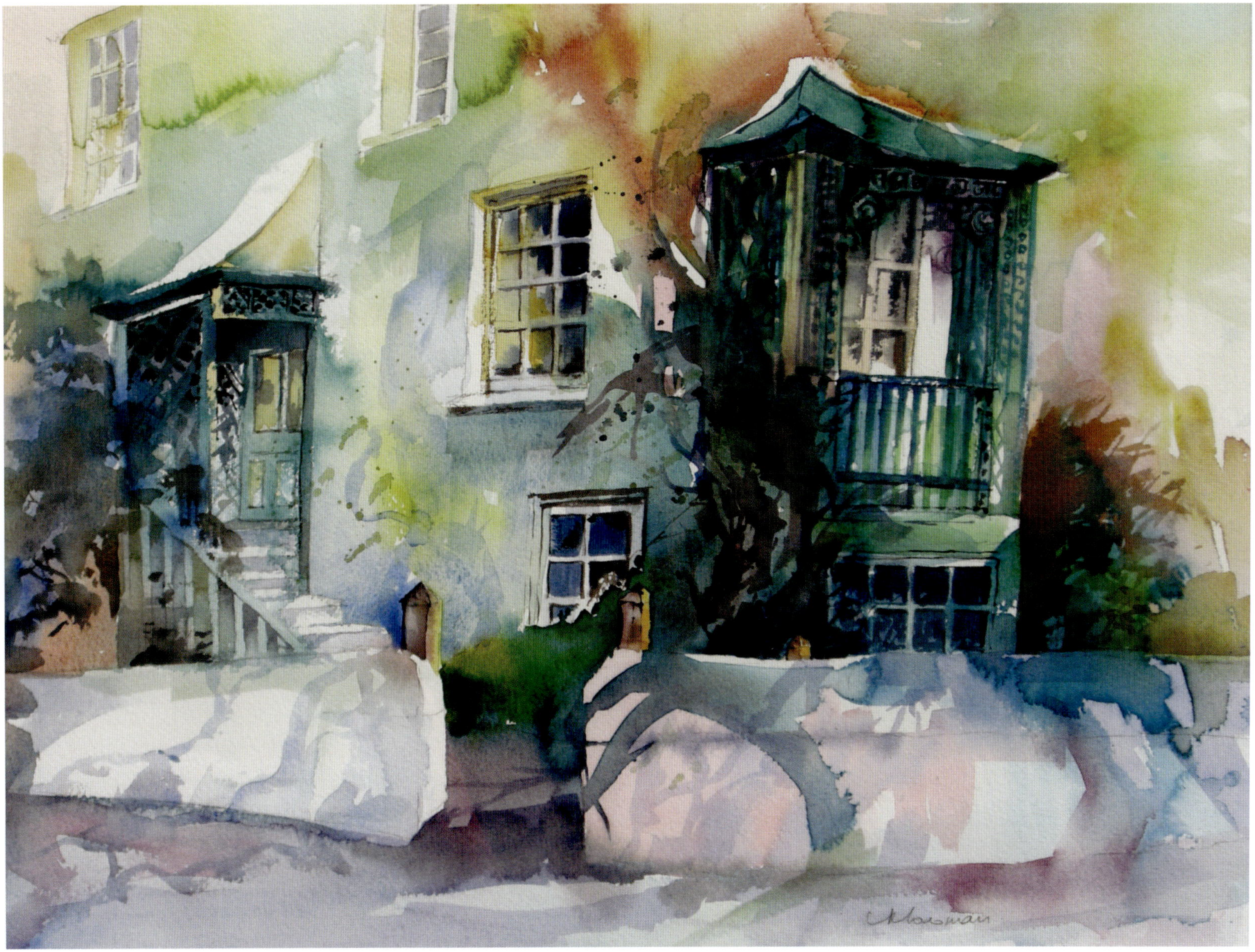

The Green Door, watercolour, 16 x 12 in

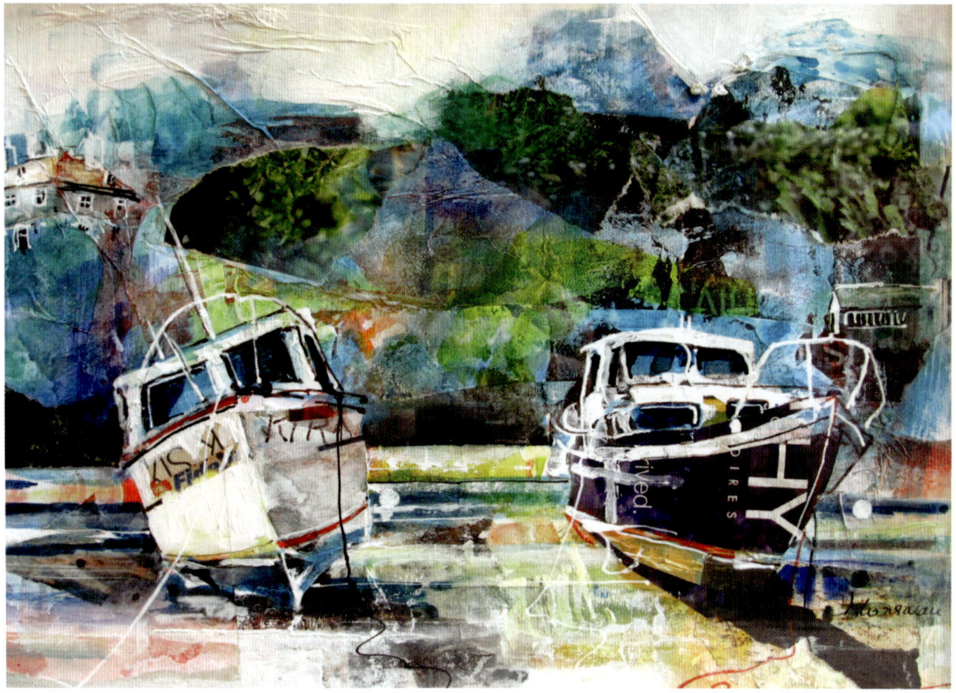

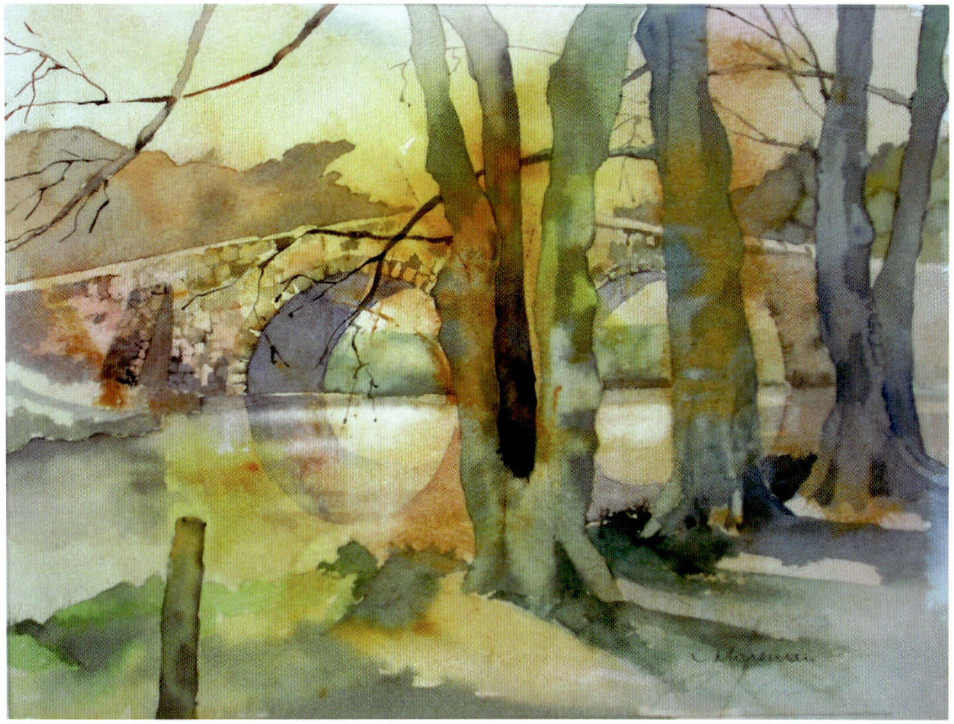

Left in the Lurch,
mixed media, 15 x 11 in

A Walk by the River,
watercolour, 14 x 10 in

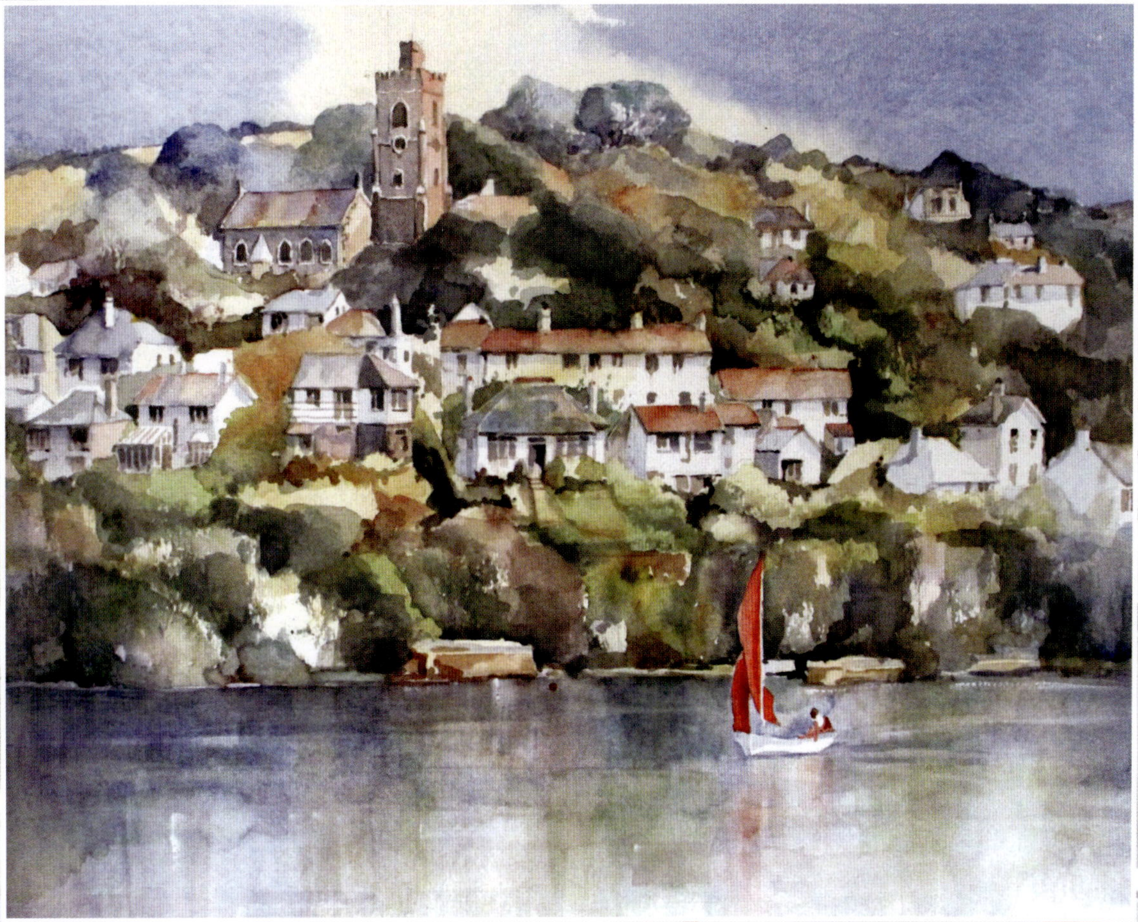

Newton Creek Sailing, watercolour, 22 x 18 in

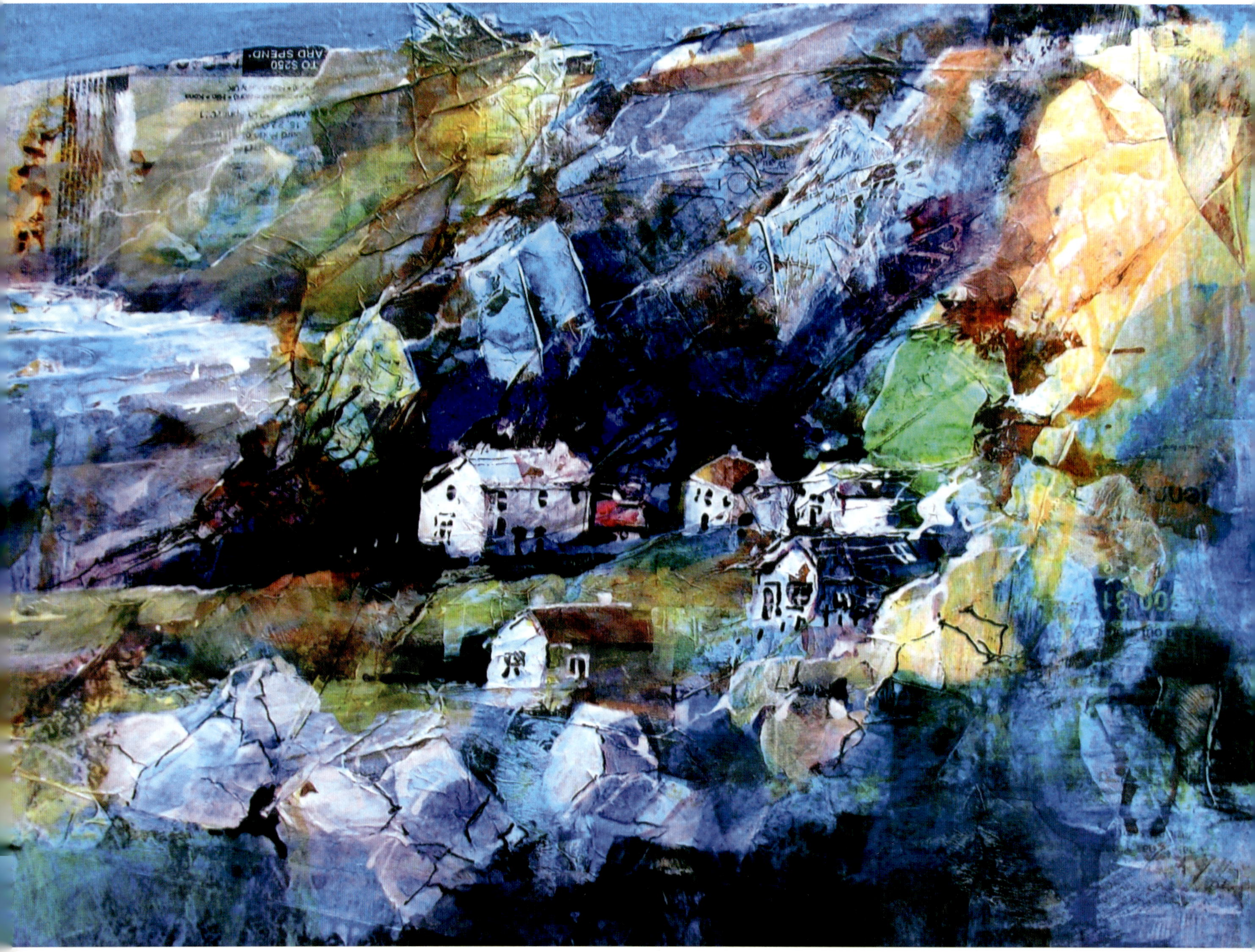

The Red Boat,
mixed media, 12 x 16 in

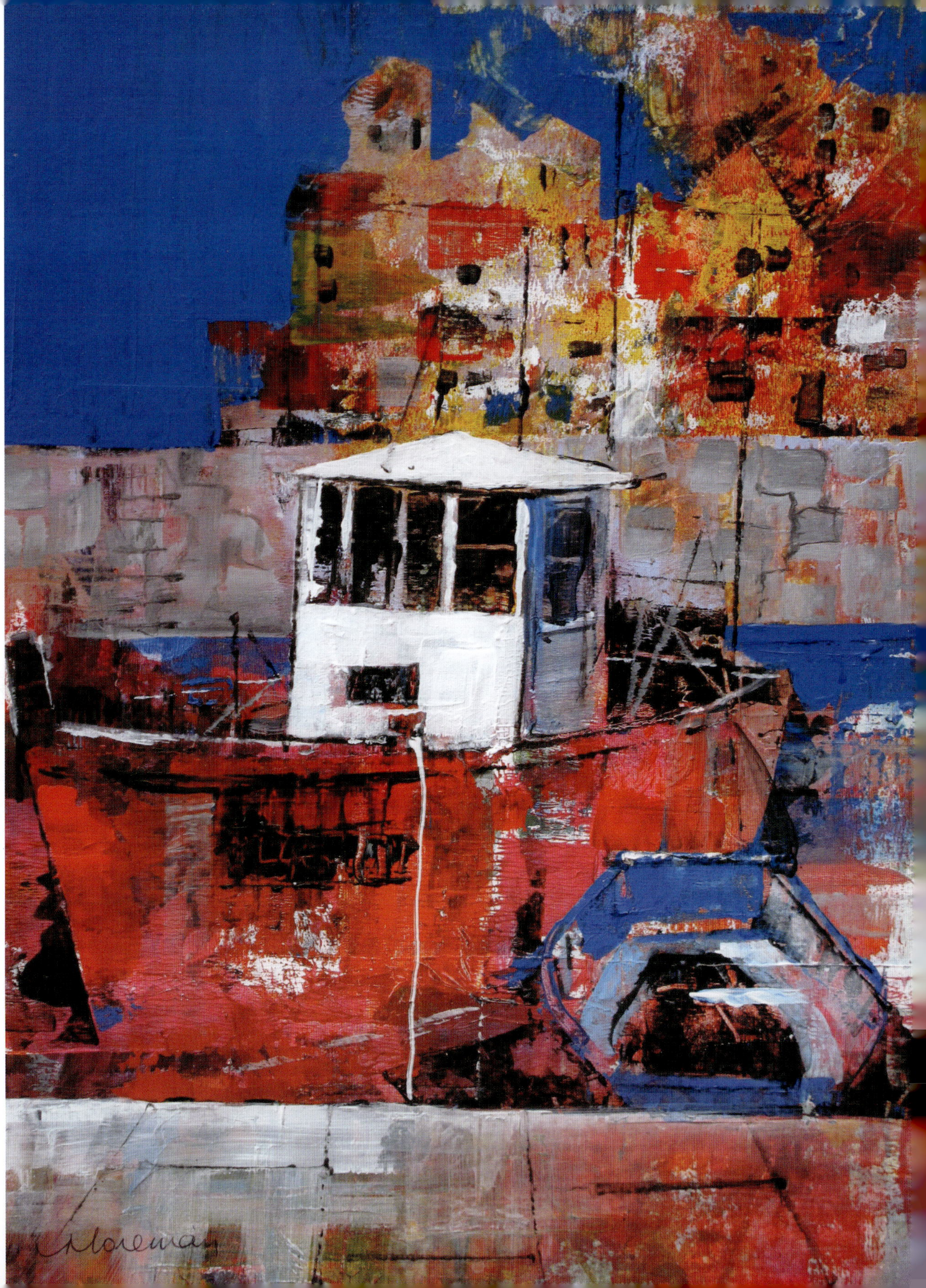

The Cornish Cove,
mixed media, 17 x 12 in

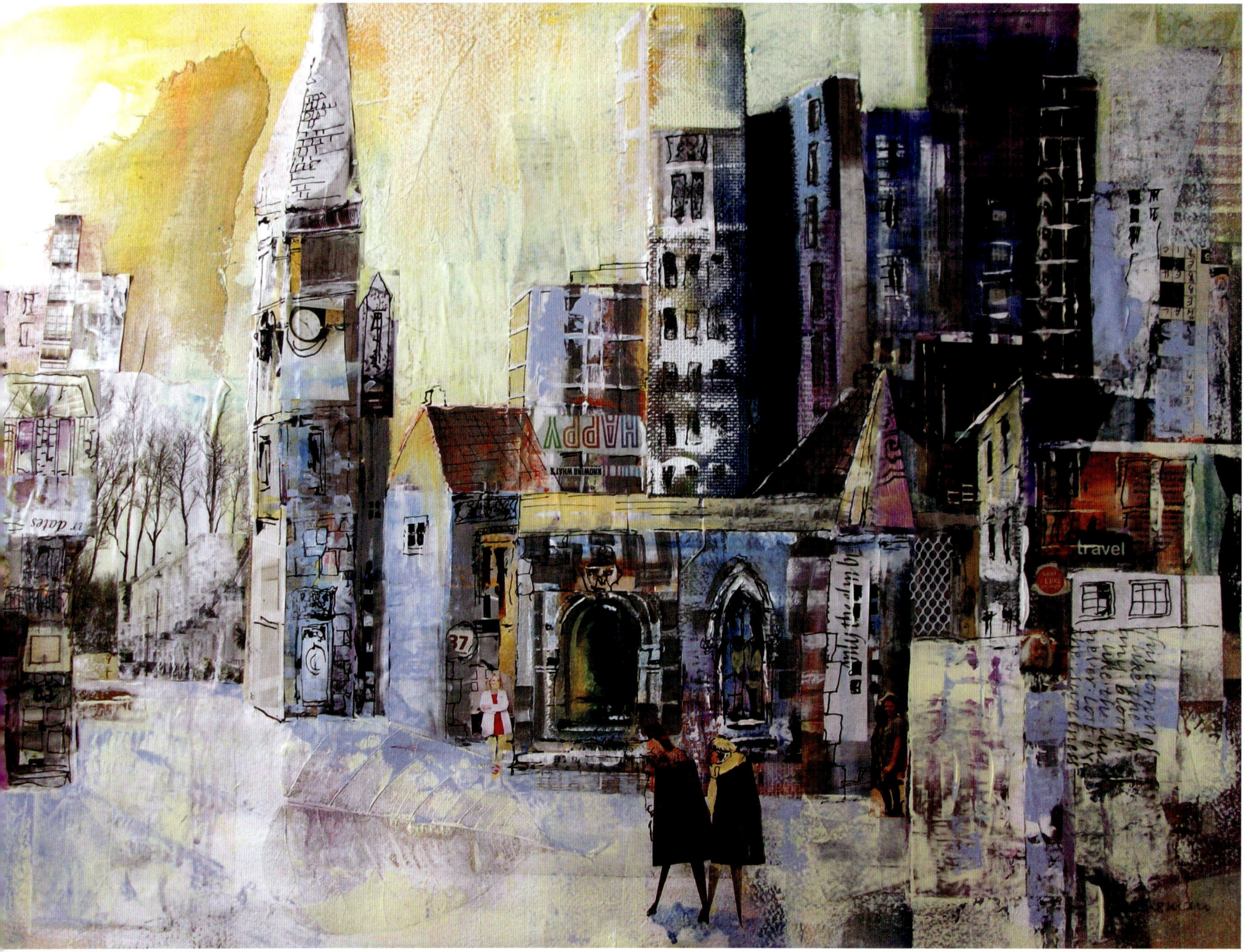

Chattering on a Cold Morning, collage, 25 x 19 in

Clapper Bridge, mixed media, 19 x 14 in

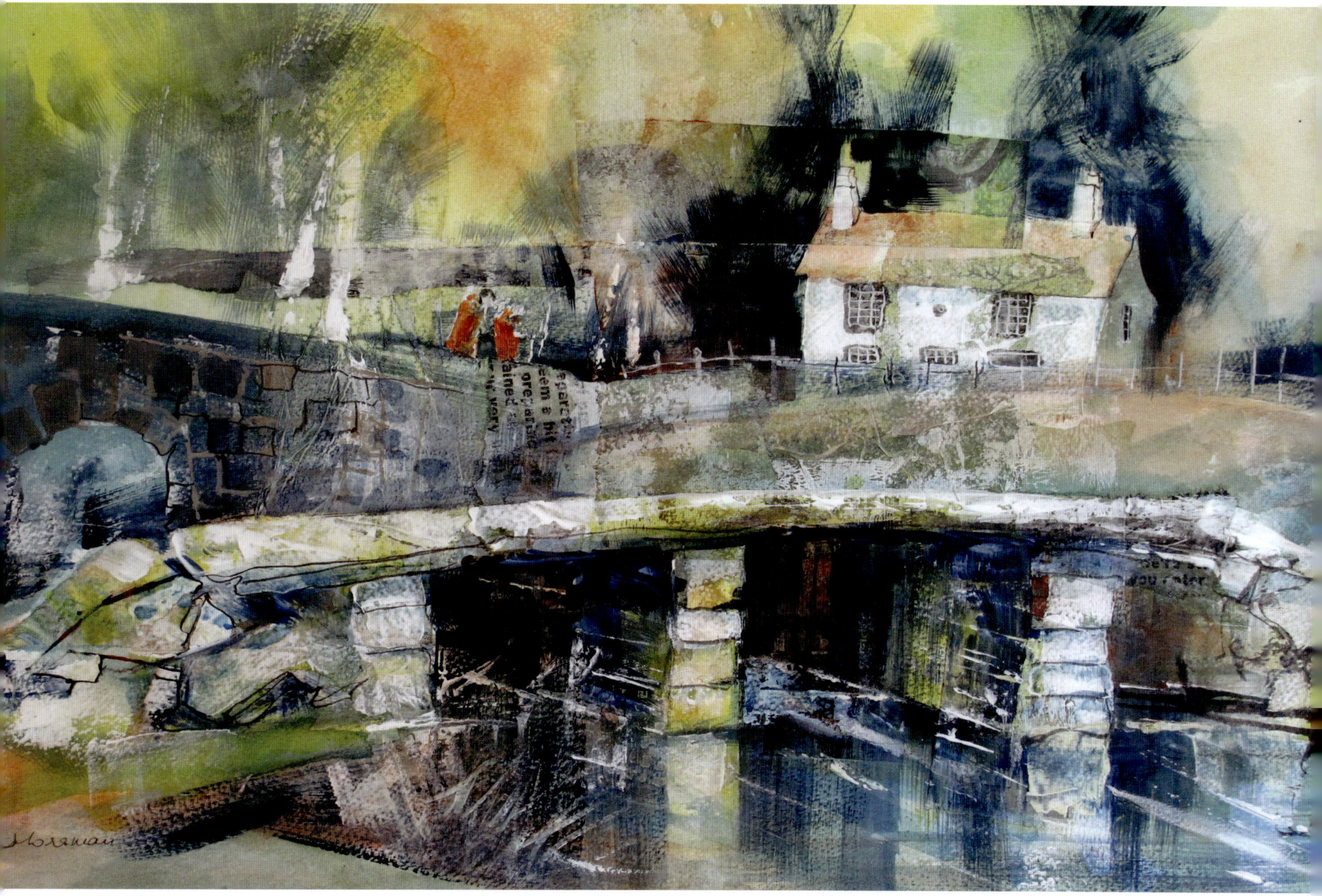

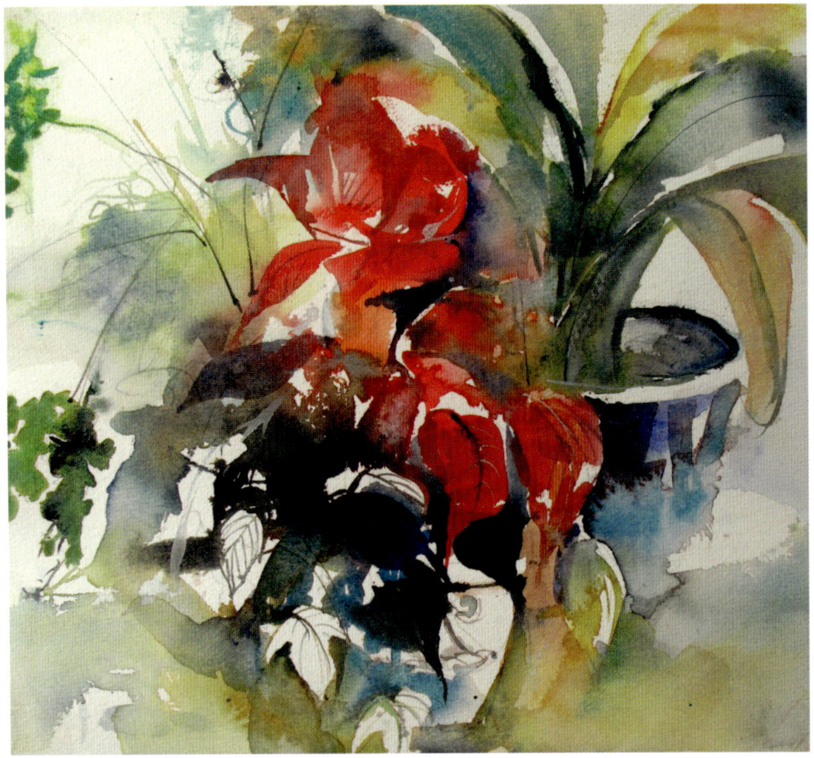

Pot Plant, watercolor, 15 x 15 in

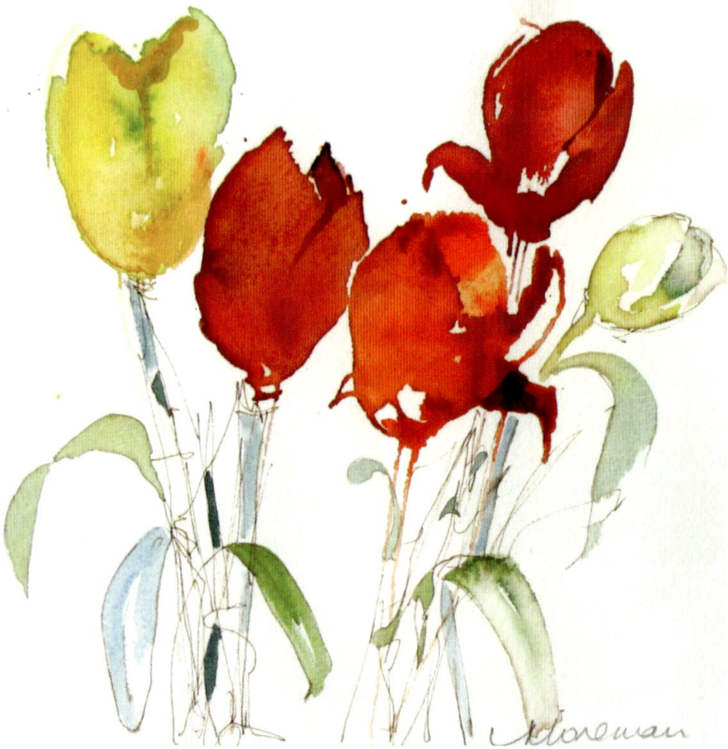

Tulips, watercolour, 8 x 8 in

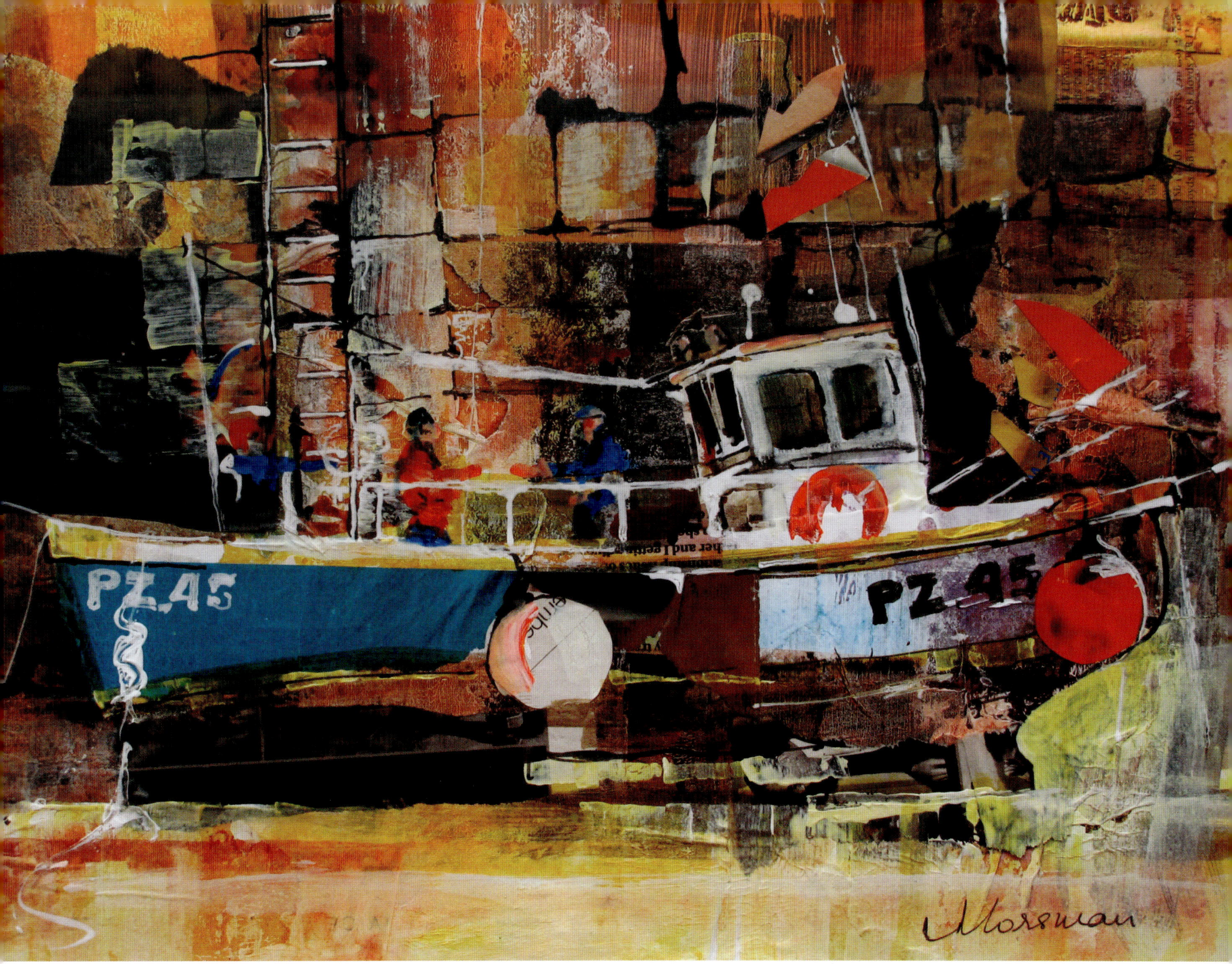

Men who Bait, mixed media, 18 x 16 in

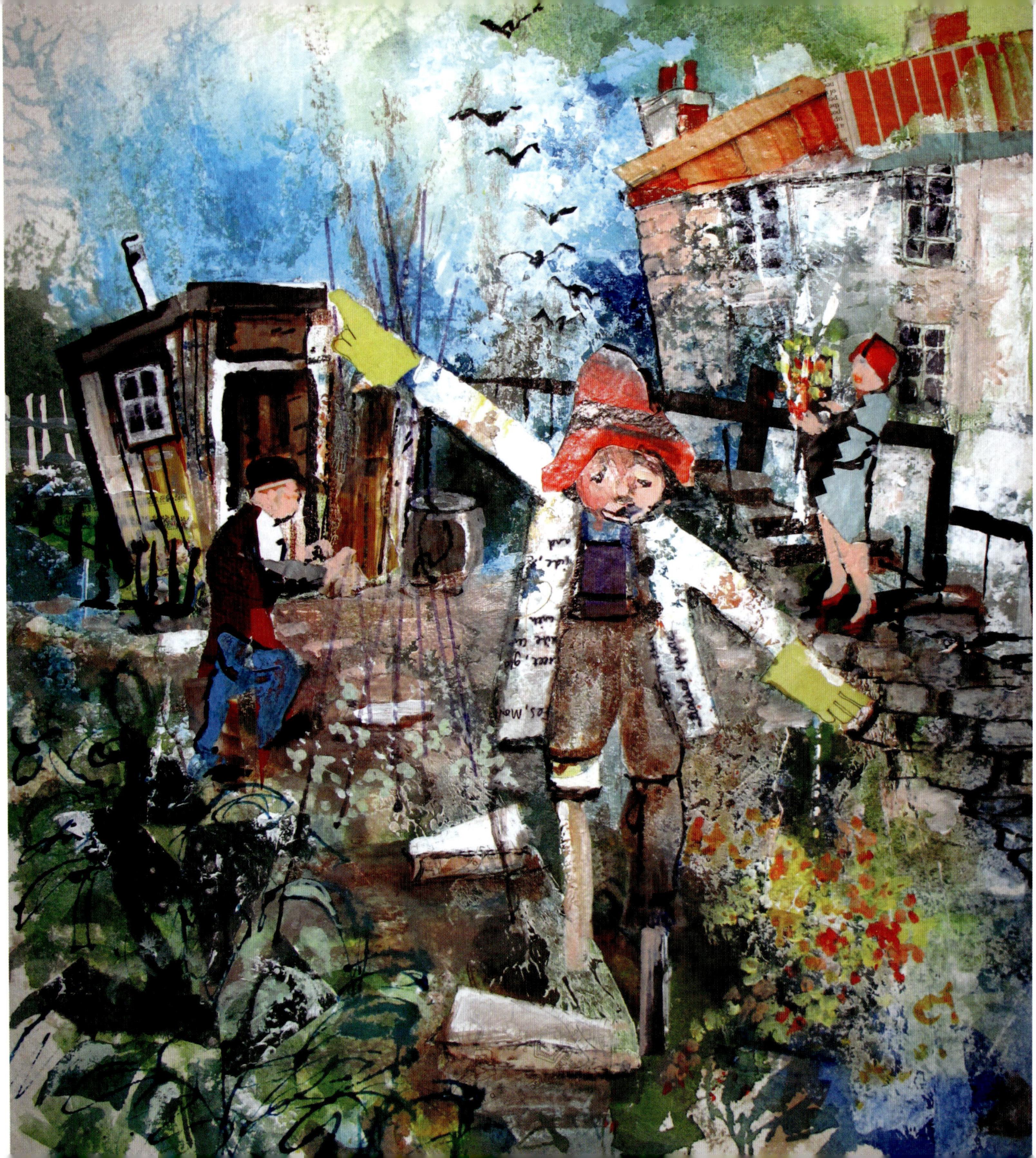

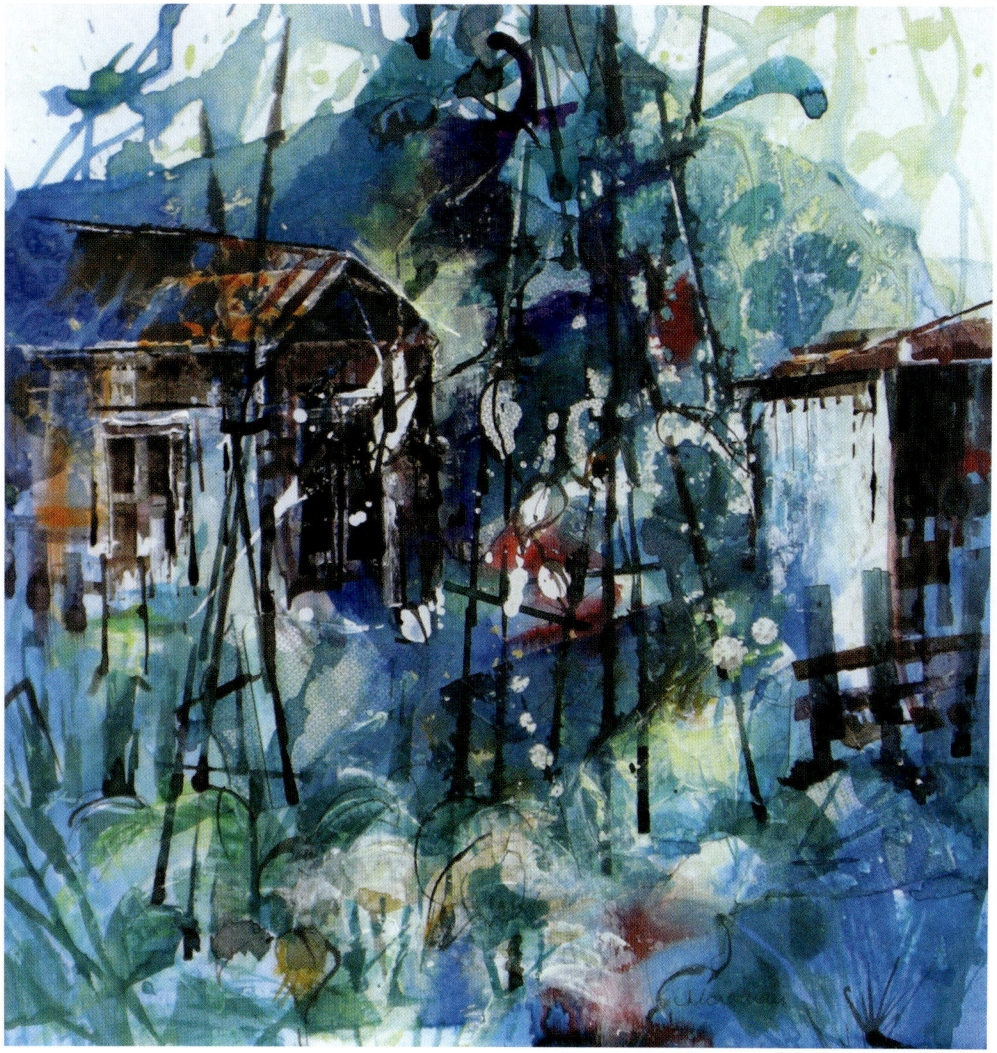

Runner Beans, mixed media, 14 x 14.5 in

Marigolds, mixed media, 20 x 18 in

There is something about an allotment that is always appealing, especially if there is a scarecrow or a hut.

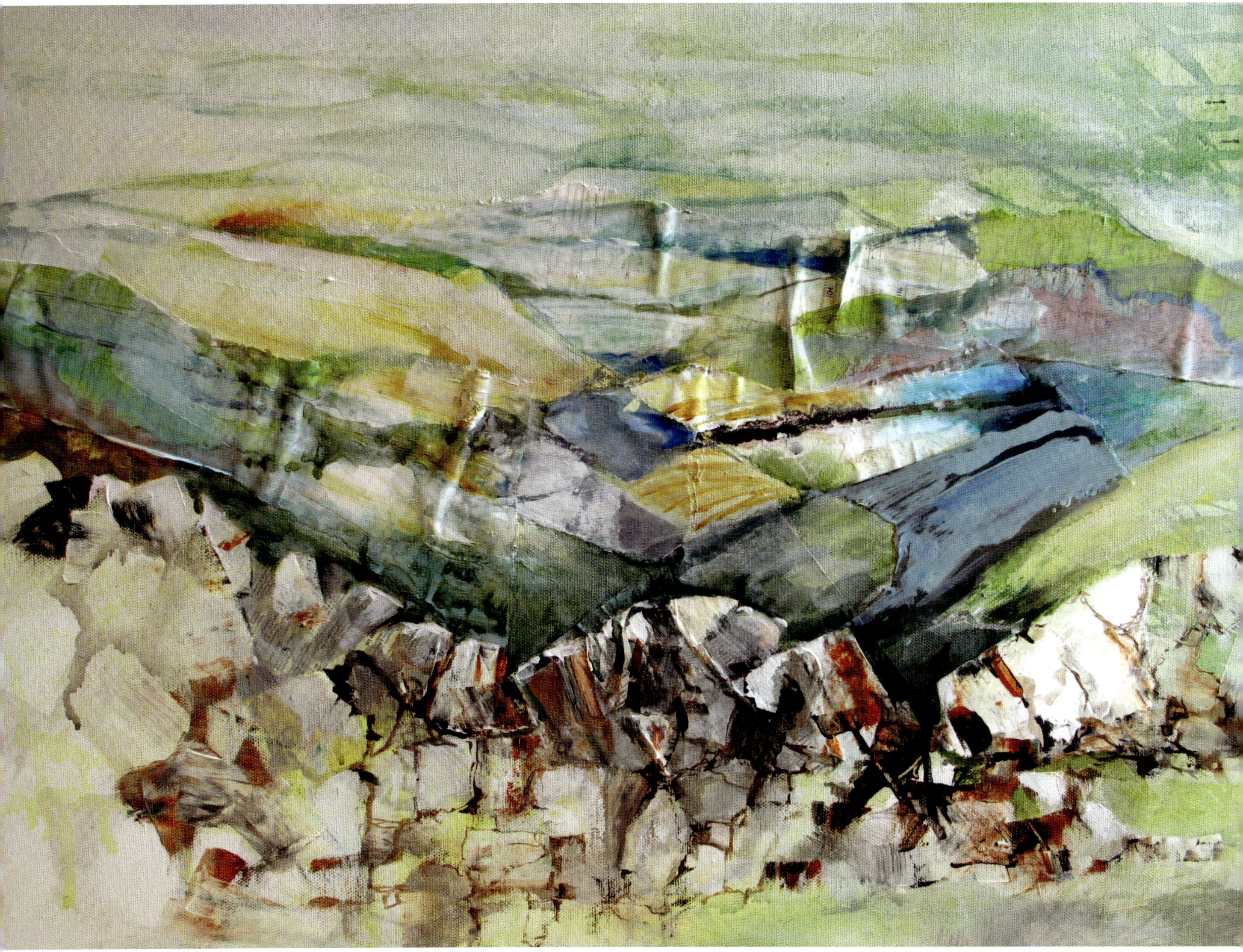

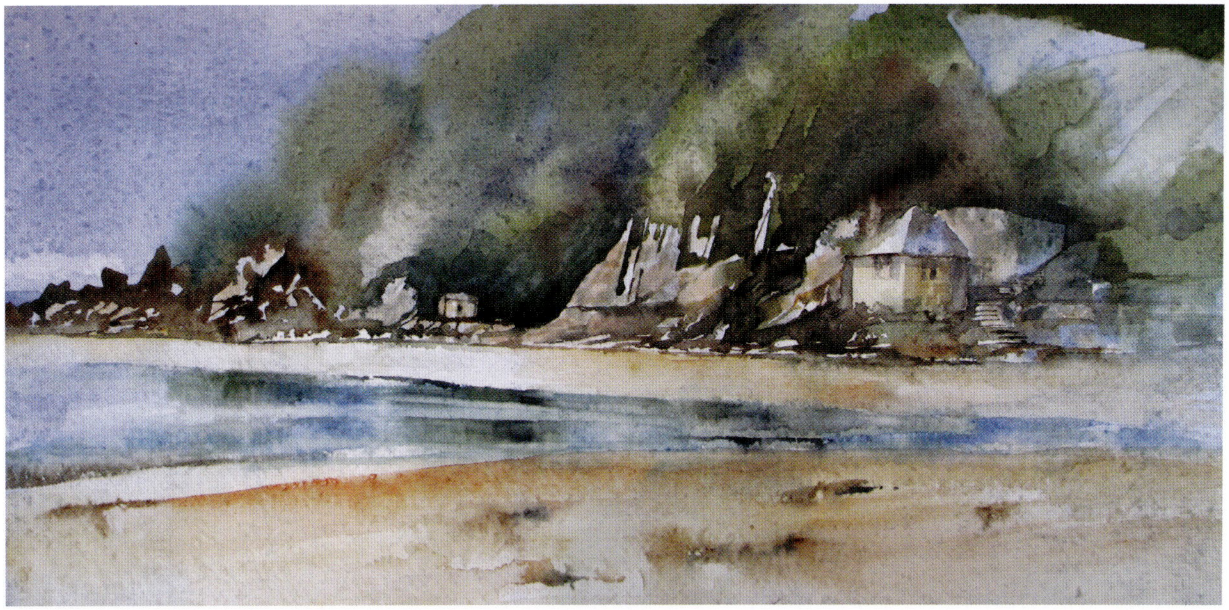

On the Plym, watercolour, 12 x 10 in

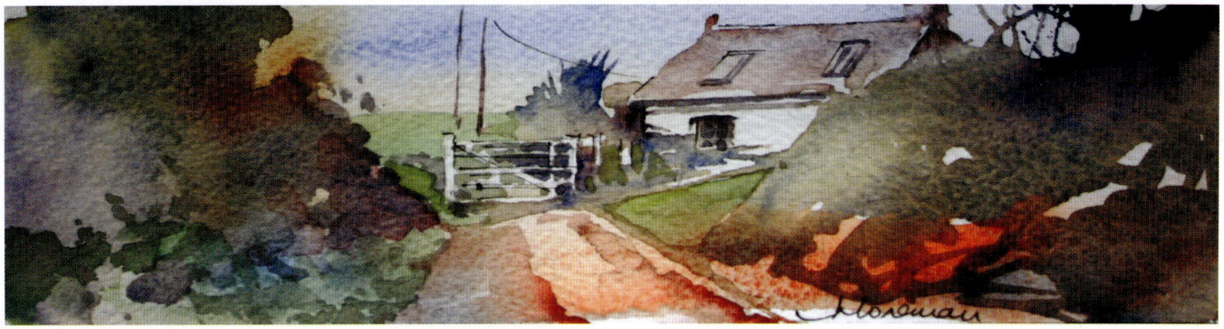

Wembury Walk, watercolour, 9 x 5 in

Over the Wall, mixed media, 18 x 14 in

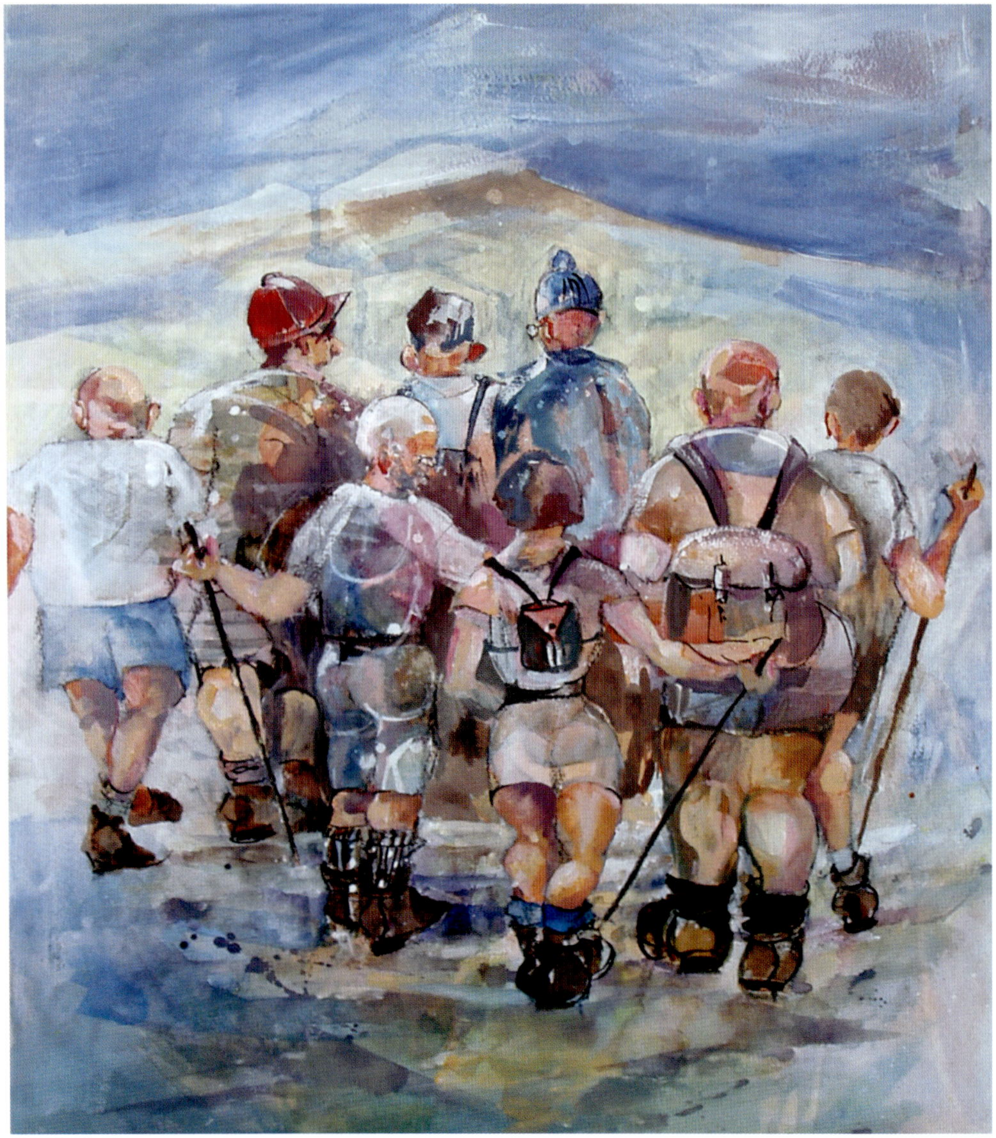

The Ramblers, watercolour, 20 x 33 in

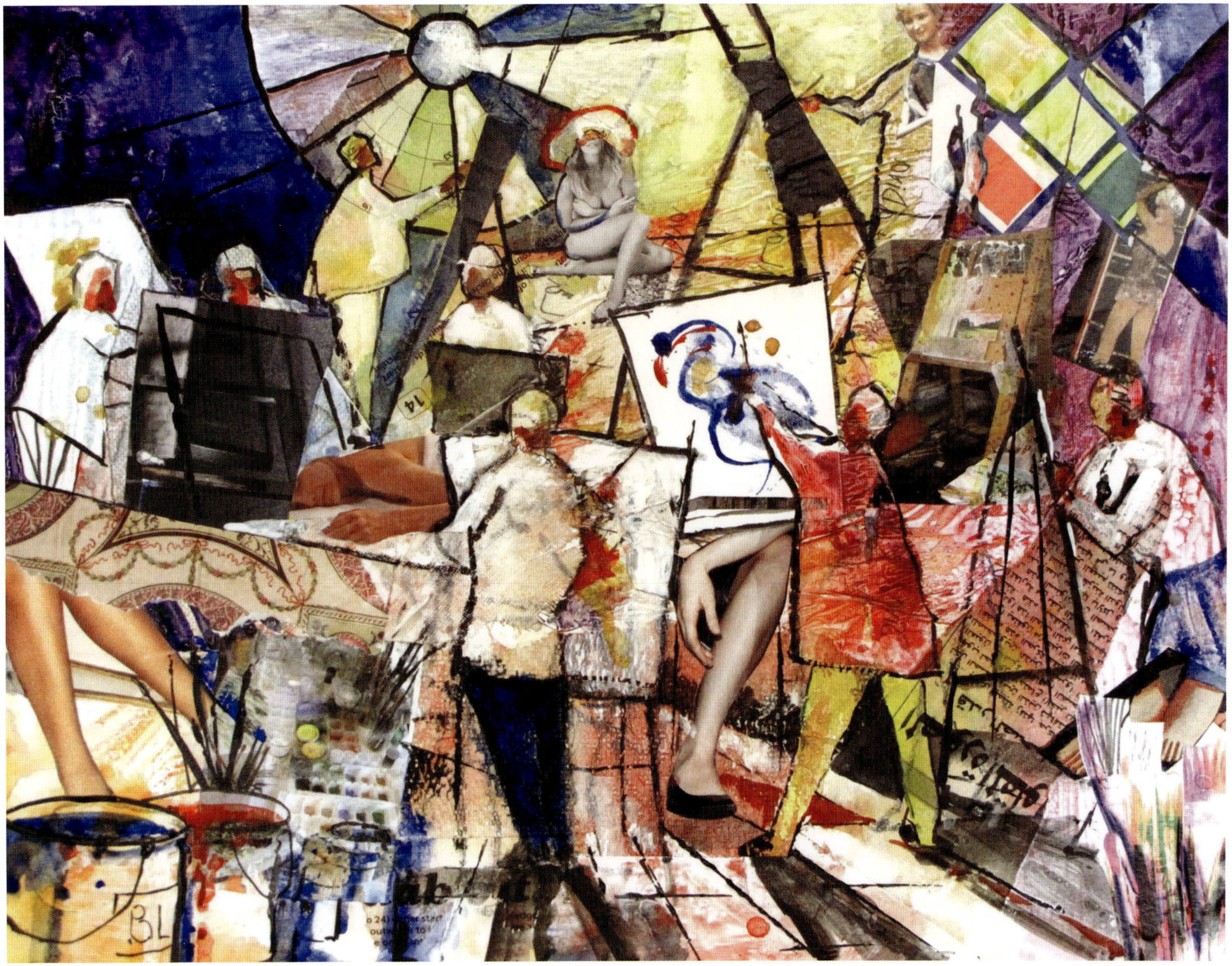

Stained Glass Life Class, collage, 18 x 15 in

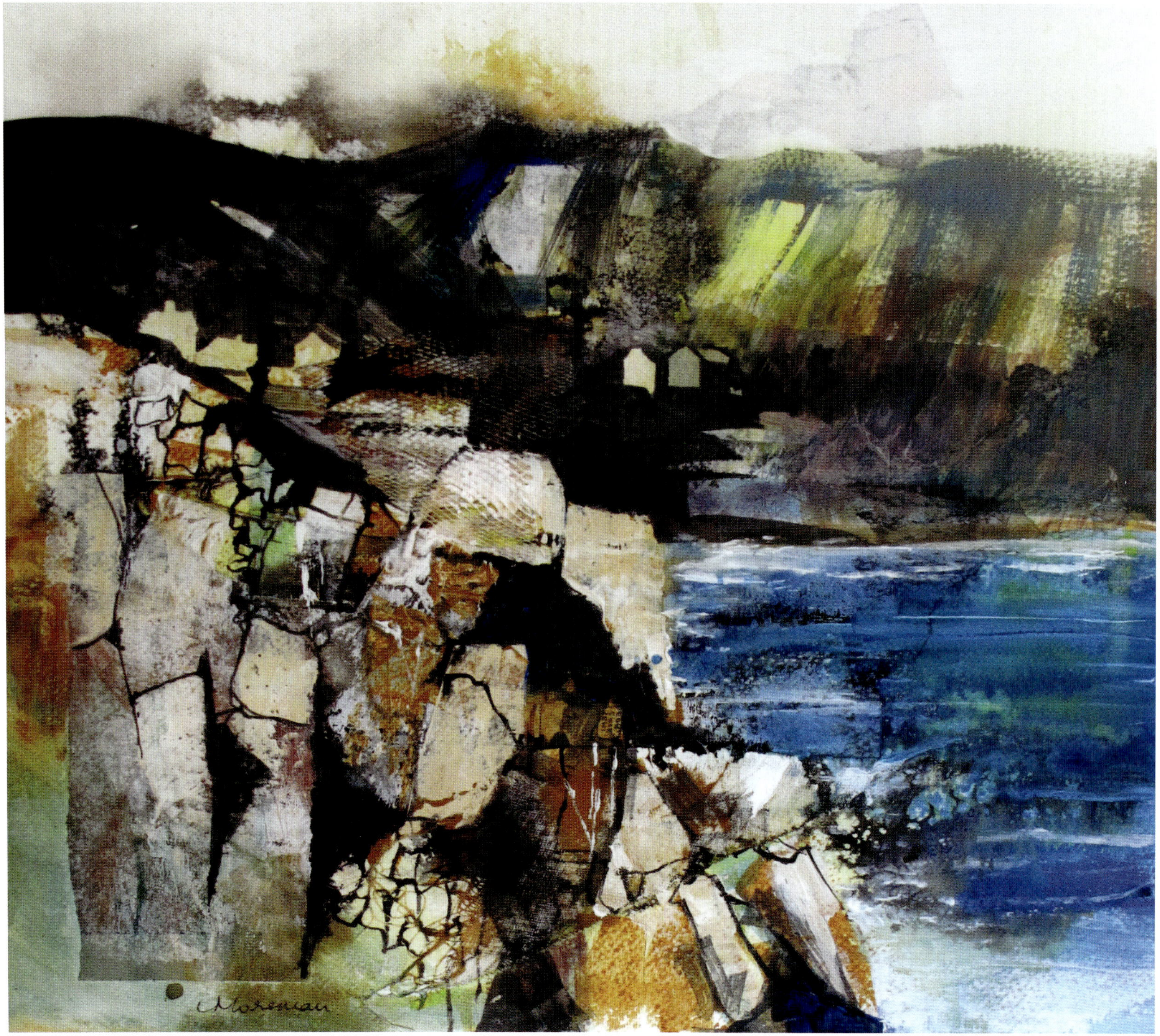
Morsman

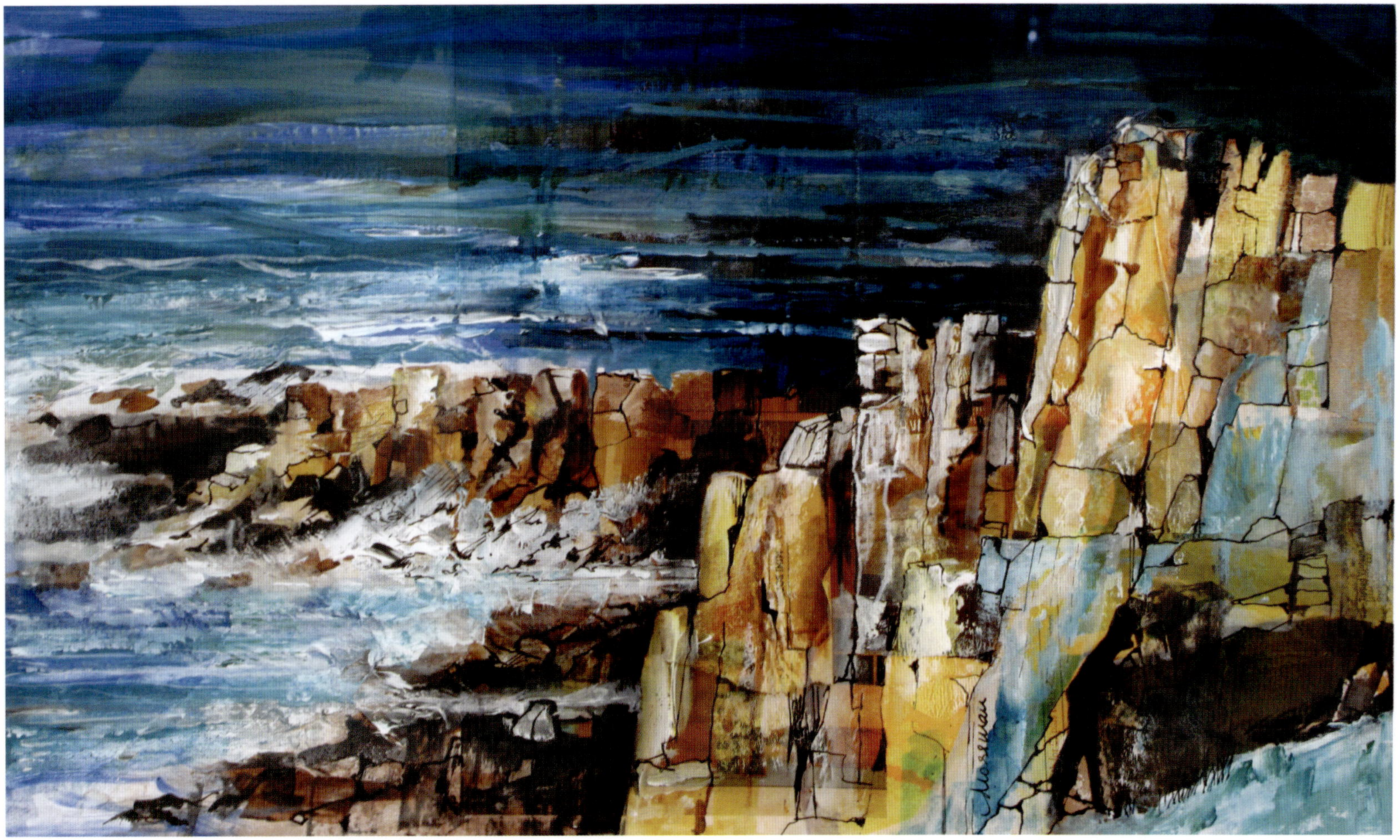

Land's End, mixed media, 16 x 13 in

Quarry Cottages, mixed media, 13 x 12 in

The Ladybird, watercolour, 16 x 13 in

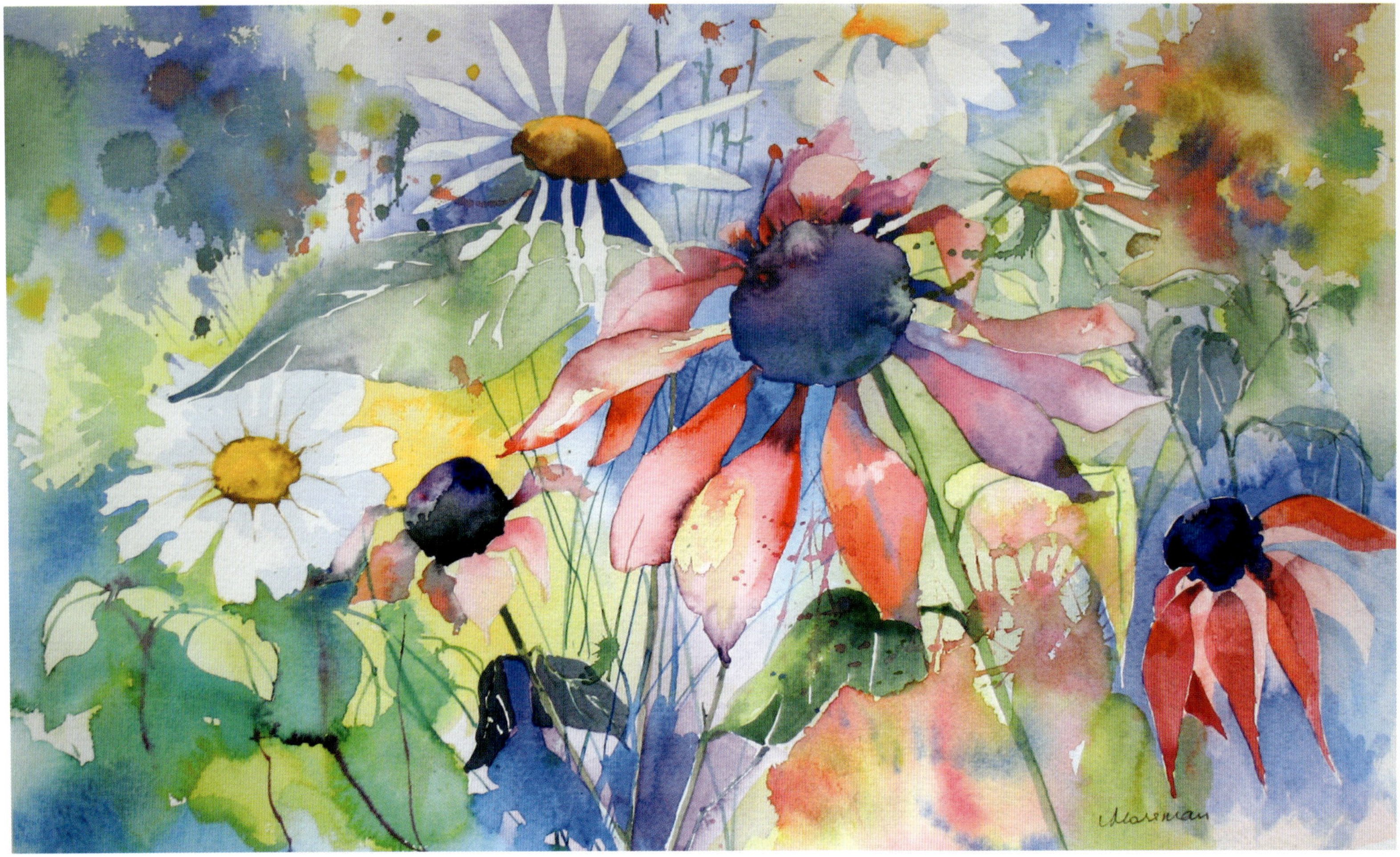

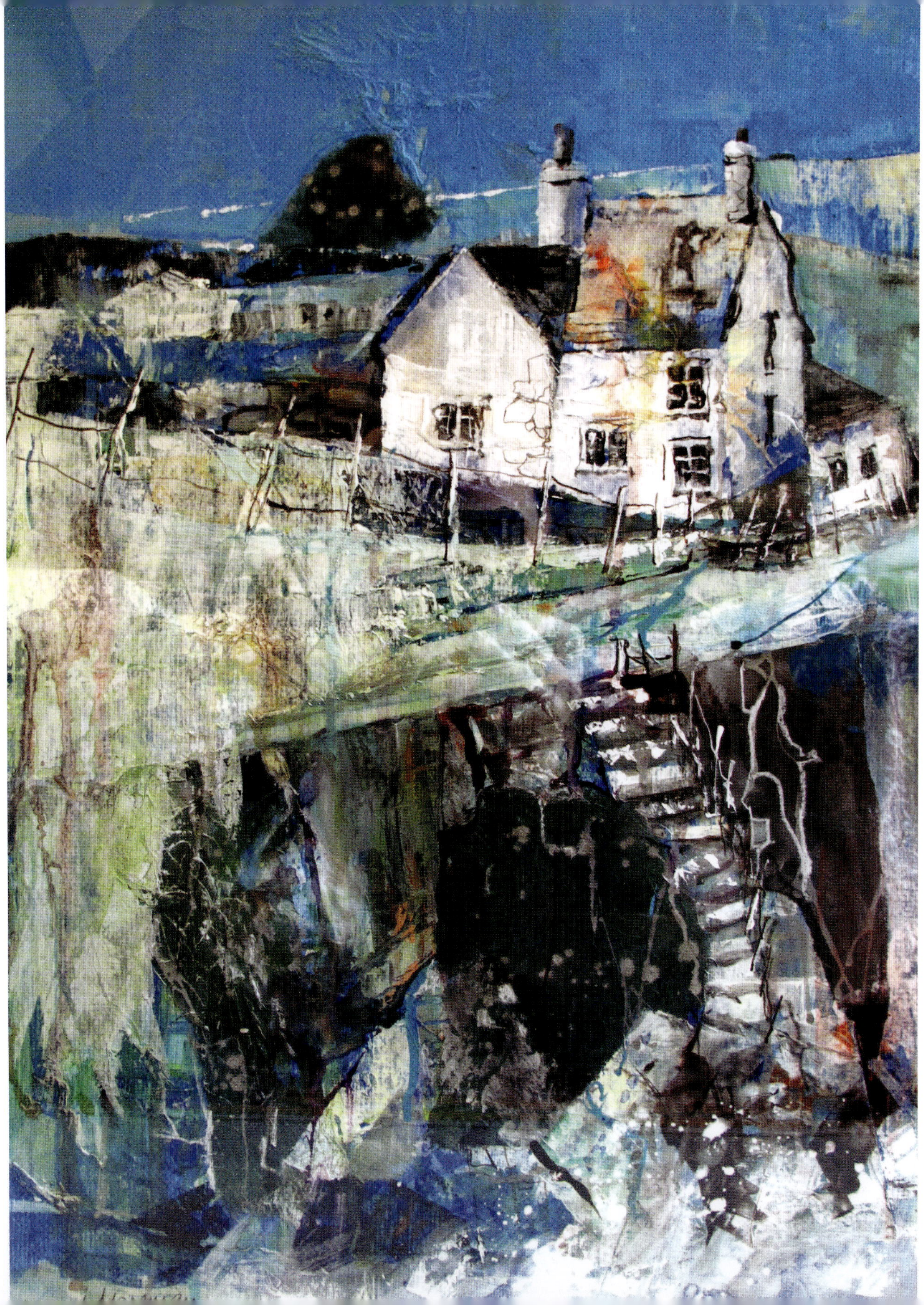

Closer to the Edge,
mixed media, 18 x 24 in

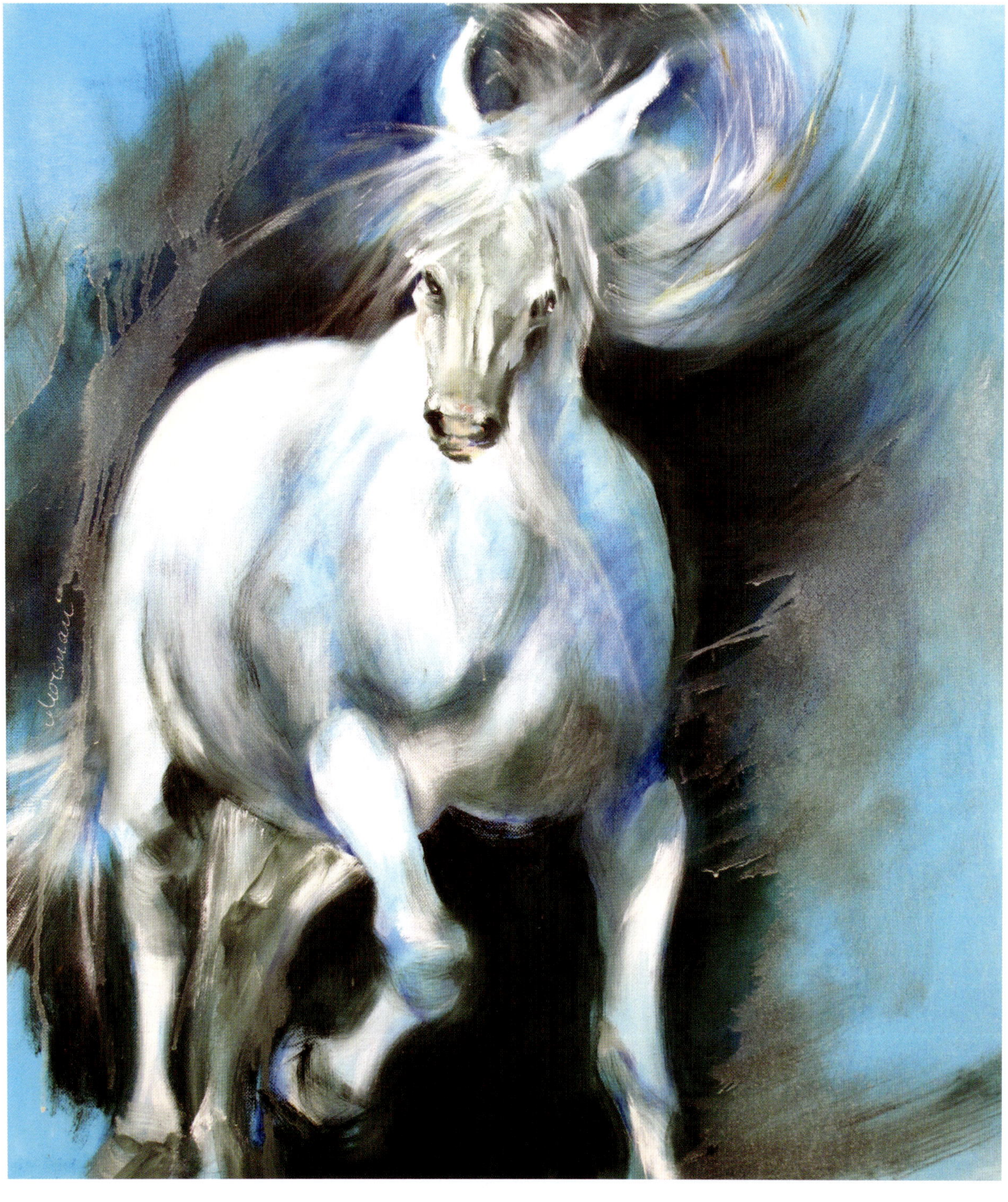

Flying Mane,
acrylic, 17 x 20 in

North Cornish Coast,
mixed media, 18 x 15 in

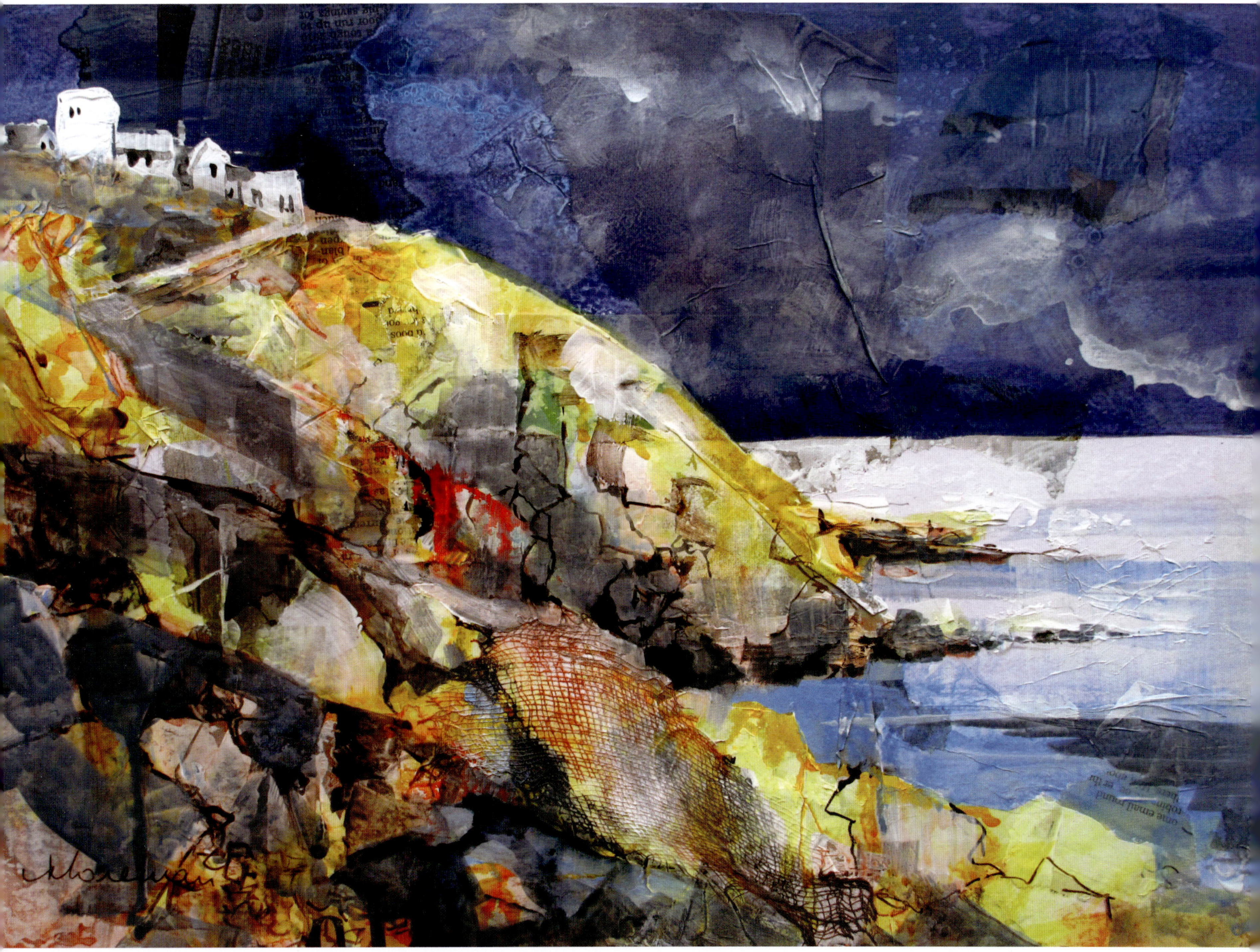

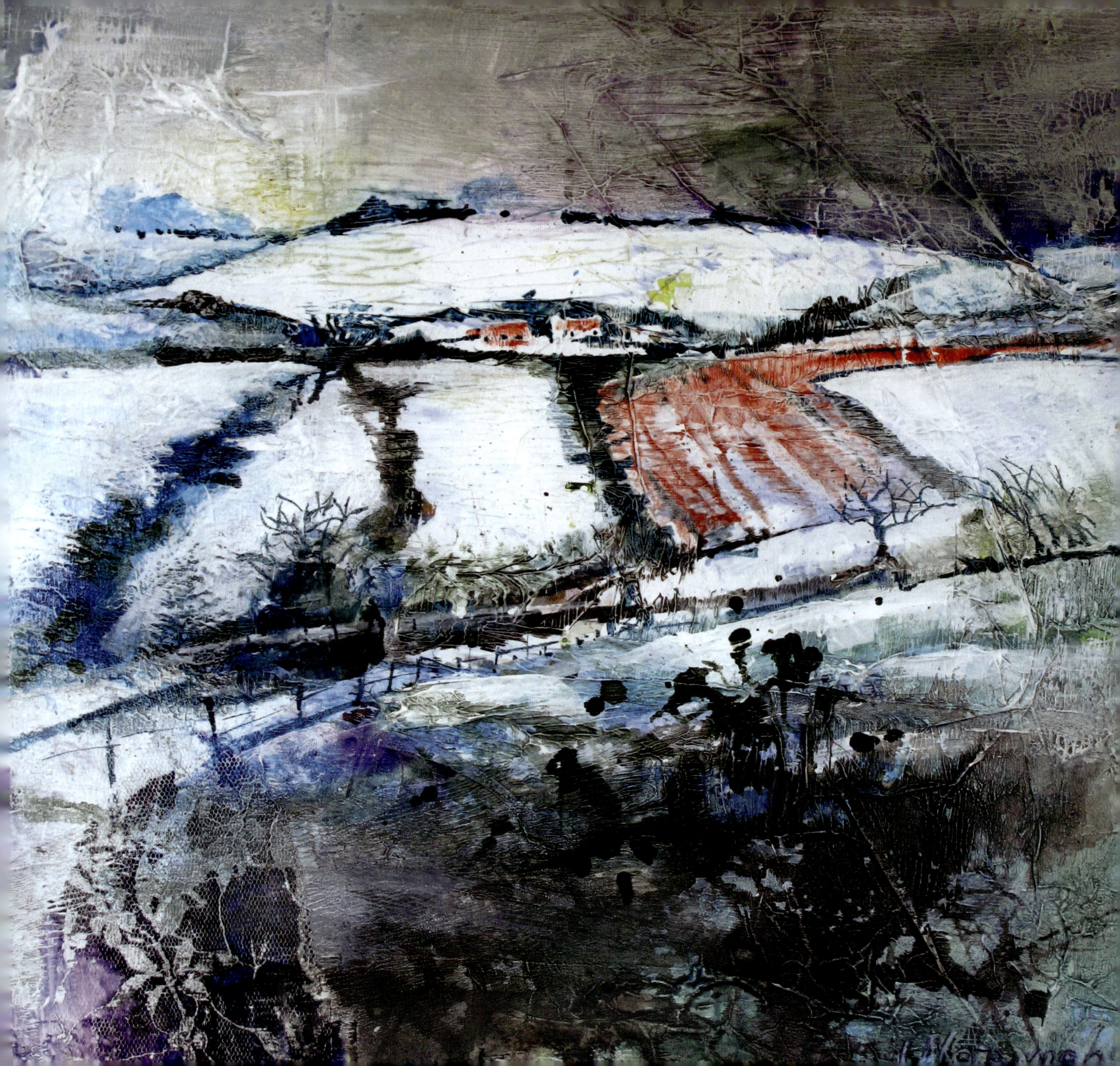

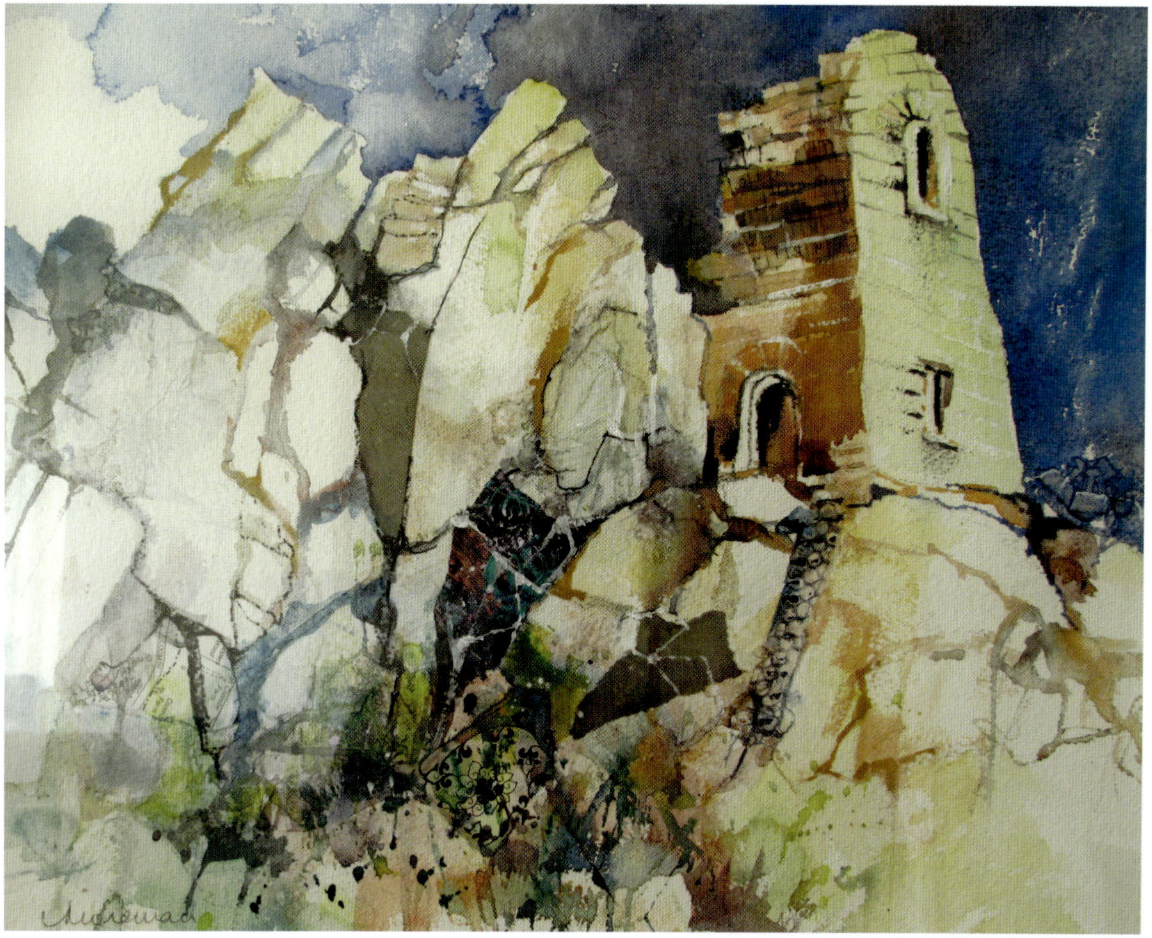

Hermit's Rock, watercolour, 17 x 13 in

Winter on the Hill, mixed media, 16 x 12 in

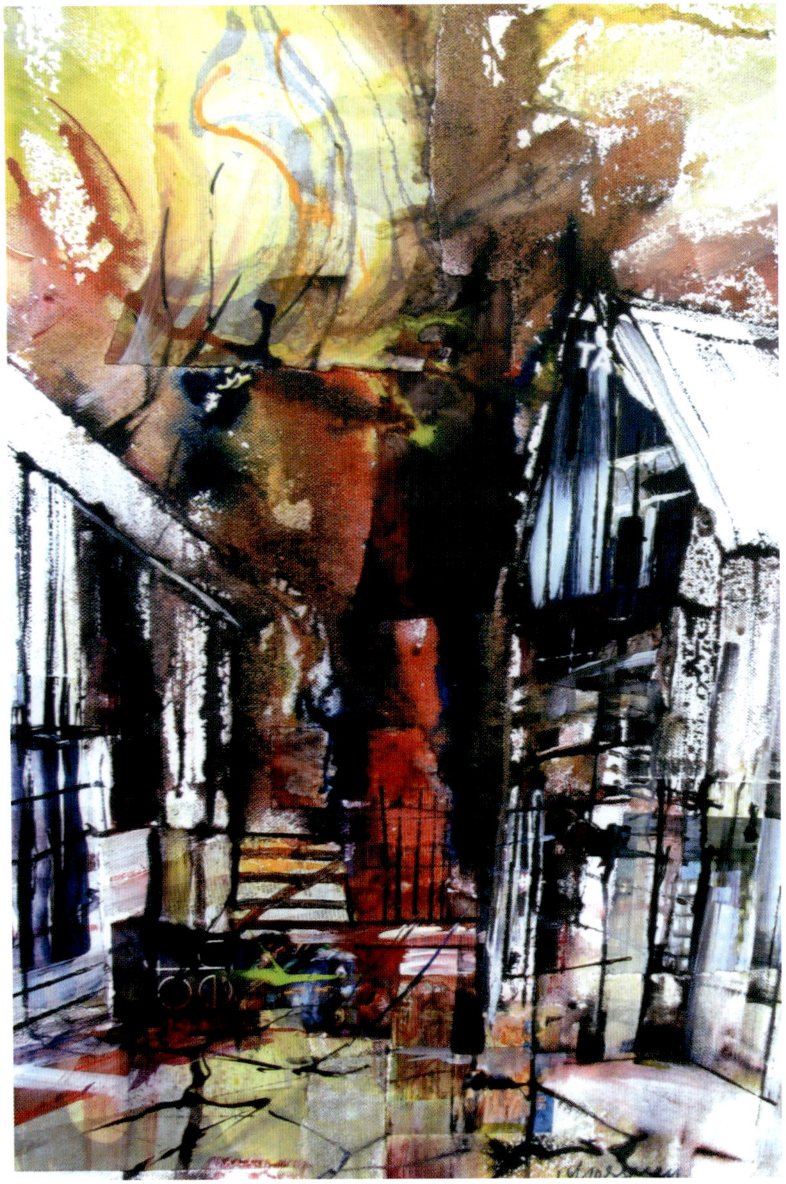

Abandoned Stables, mixed media, 13 x 18 in

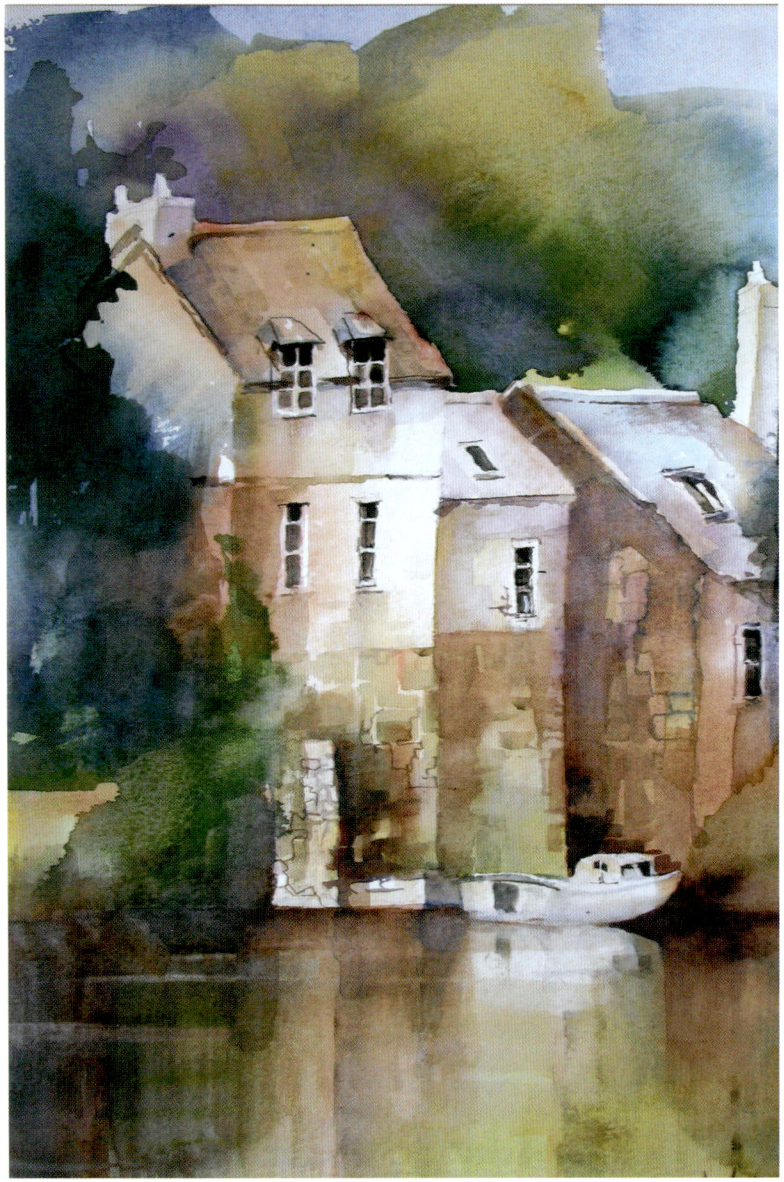

Mooring by the Backdoor, watercolour, 11 x 15 in

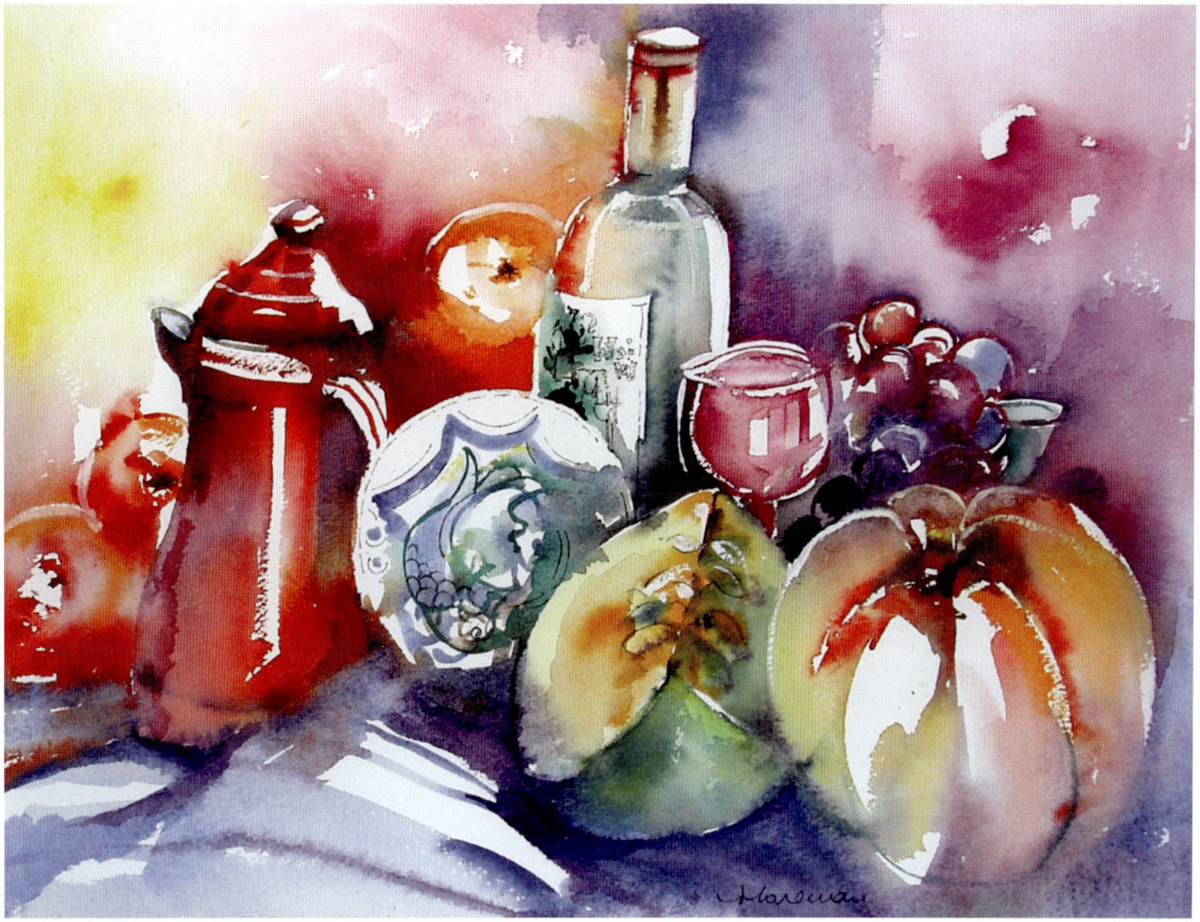

Fruit and Wine, watercolour, 14 x 16 in

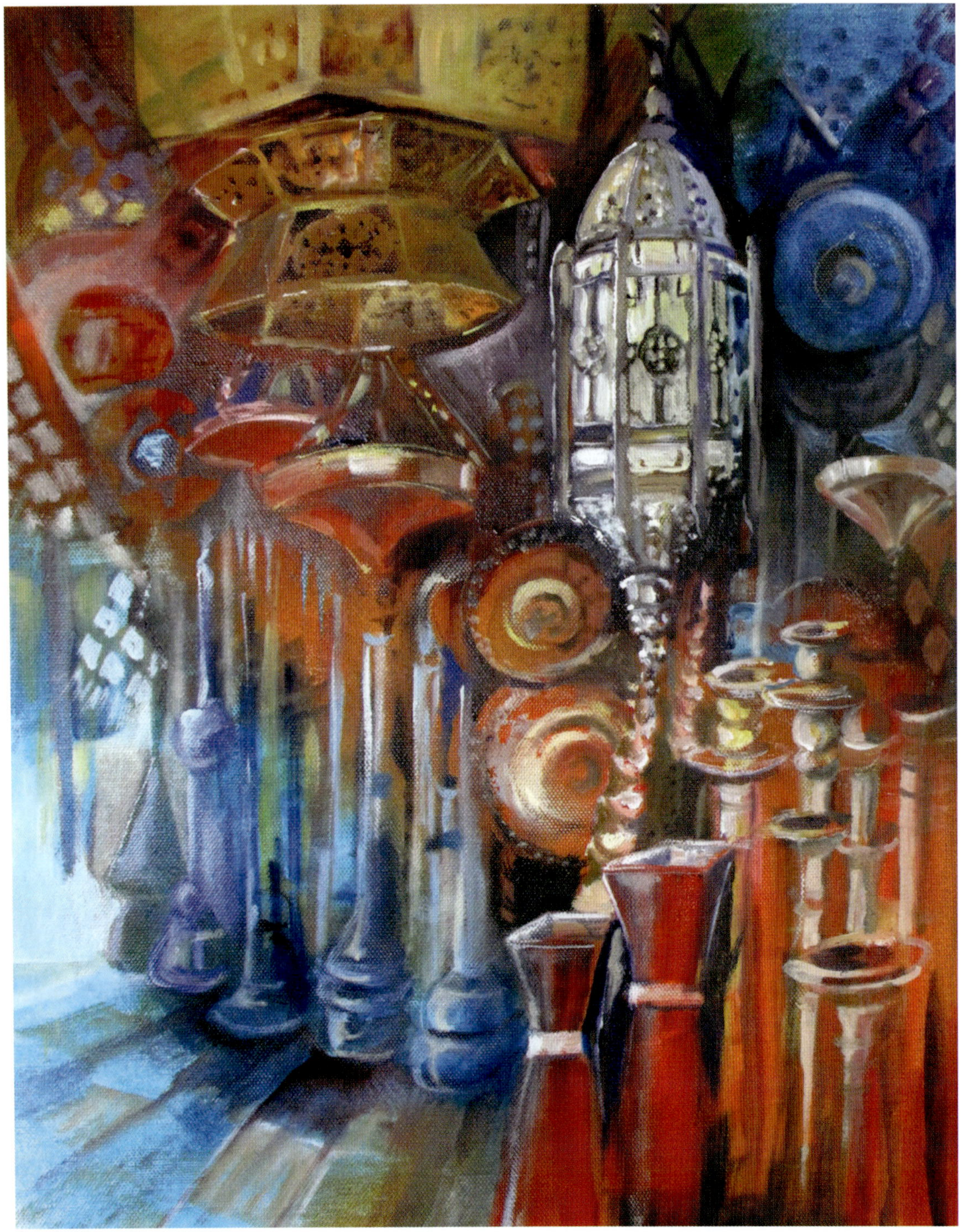

Lamps in the Souk, oil, 20 x 16 in

A shop in Fès, Morocco which was filled with lamps of every description.

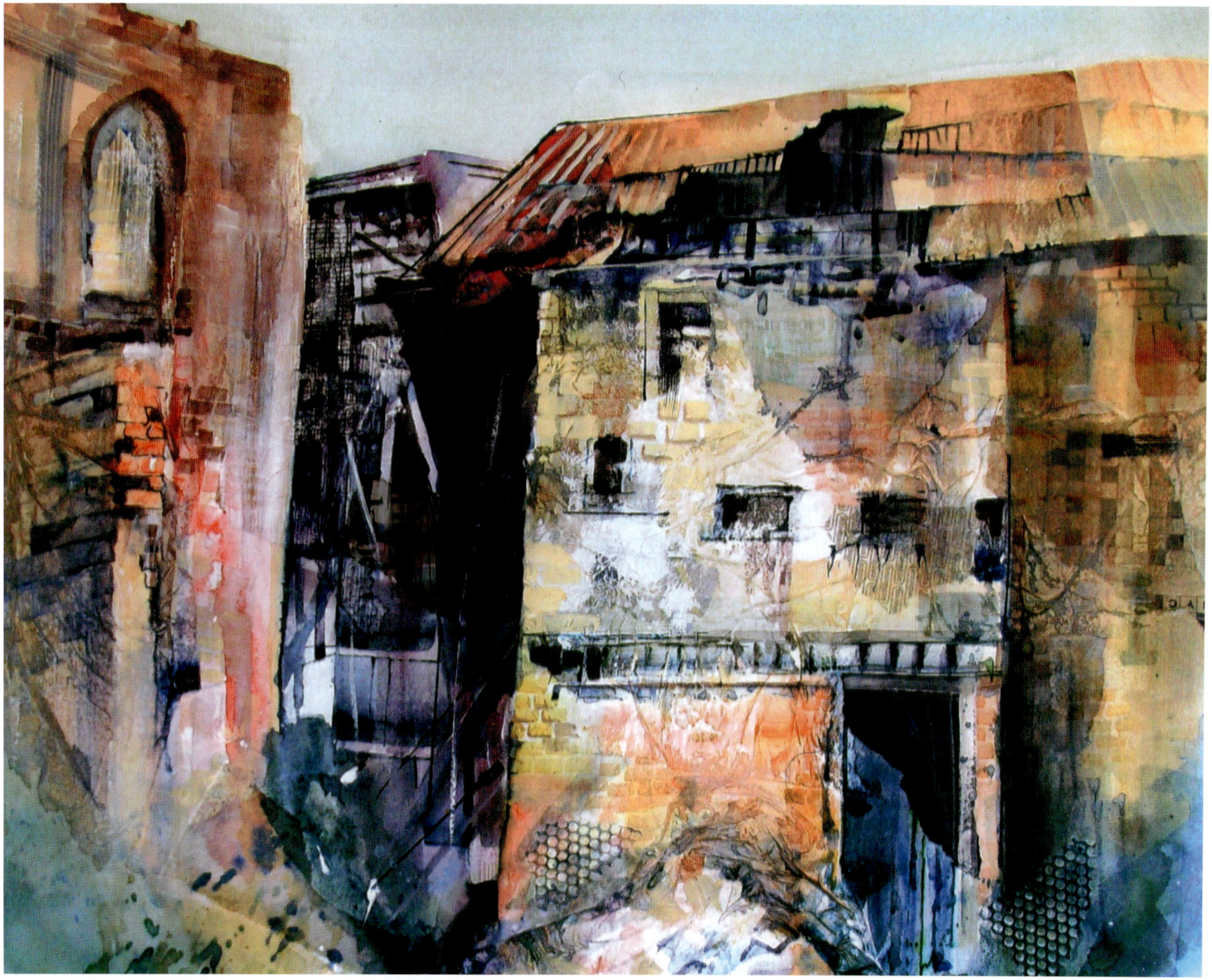

Dereliction, mixed media, 19 x 16 in

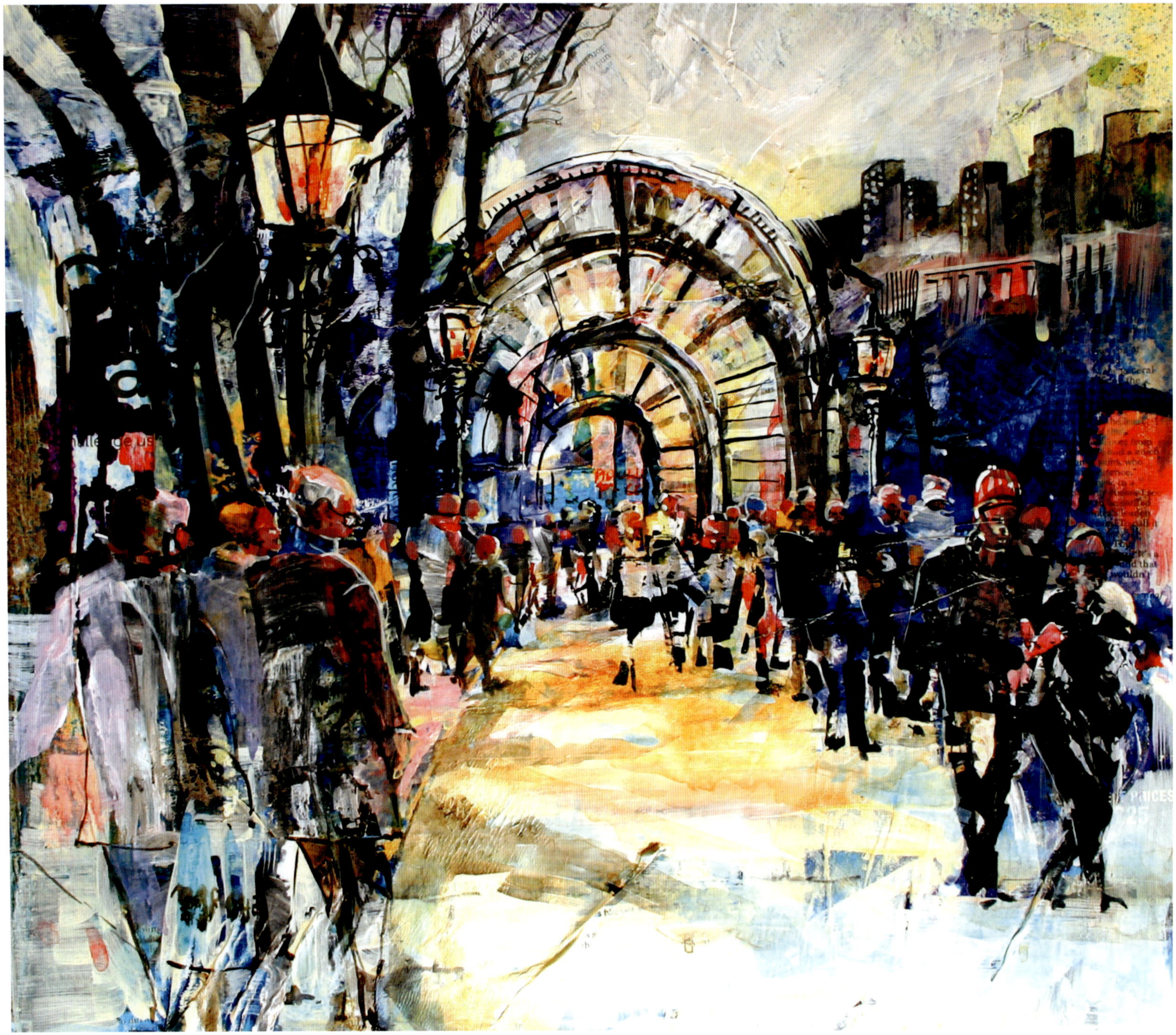

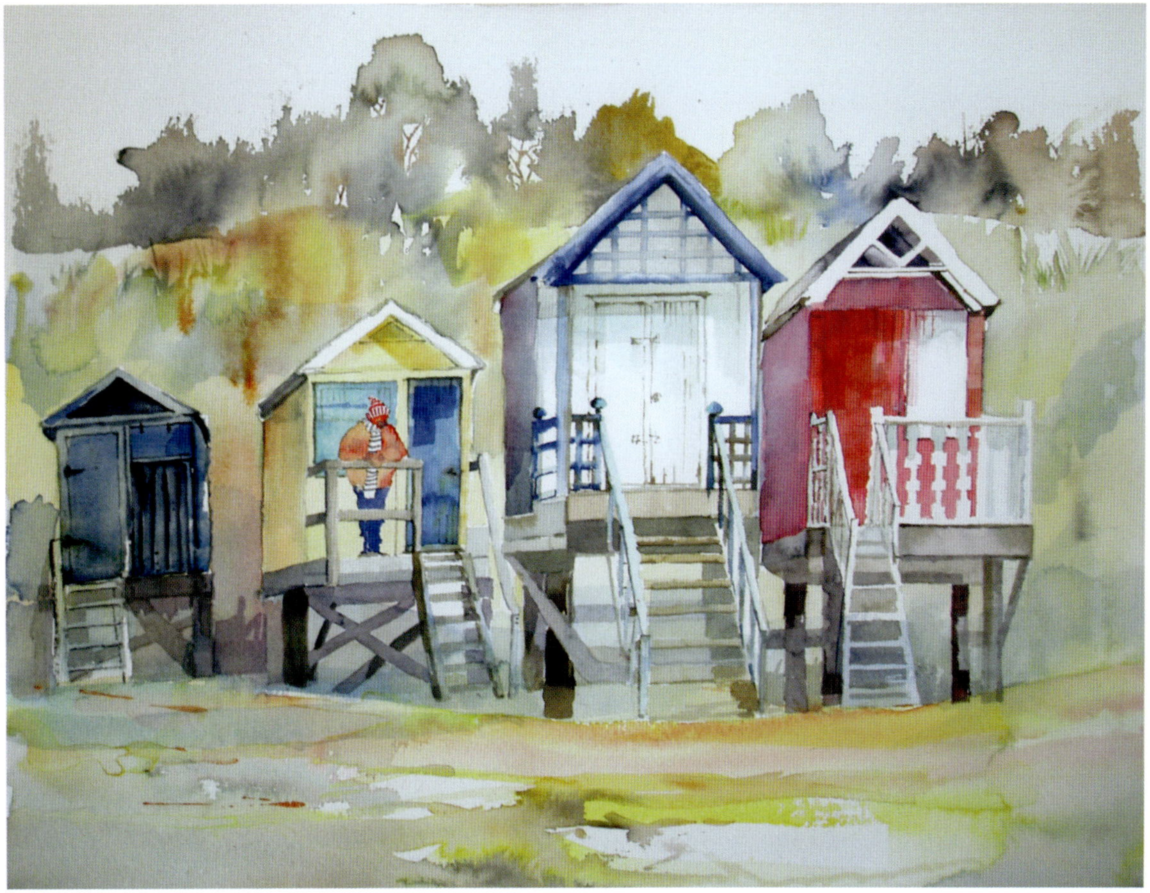

Too Cold Today!, watercolour, 15 x 12 in

Les Halles, mixed media, 22 x 20 in

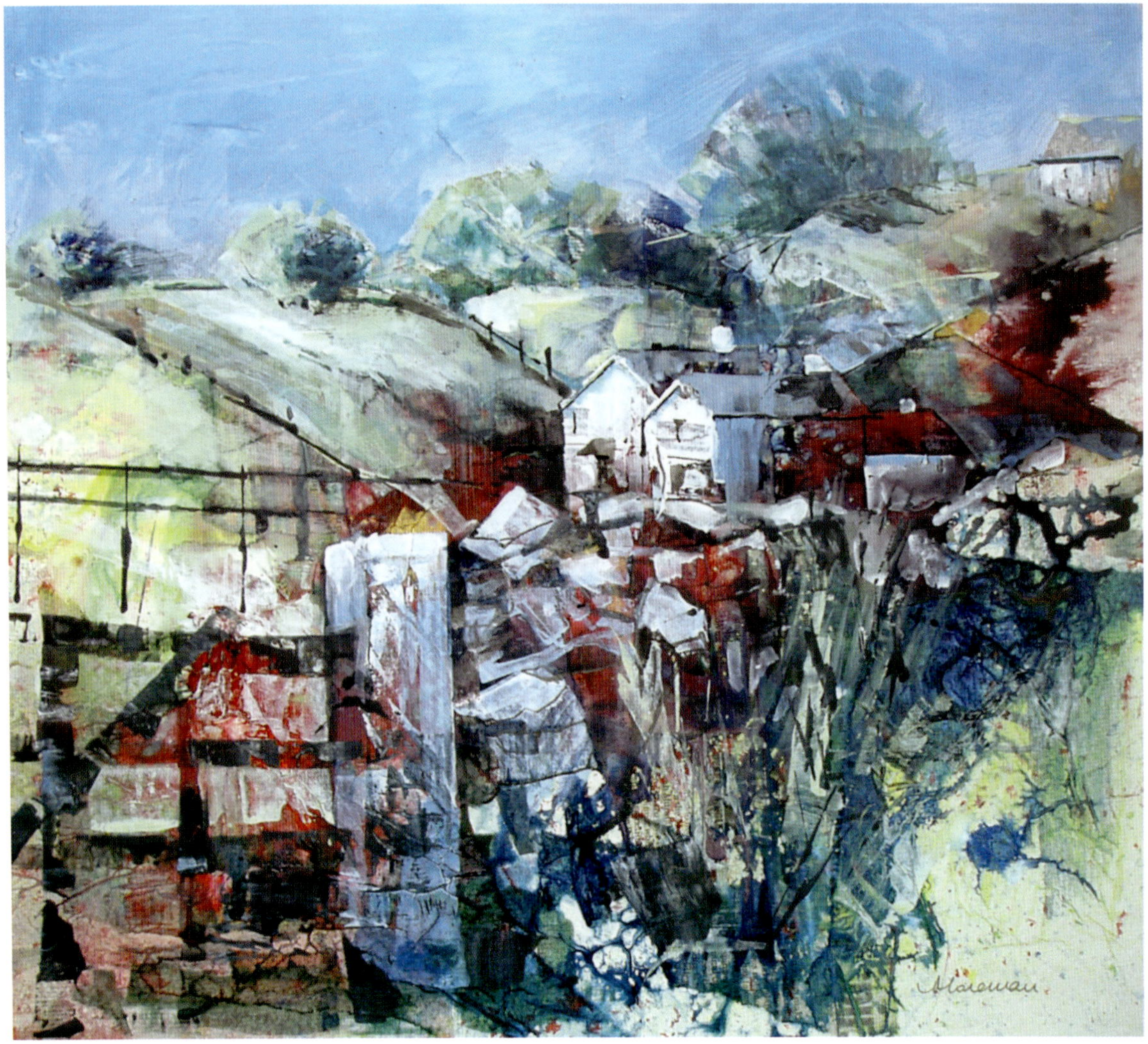

Over the Gate, mixed media, 15 x 12 in

Blue Boat, mixed media, 24 x 20 in

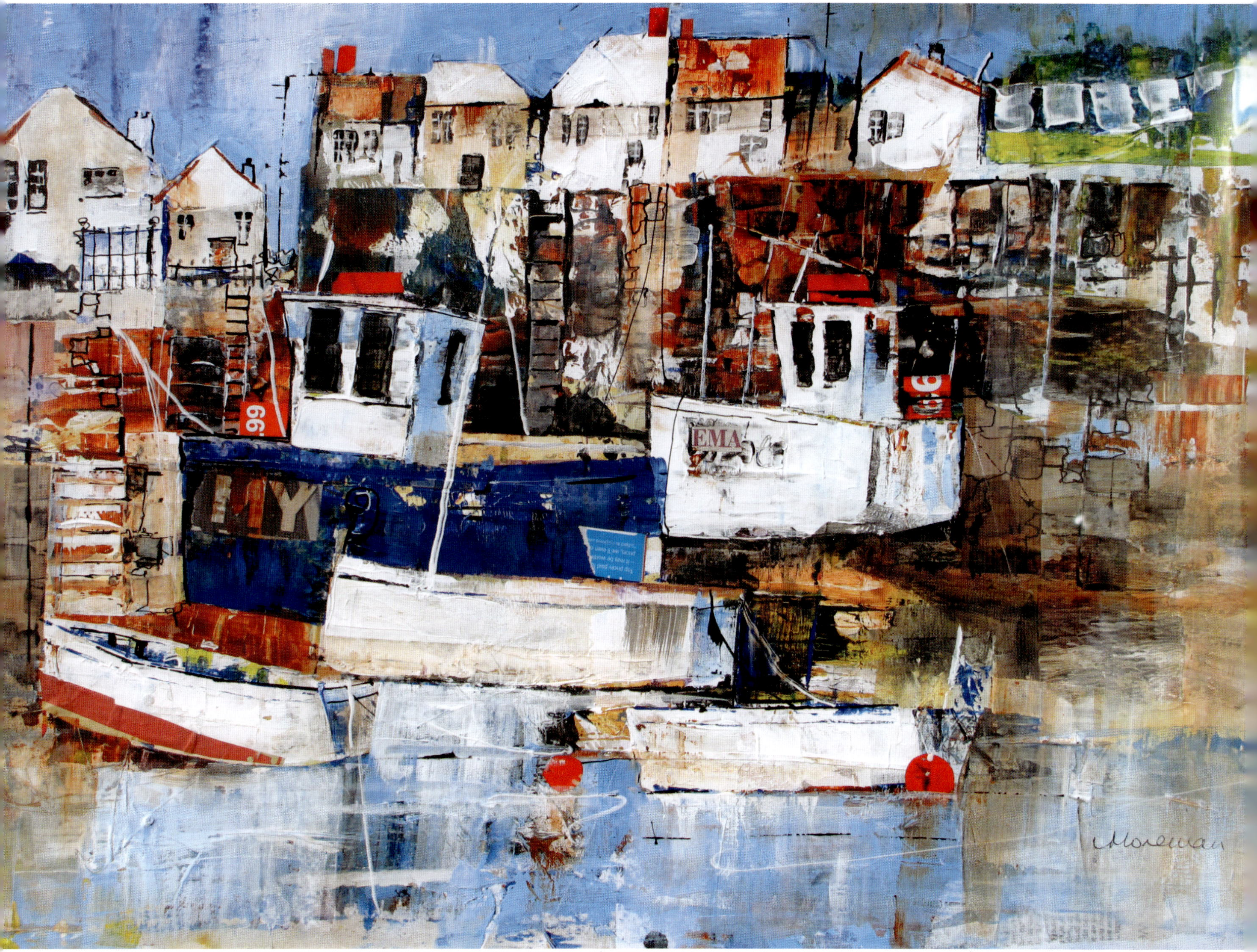
99
EMA

Pope's Quay, Noss Mayo,
mixed media, 18 x 14 in

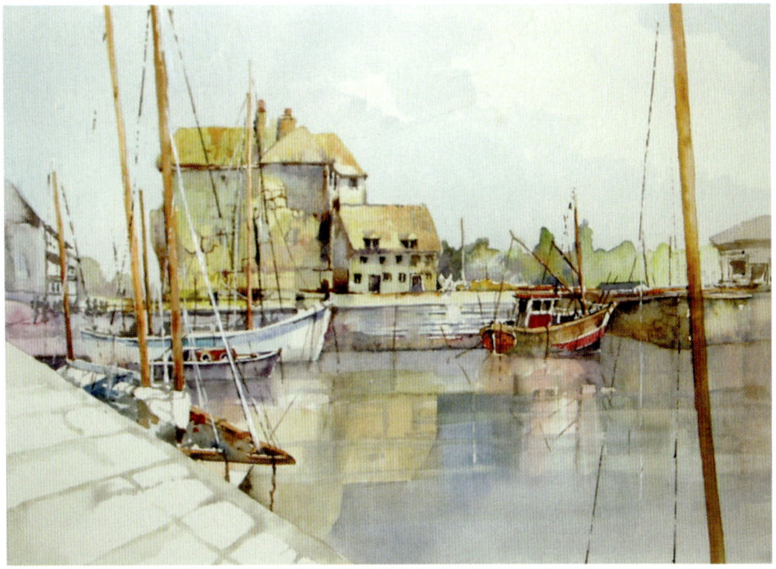

Honfleur, watercolour, 12 x 10 in

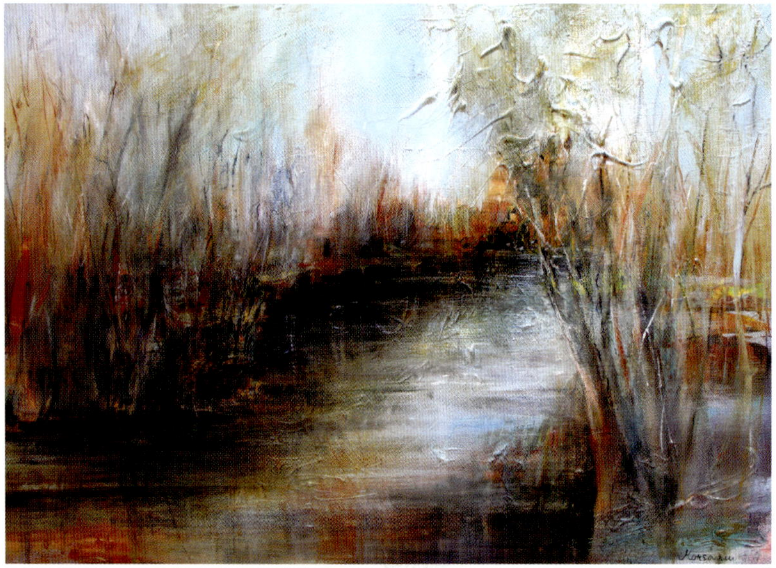

Texture from a previously painted picture on a large canvas using a loose approach with watery acrylic, 26 x 30 in.

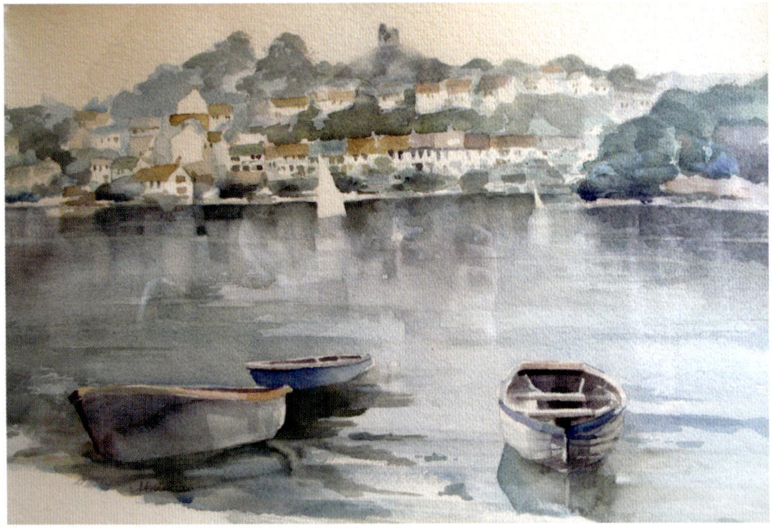

Sailing By, watercolour, 14 x 12 in

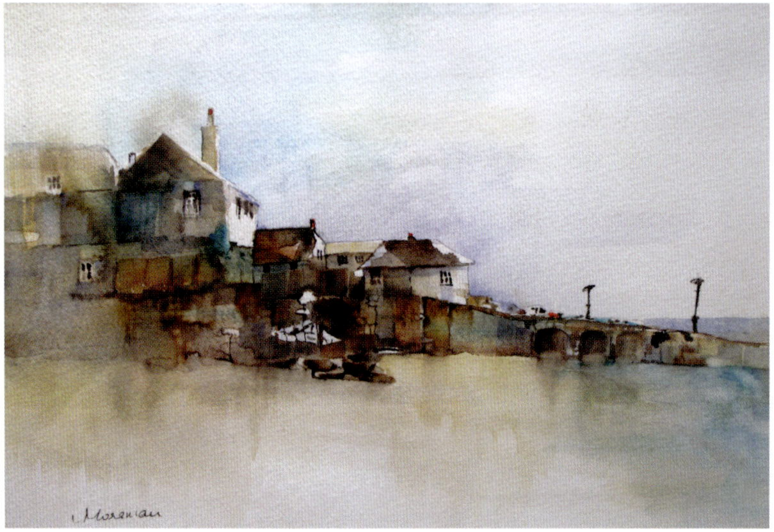

Saltash, watercolour, 15 x 12 in

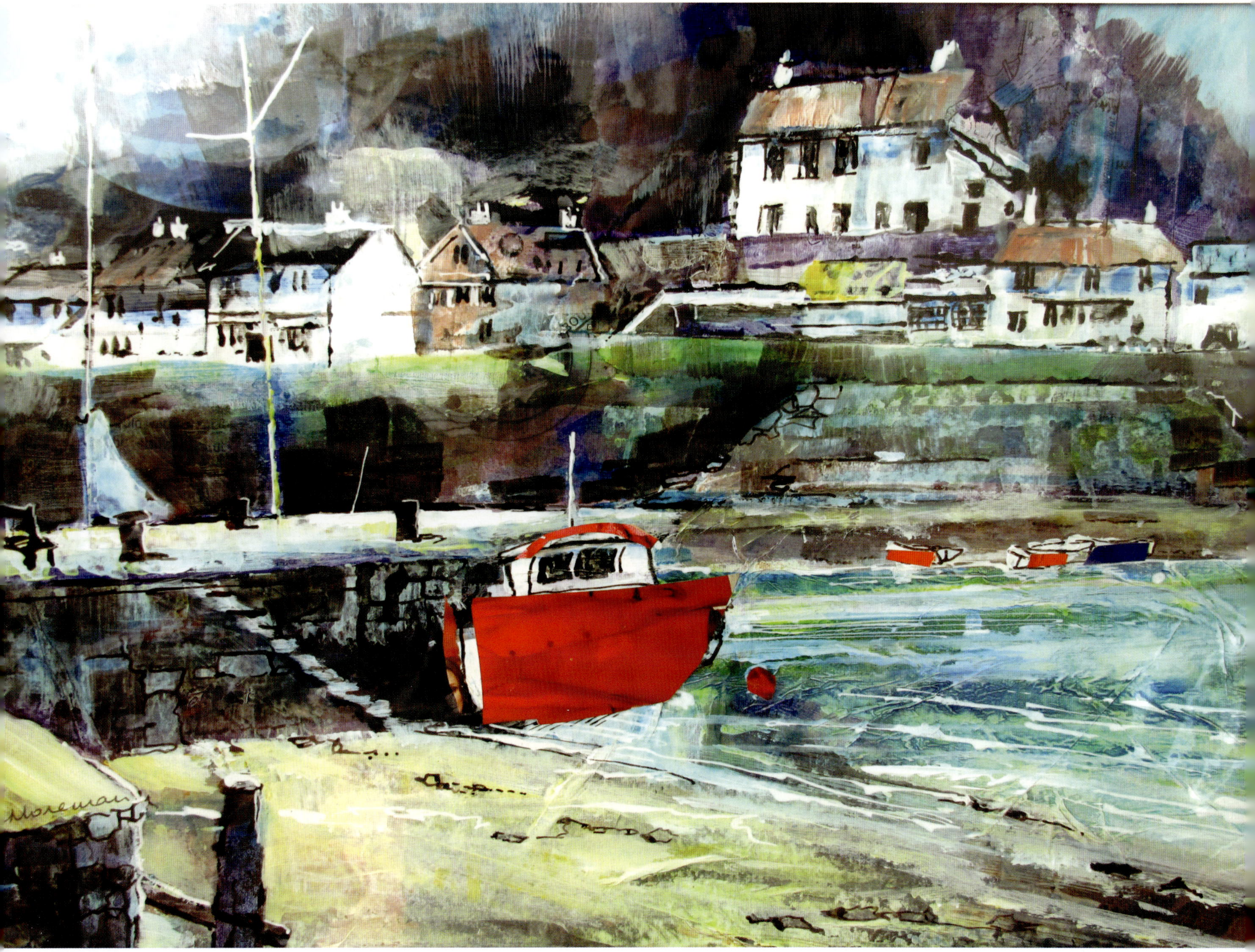

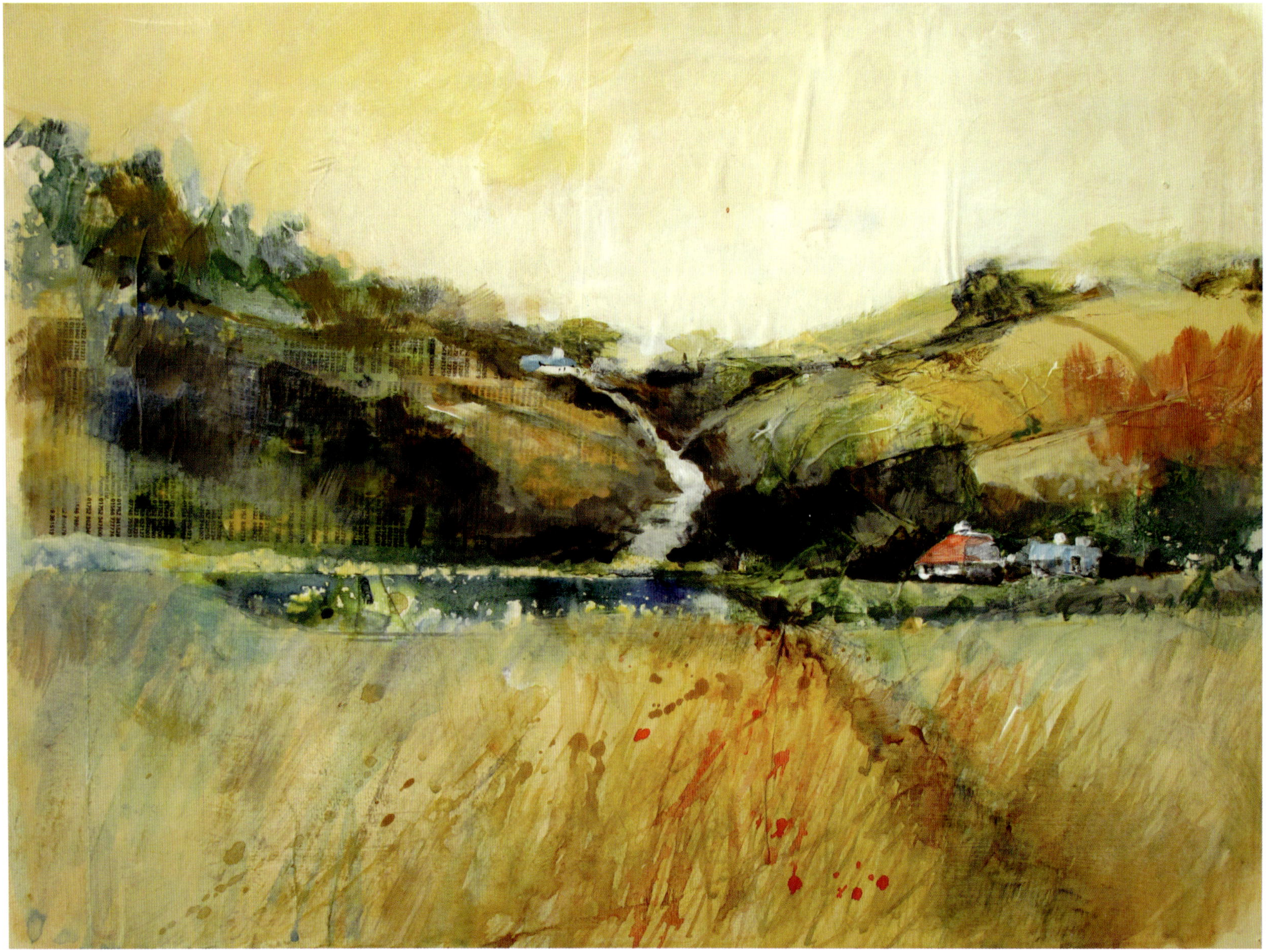

Poppyfield, mixed media, 17 x 14 in

Three Looking to Escape, watercolour, 12 x 12 in

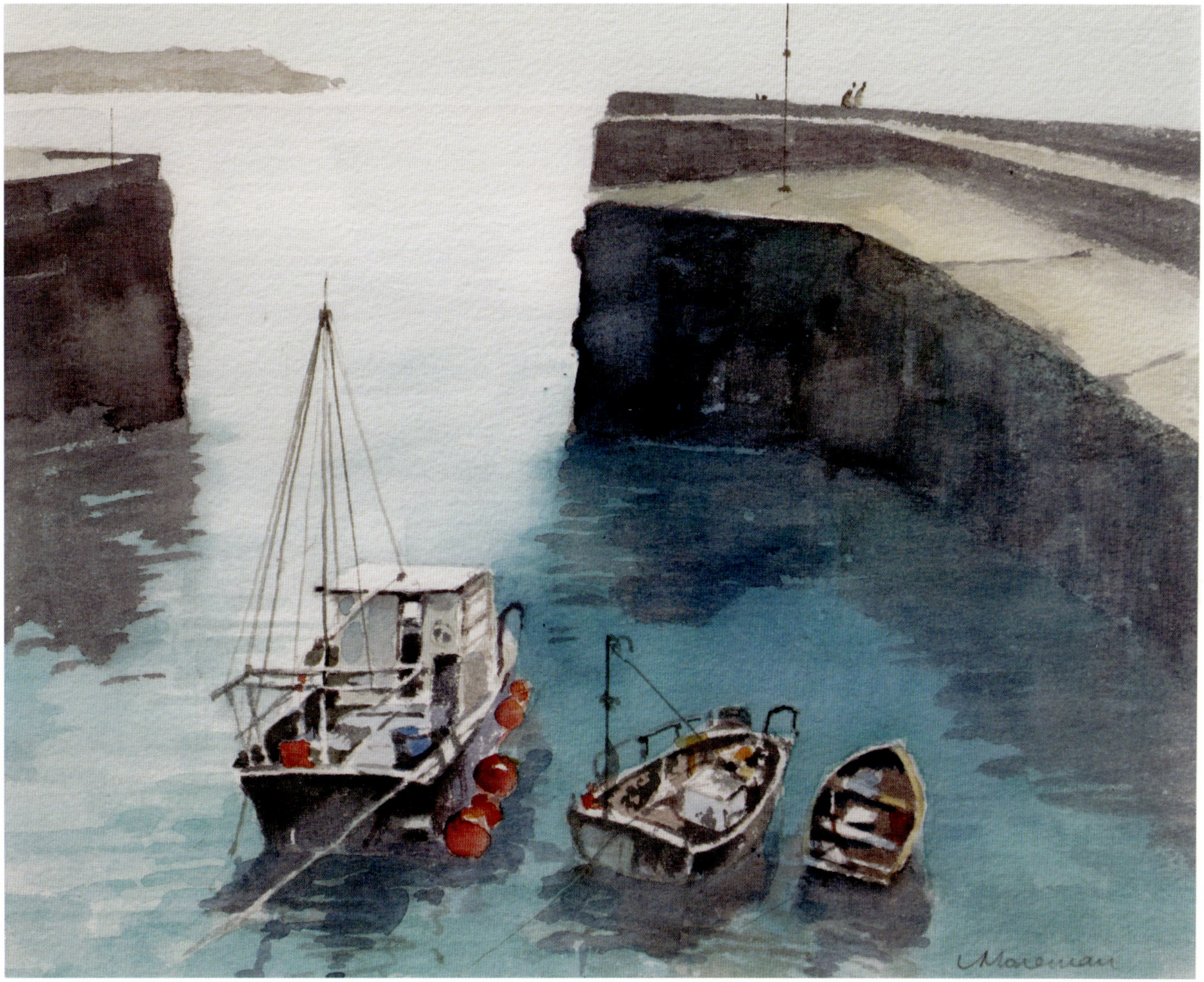

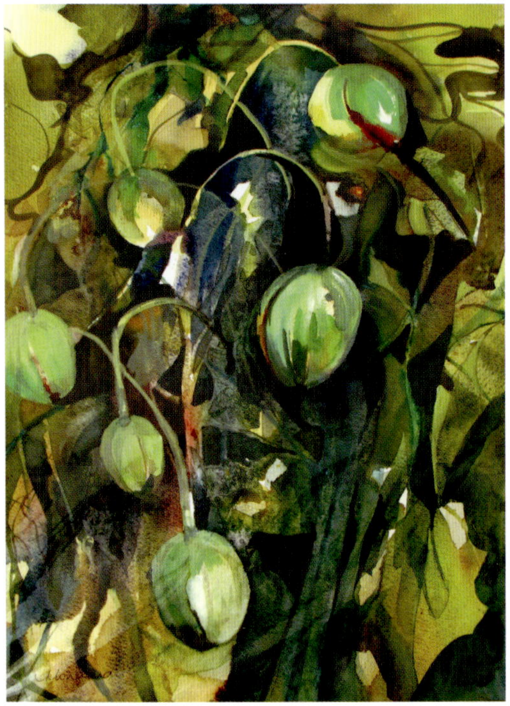

Poppyheads, watercolour, 14 x 22 in

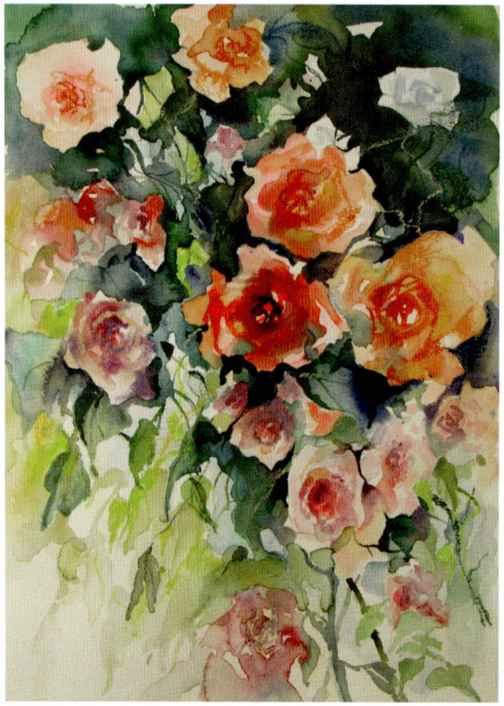

Roses I, watercolour, 12 x 15 in

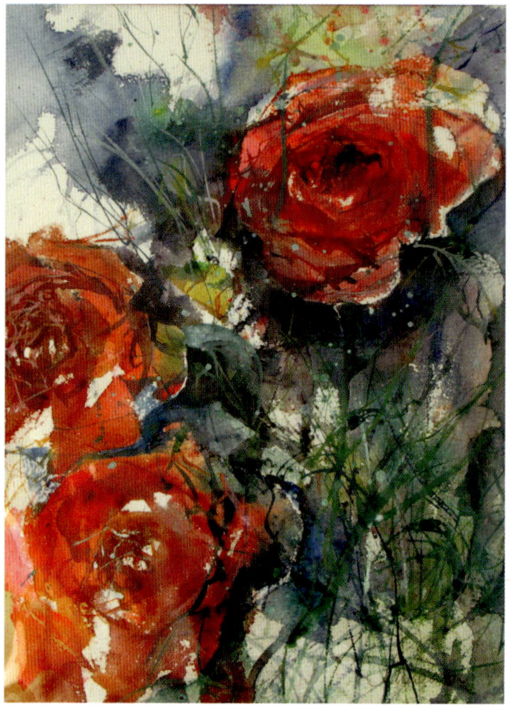

Roses II, watercolour, 17 x 19 in

Riverside Road East,
collage, 20 x 20 in

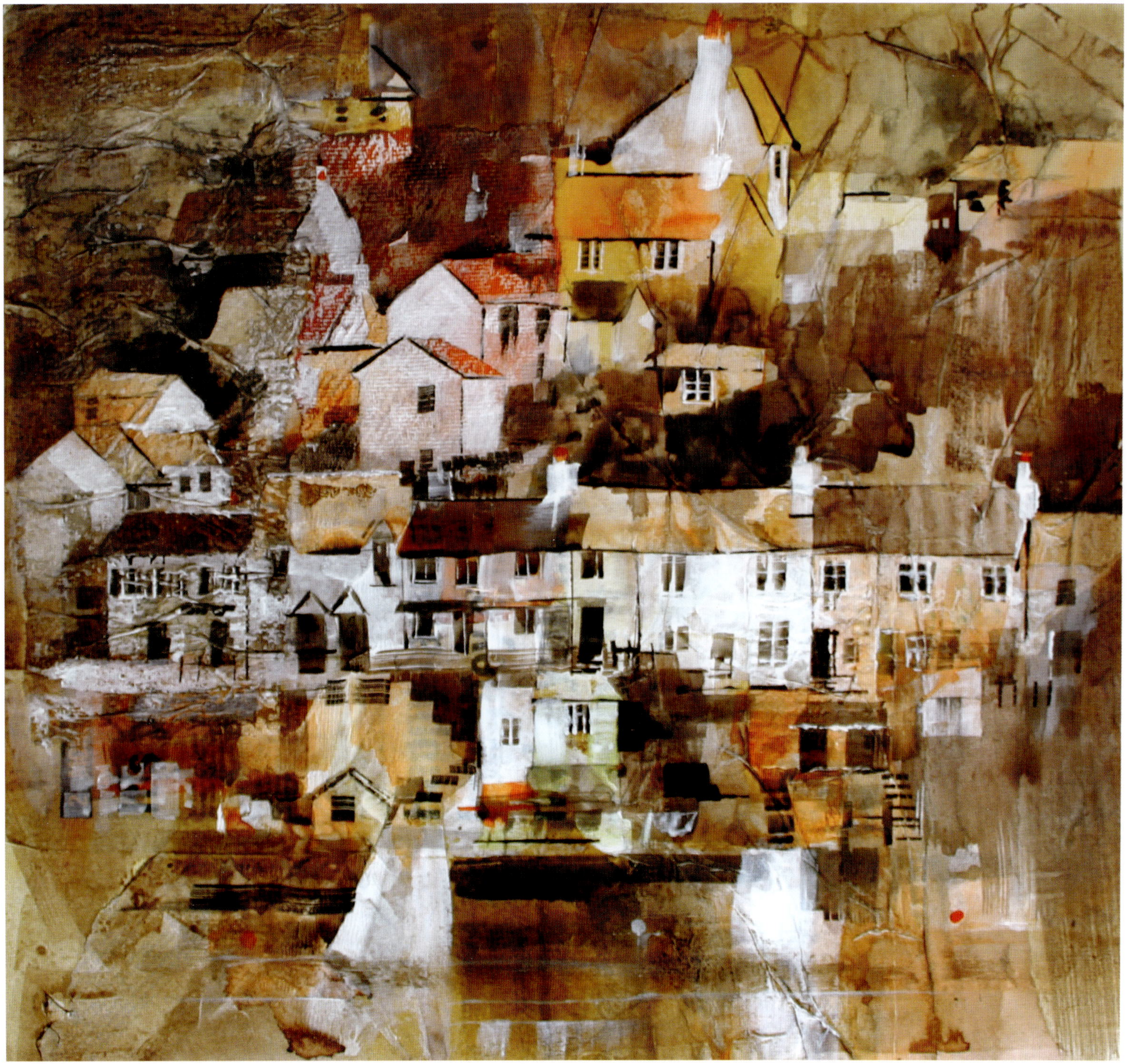

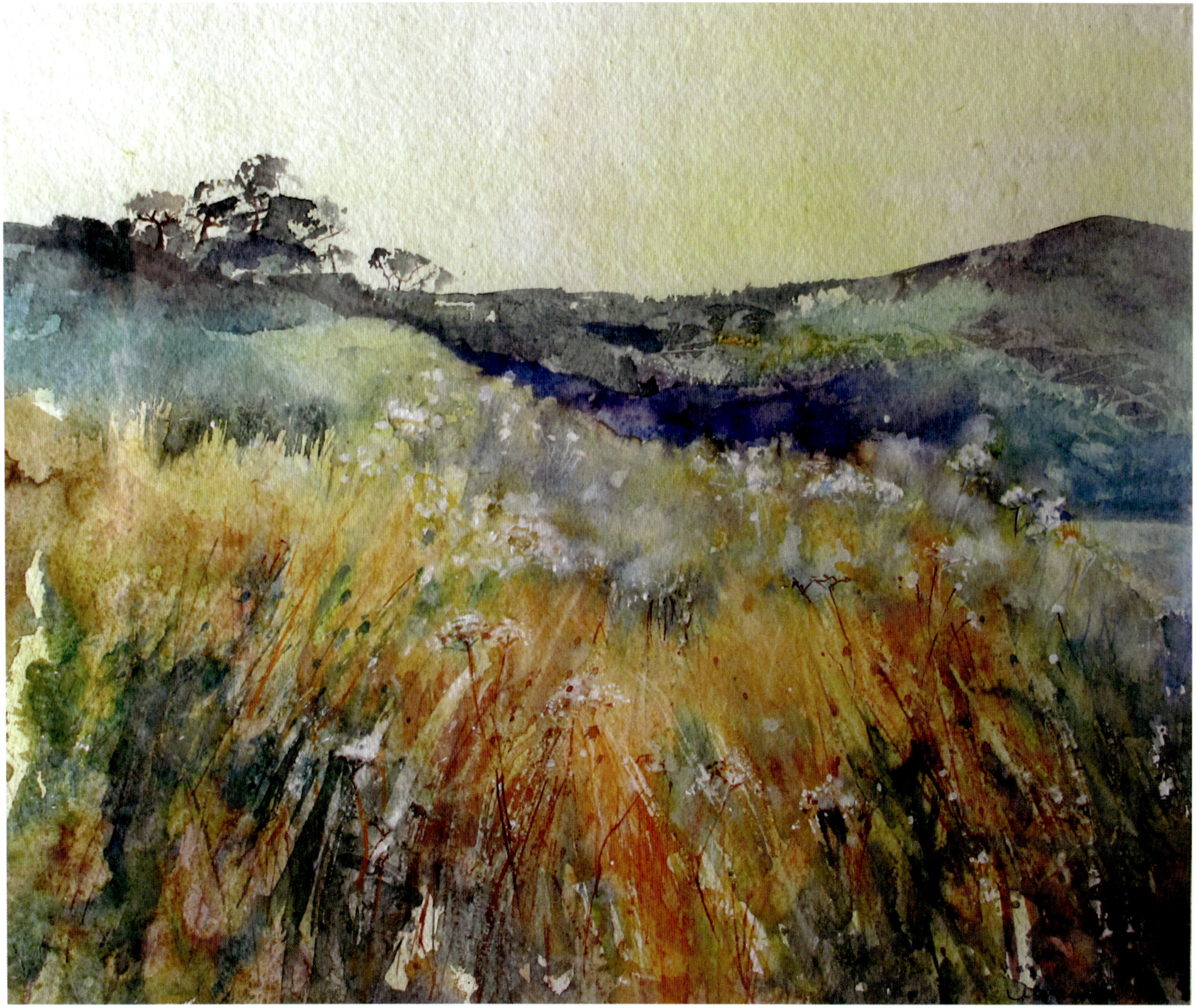

Mothecombe Meadow, watercolour, 18 x 15 in

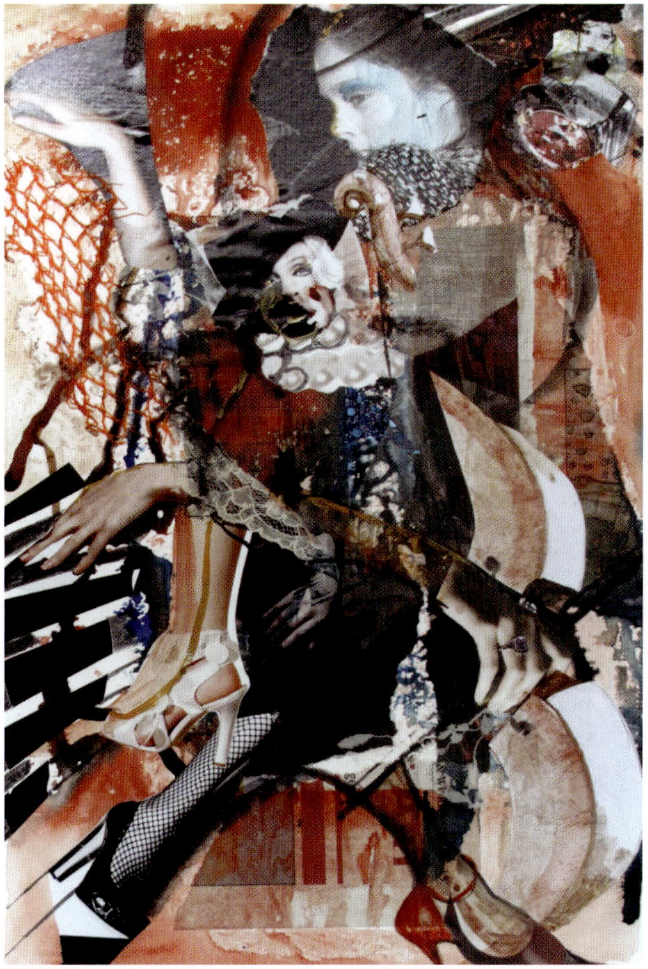

The Cellist, mixed media, 14 x 18 in

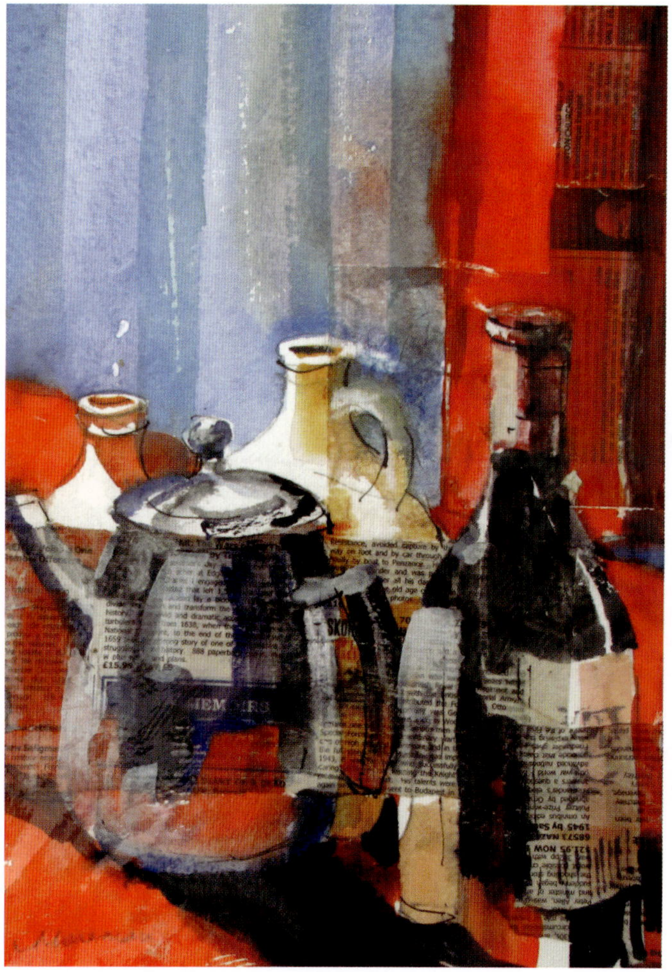

Still Life with Bottle, mixed media, 12 x 15 in

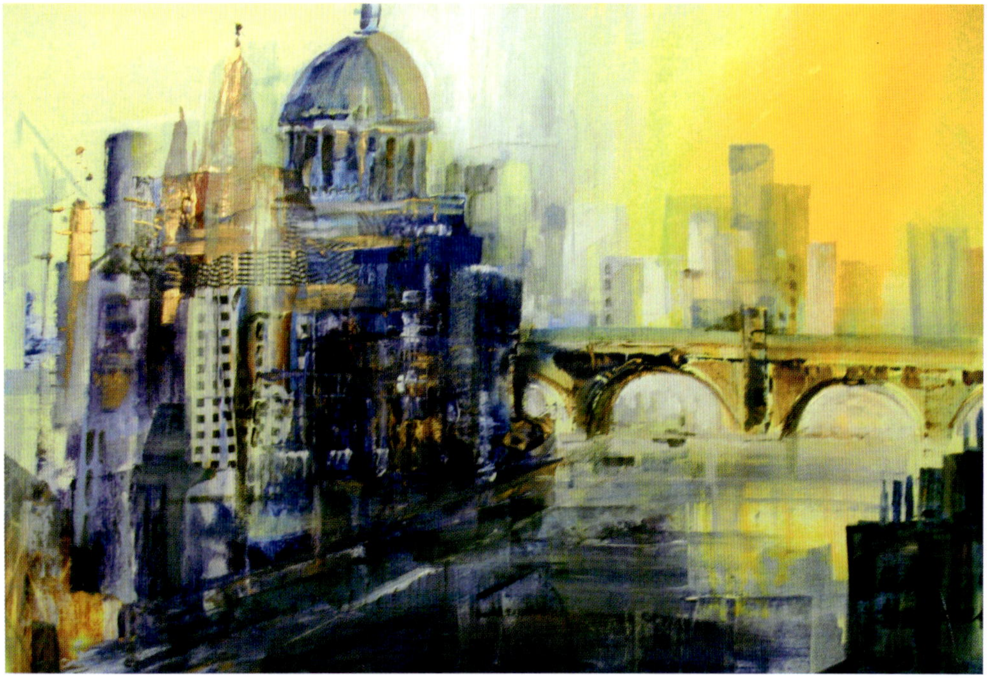

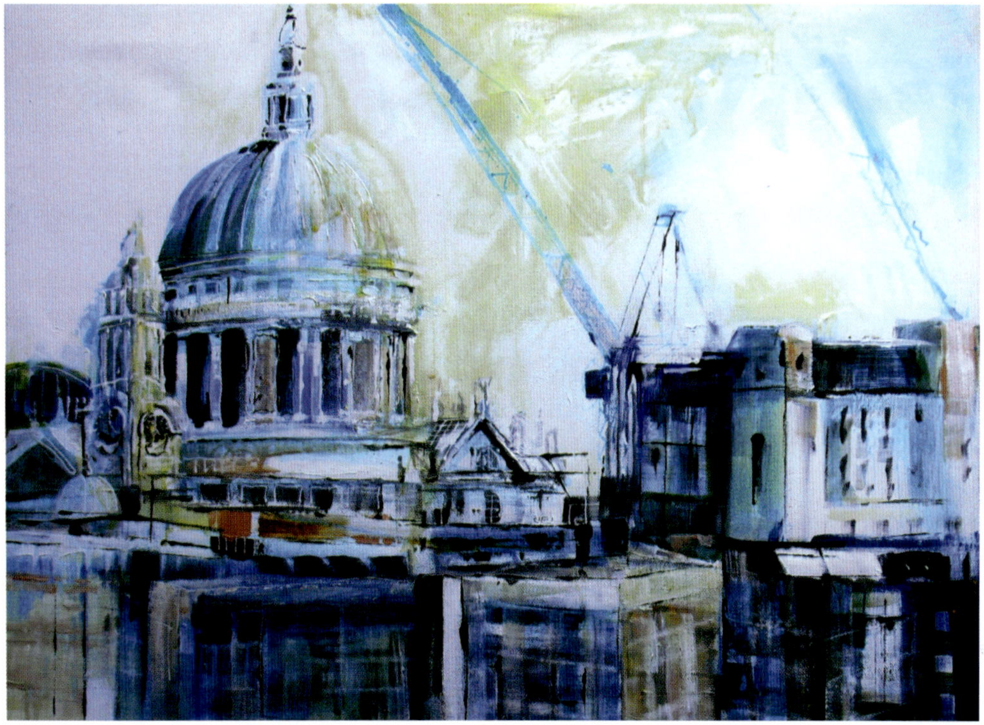

St Pauls I, mixed media, 23 x 19 in

St Pauls III, mixed media, 20 x 16 in

St Pauls II,
mixed media, 23 x 18 in

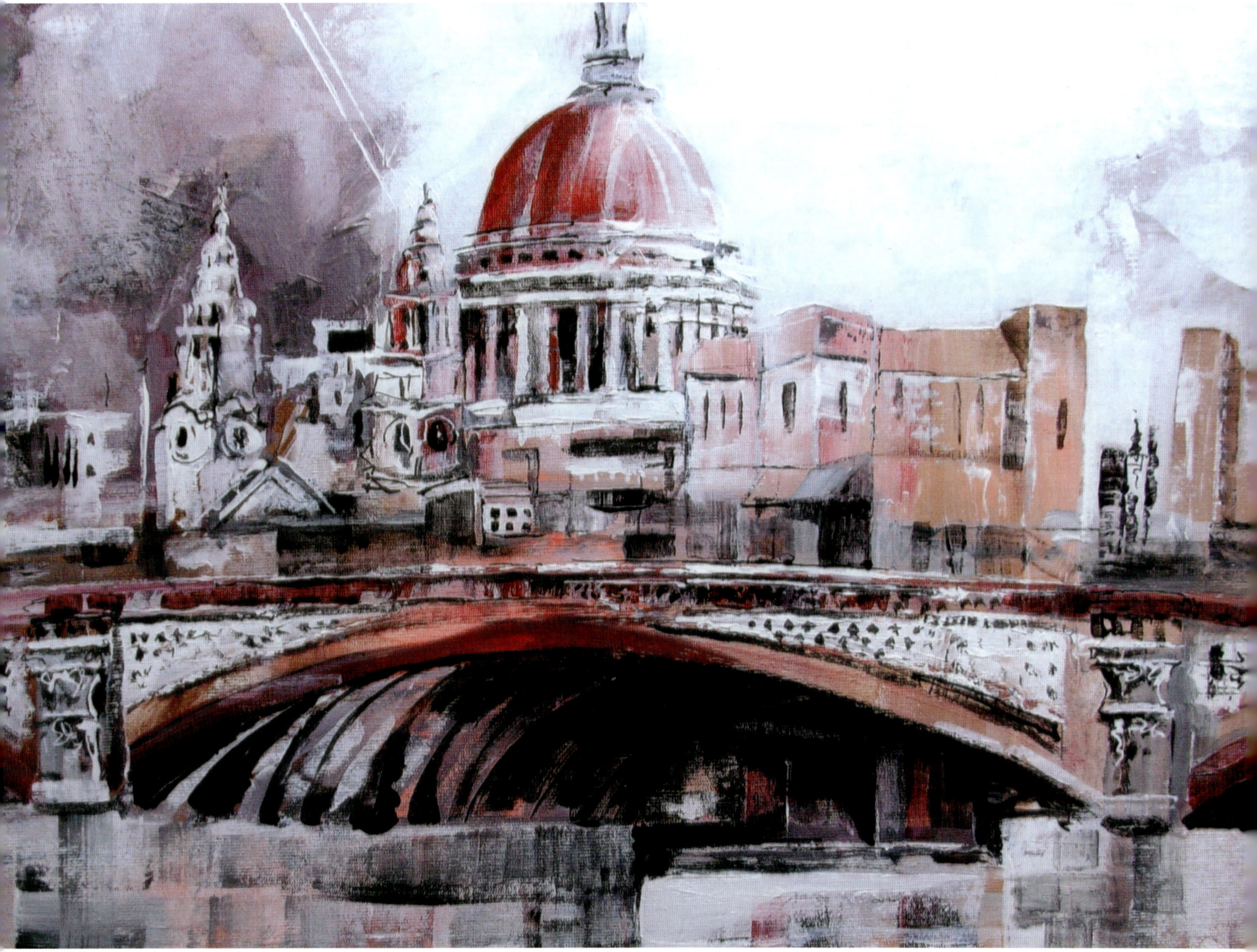

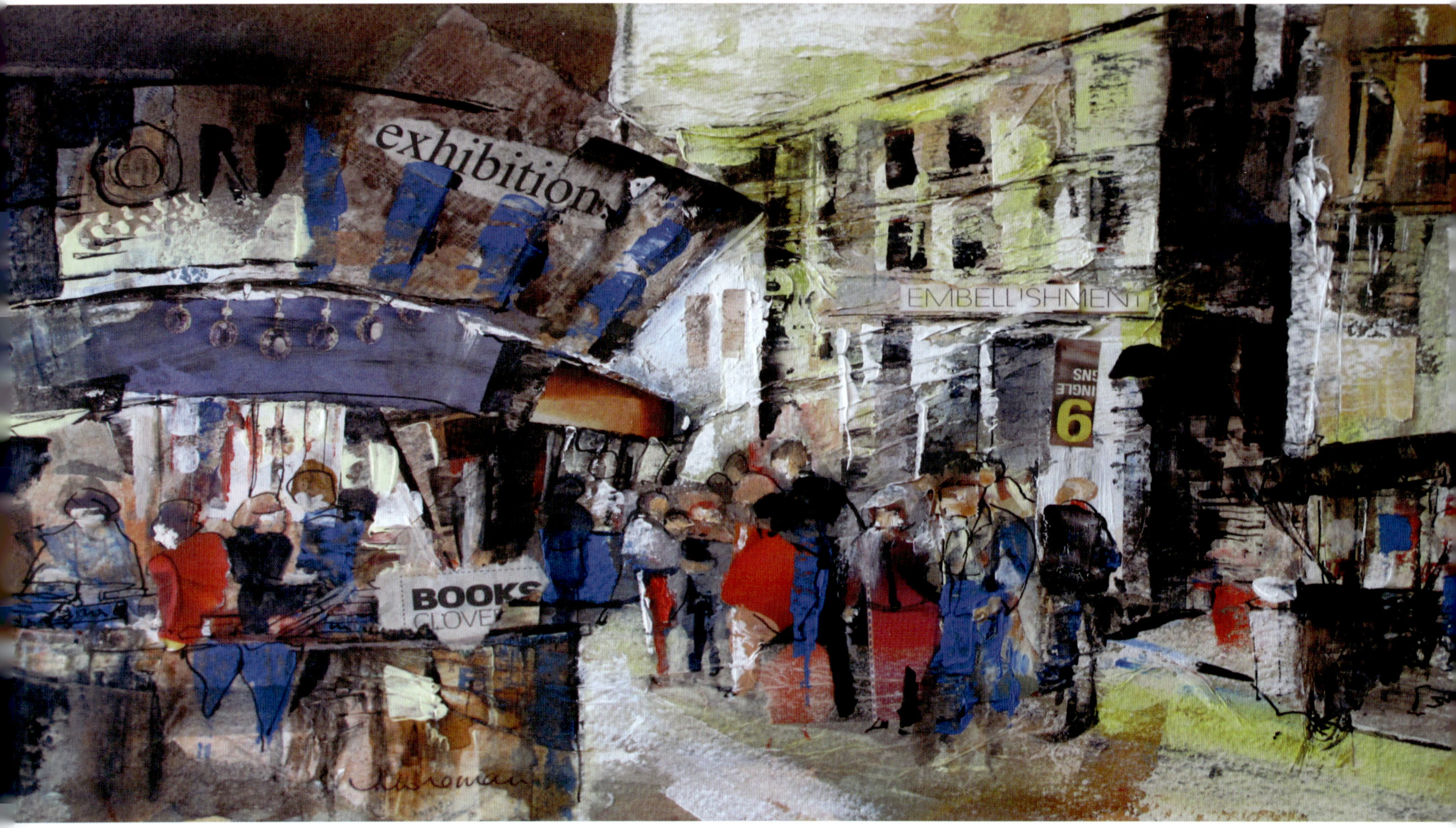

The Bookshop, collage, 19 x 13 in

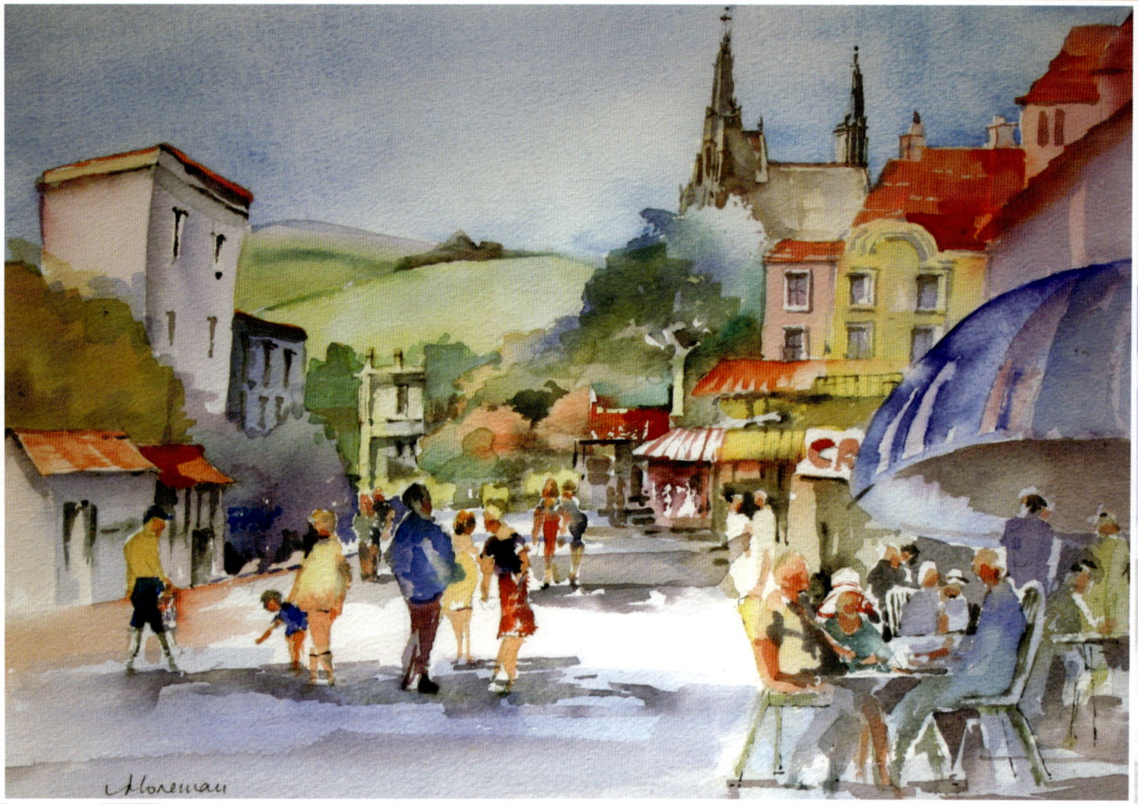

La Crêperie, watercolour, 12 x 10 in

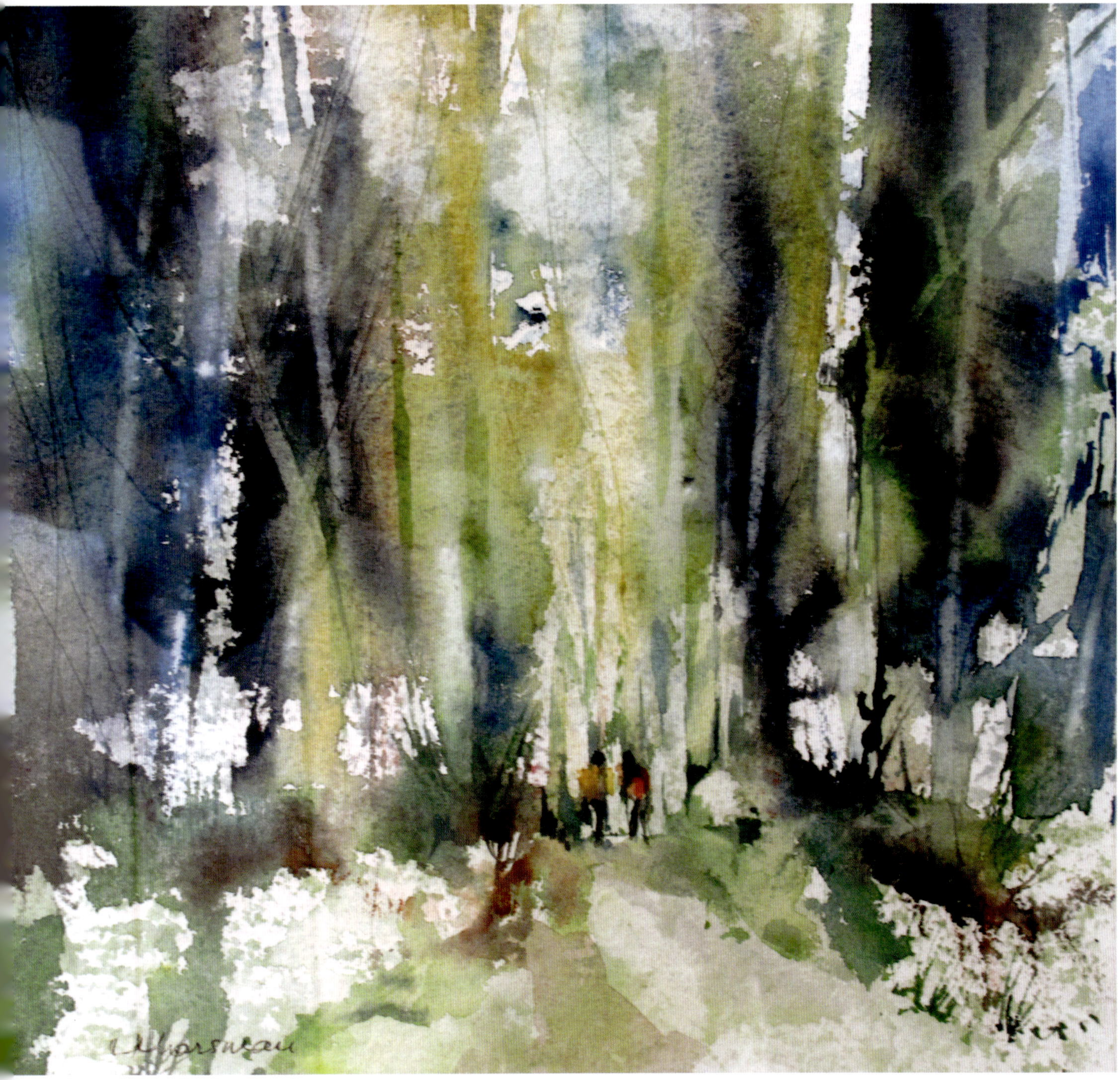

A Walk in the Woods,
watercolour, 12 x 12 in

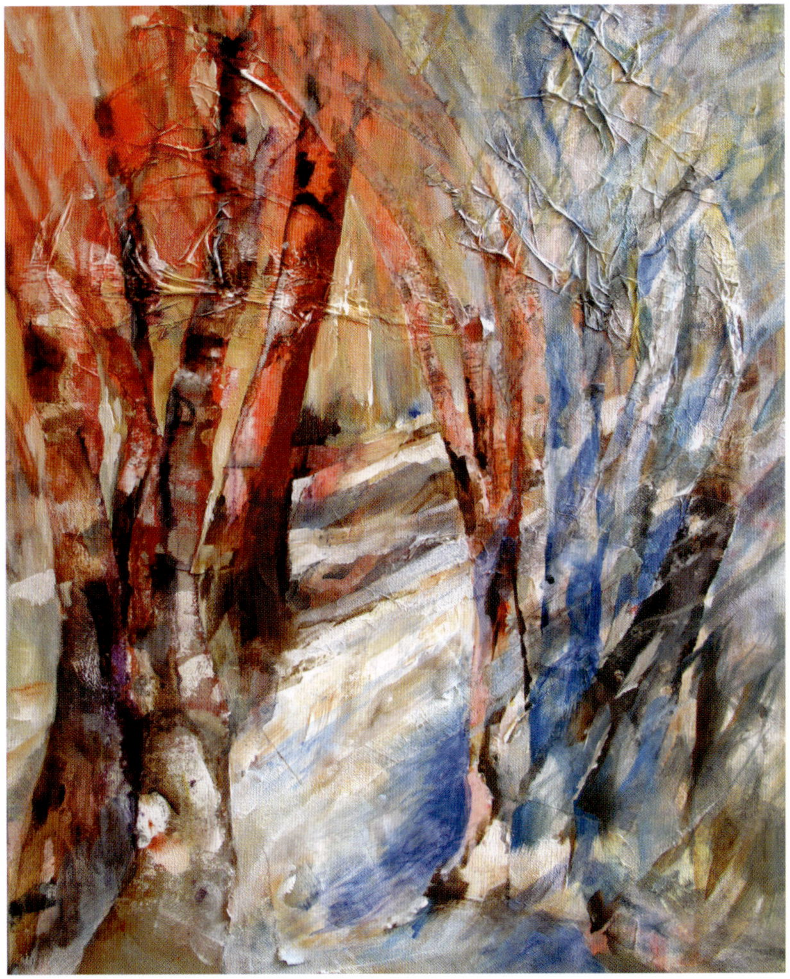

Autumn Woods, acrylic, 14 x 18 in

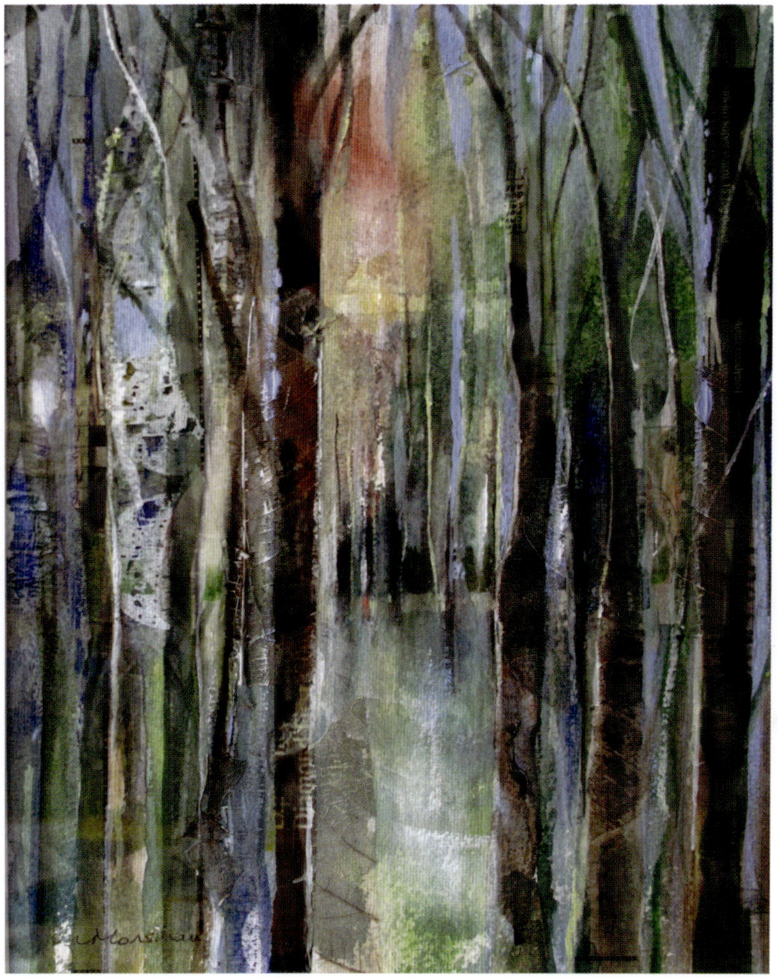

Amongst the Tall Trees, mixed media, 9.5 x 13 in

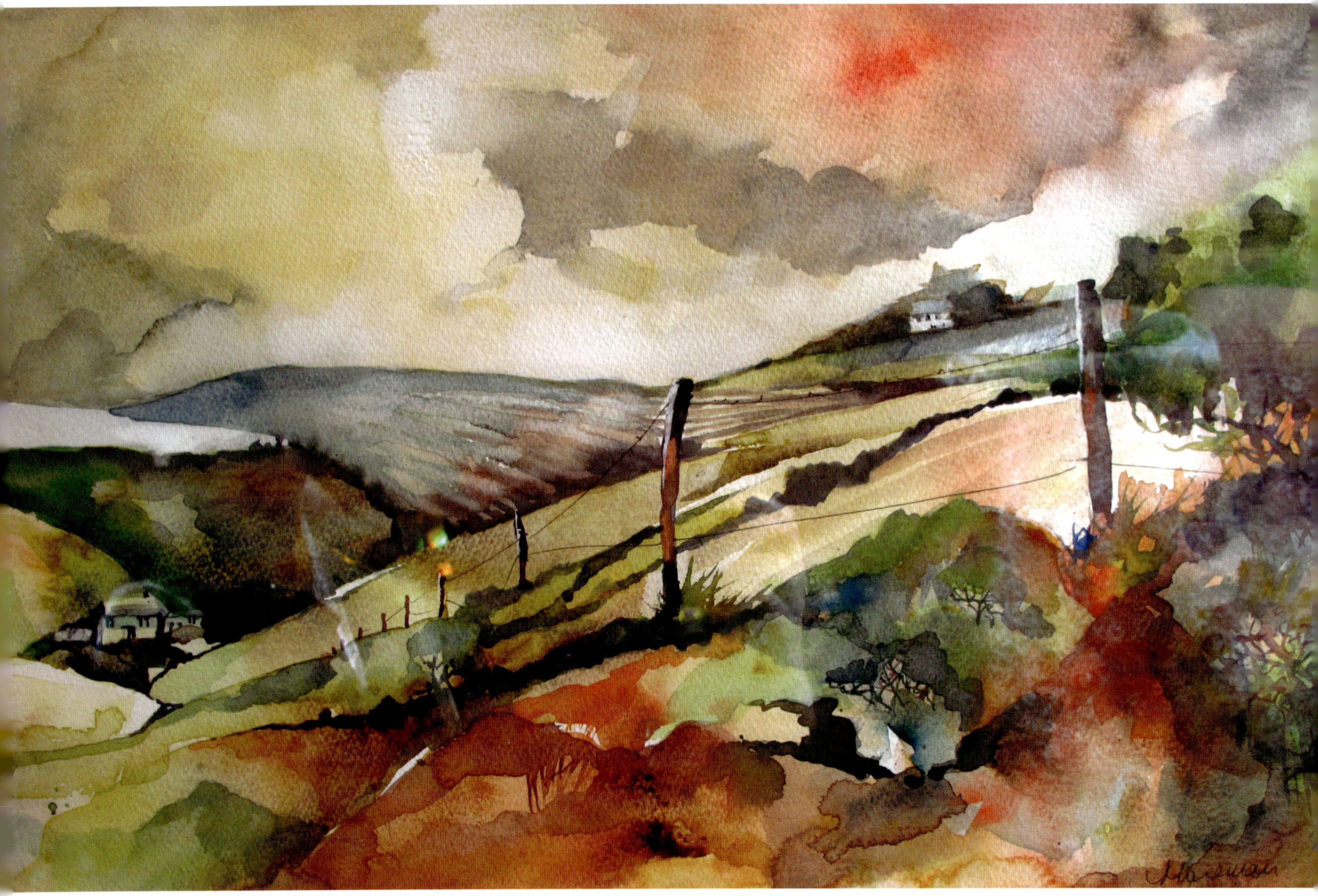

The Valley, watercolour, 15 x 11 in

The Heron, mixed media, 19 x 14 in

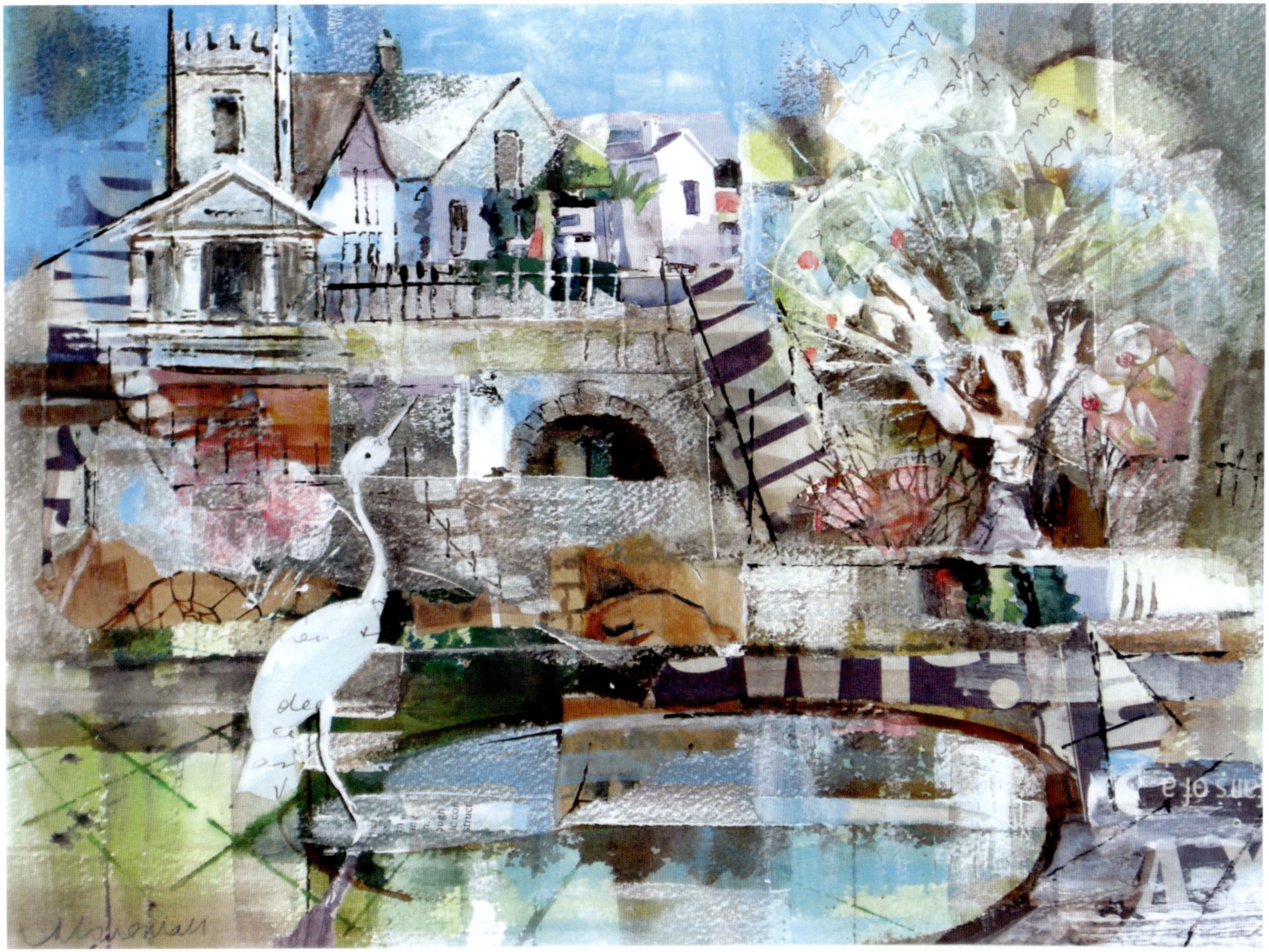

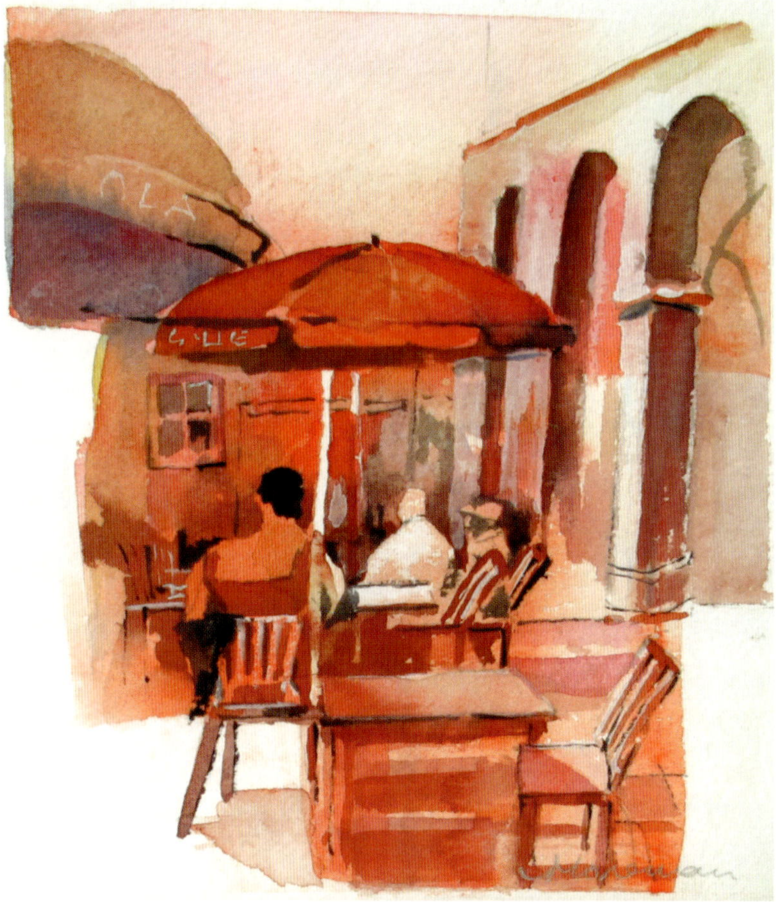

Le Café, watercolour, 8 x 10 in

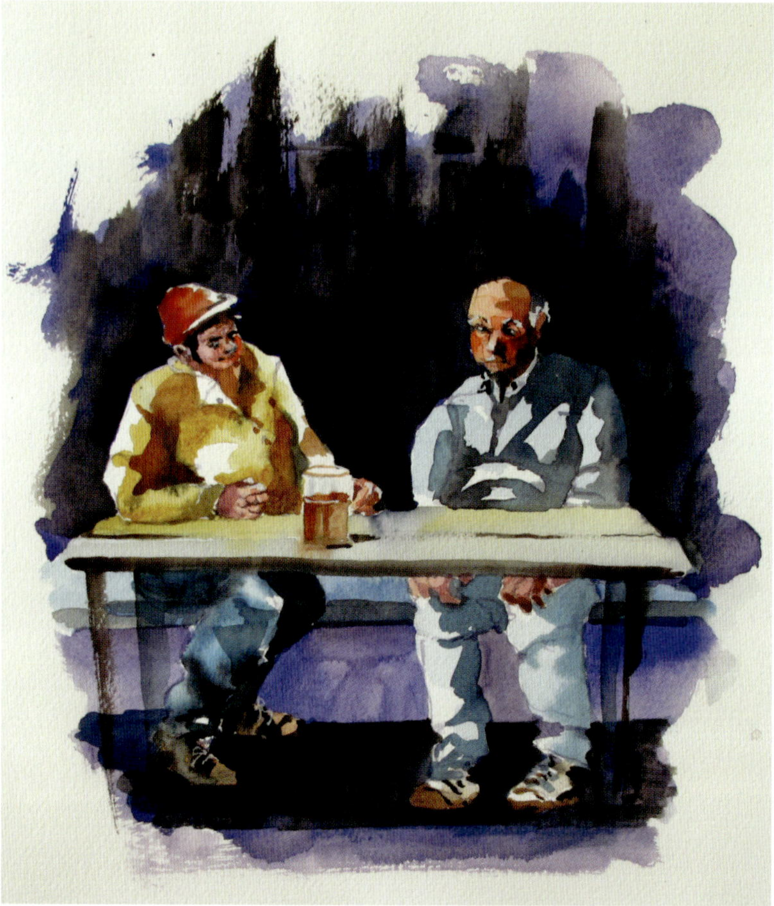

A Glass Half Full, watercolour, 9 x 11 in

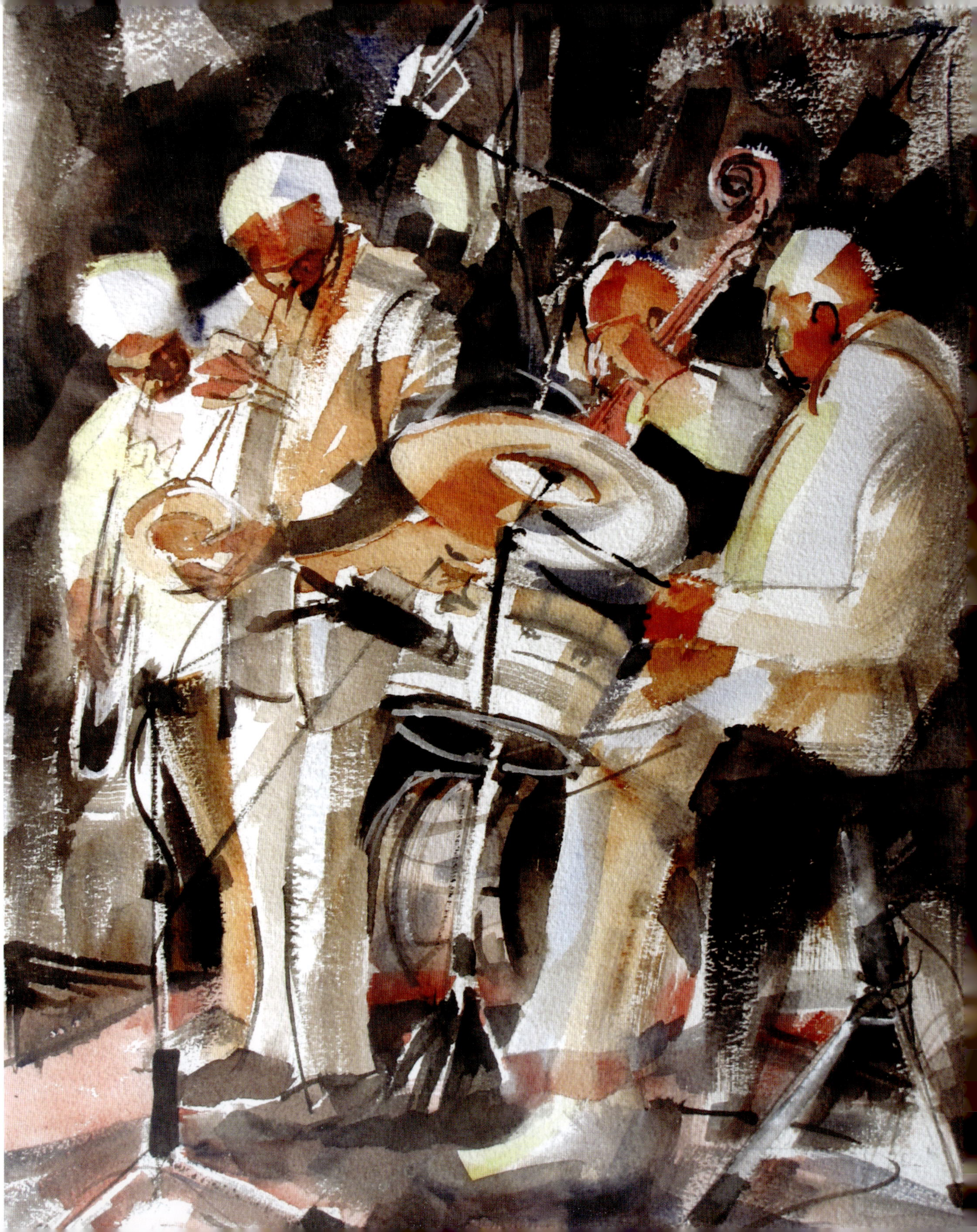

Humph and Friends,
watercolour, 14 x 19 in

A blissful summer evening in Cornwall lying on the grass listening to Humphrey Lyttelton.

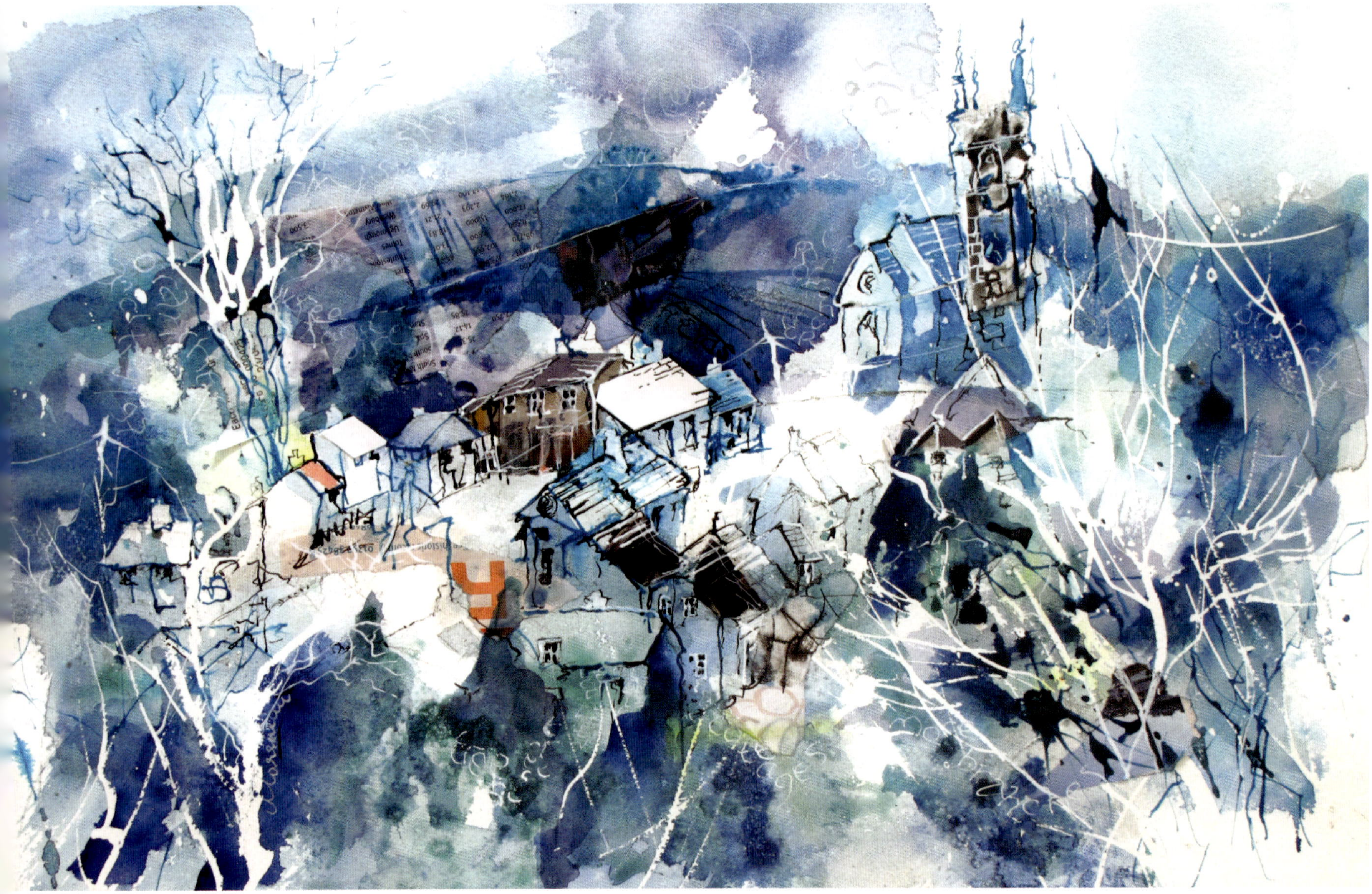

Dorset Village I, watercolour and ink, 16 x 12 in

Dorset Village II, watercolour and ink, 16 x 12 in

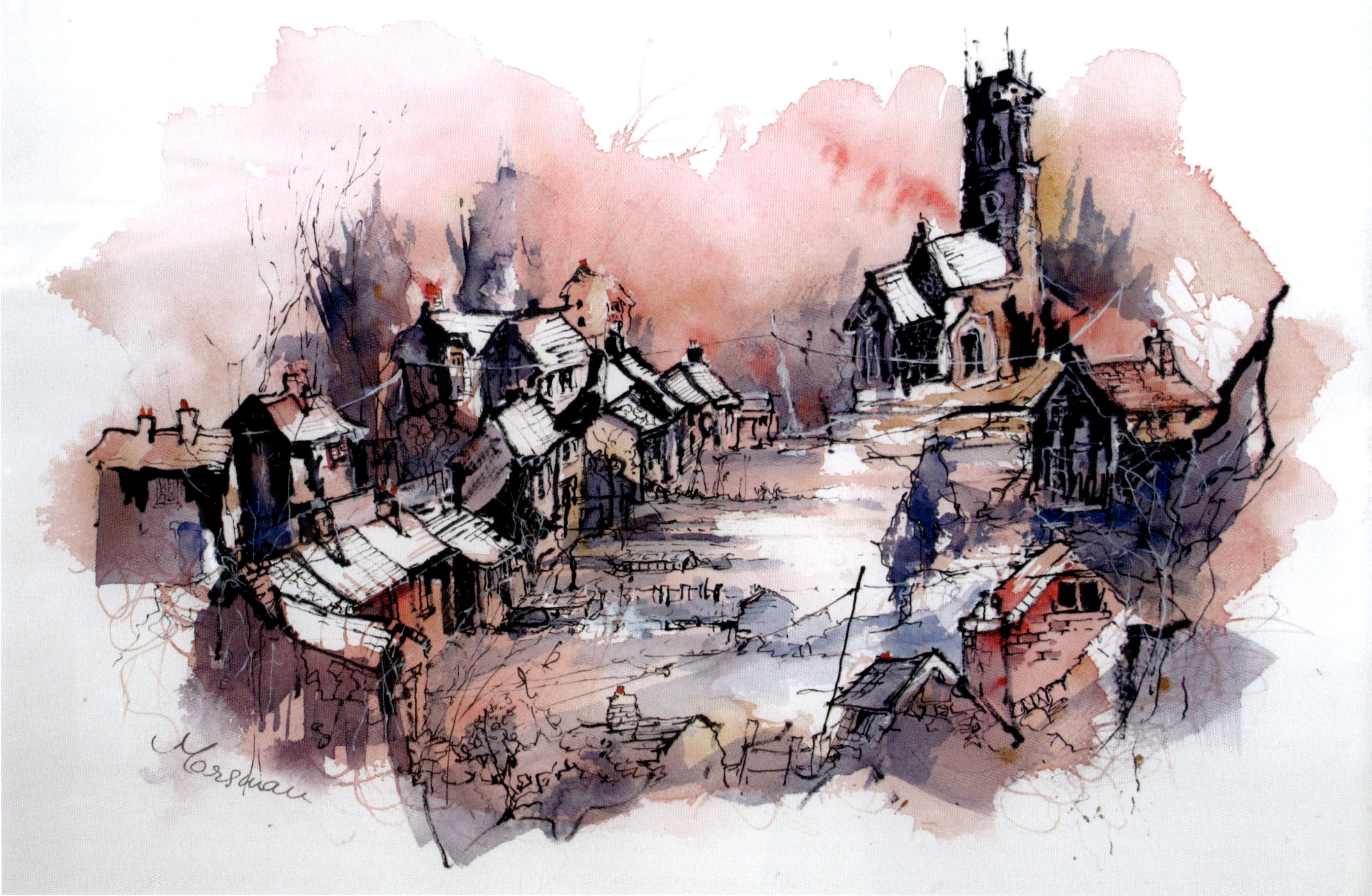

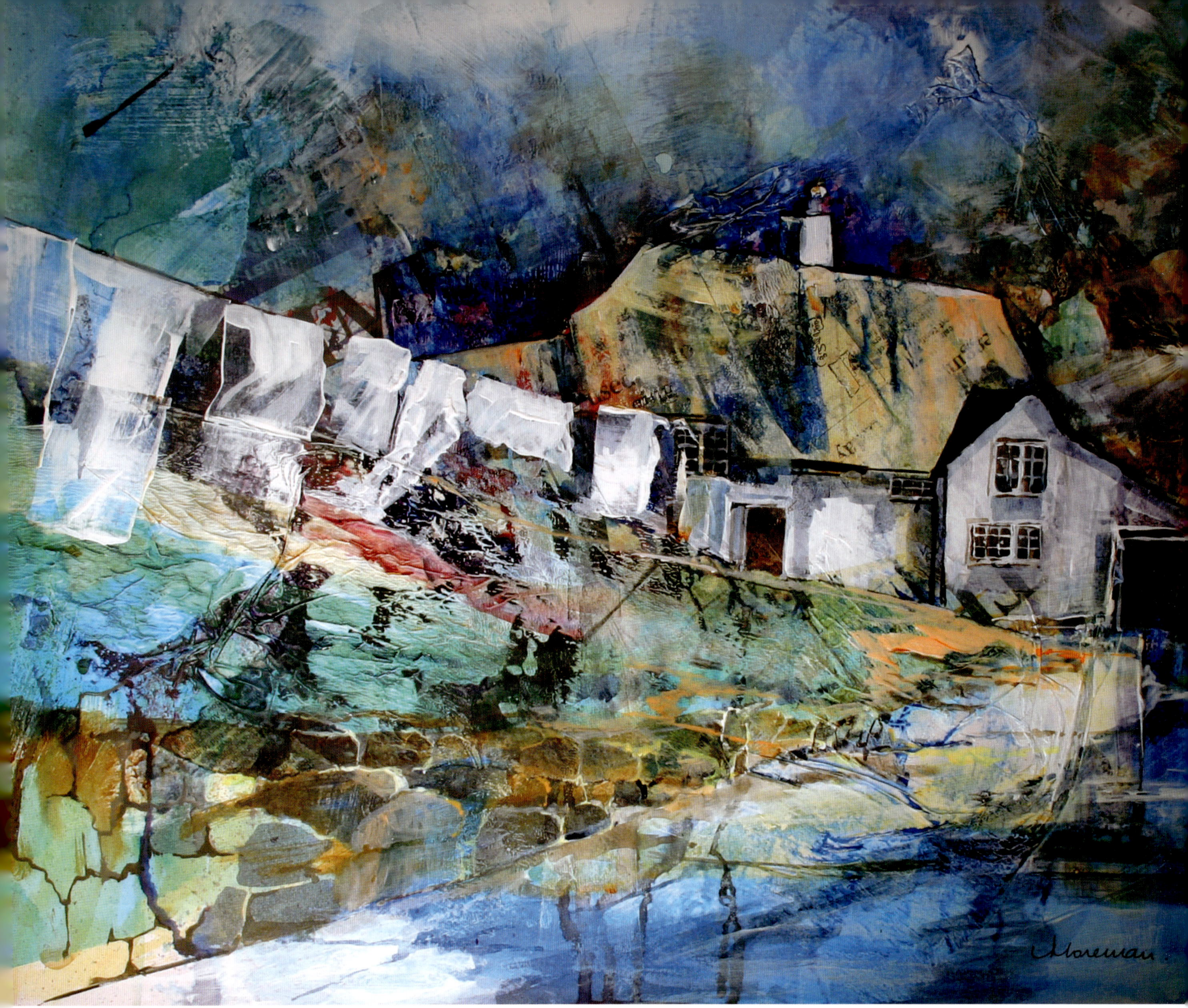
Moreman

Washing in the Wind,
mixed media, 22 x 17 in

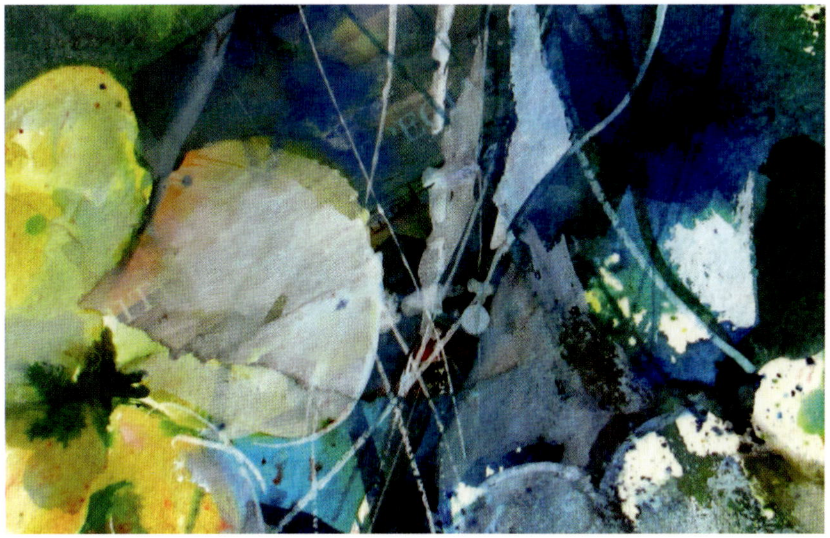

Above: *Border,*
watercolour, 9 x 6.5 in

Right: *Cherub and Tulips,*
watercolour, 6 x 14 in

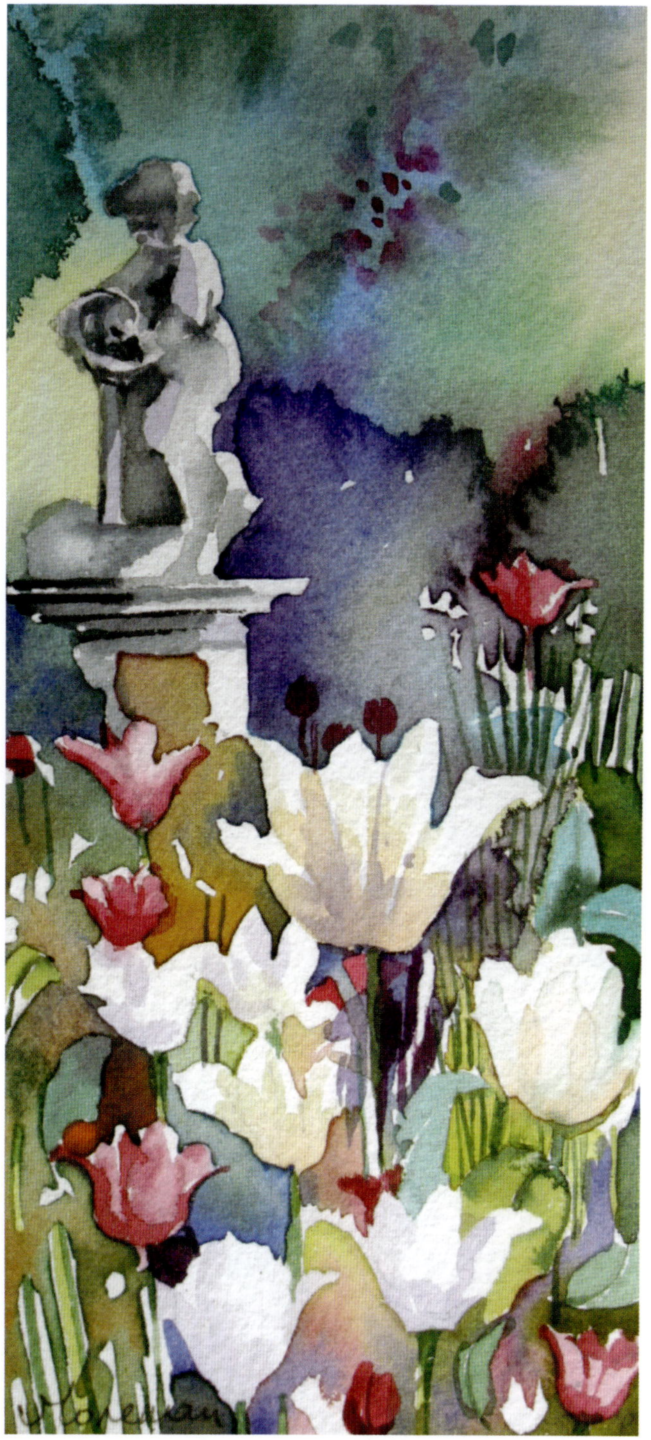

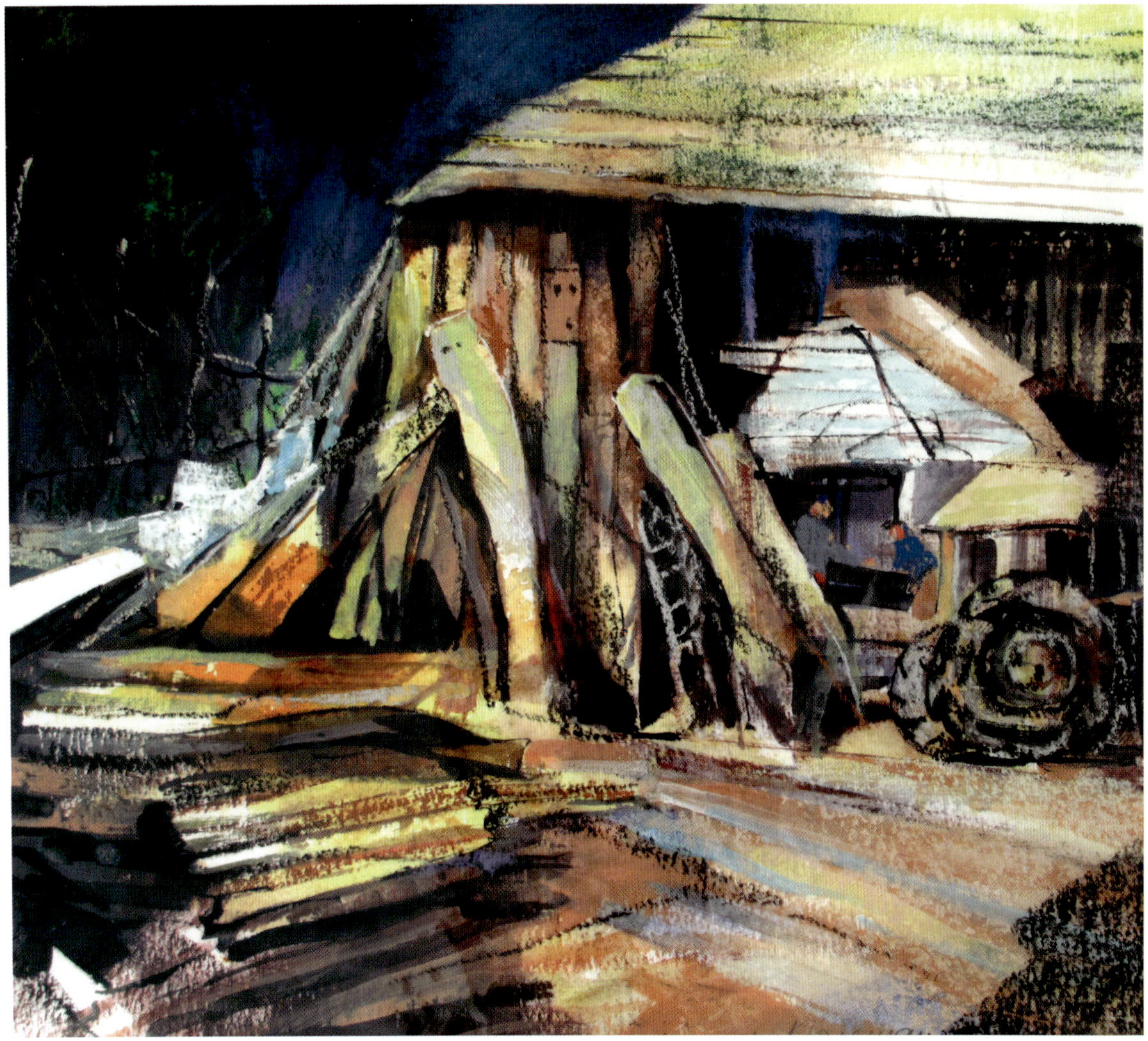

What's Going on in the Woodshed?, mixed media, 16 x 13 in

Worzel in the Bean Patch,
mixed media, 20 x 18 in

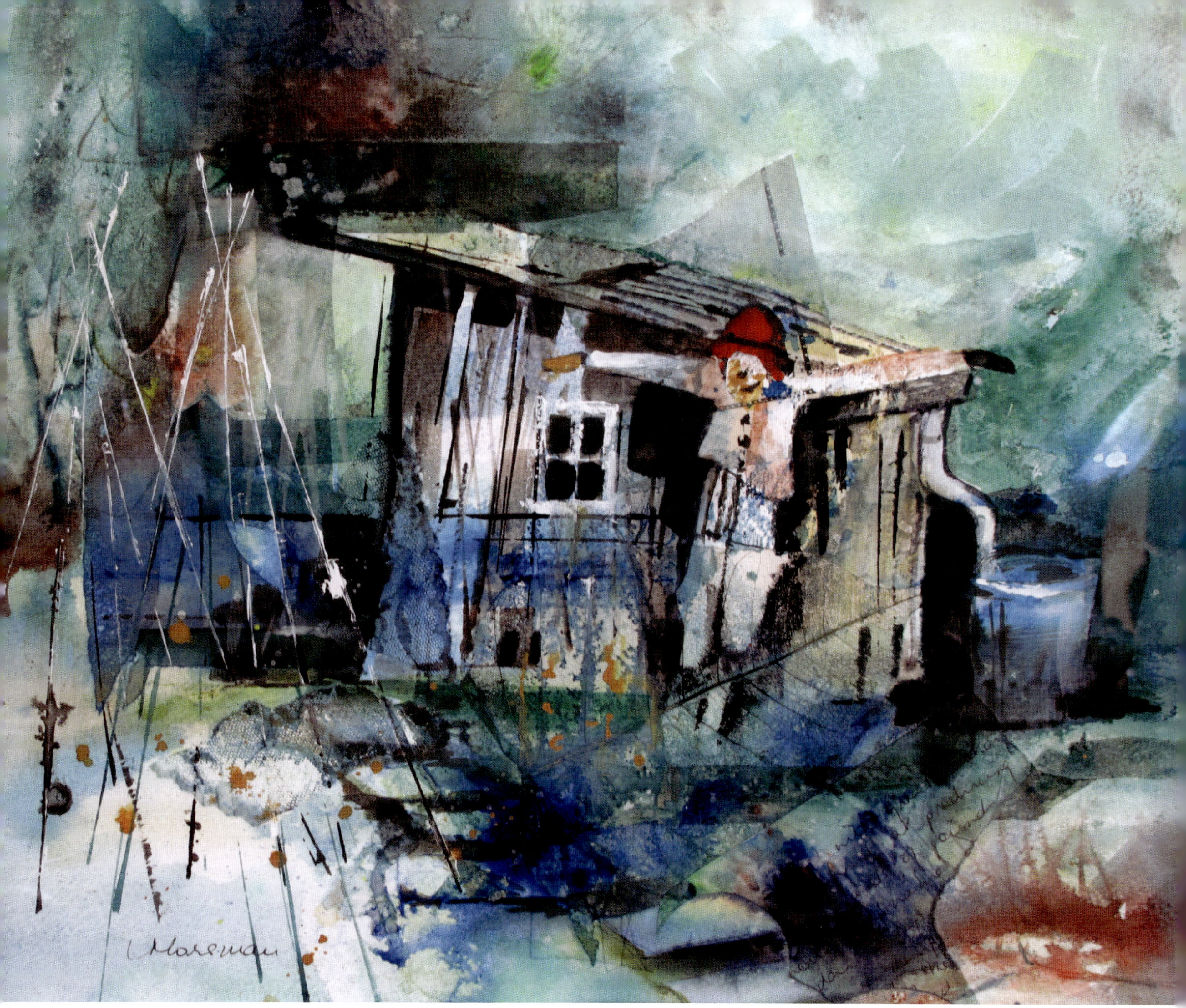

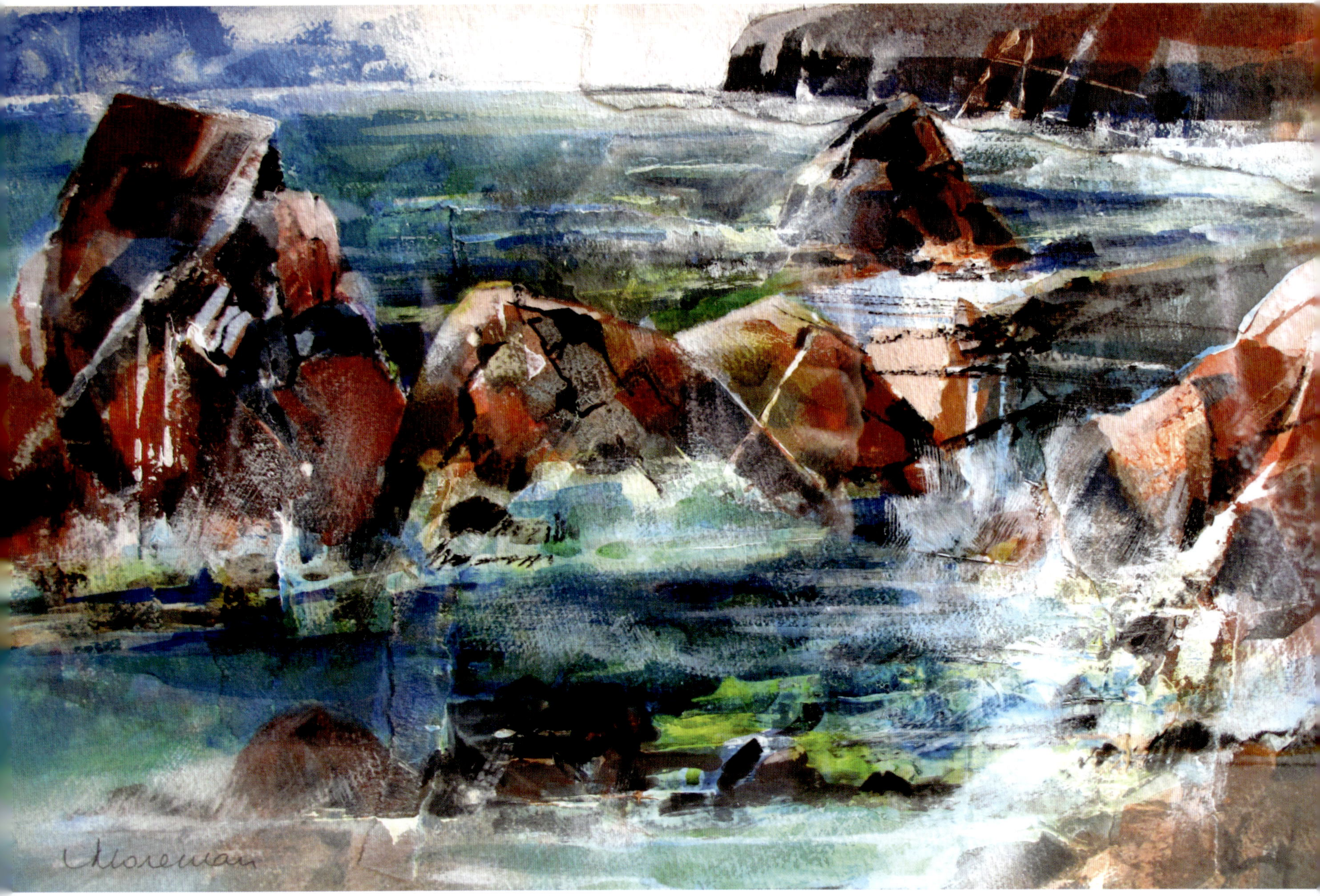

Rocks and Sea, Cornwall, mixed media, 17 x 13 in

The Viaduct, watercolour, 16 x 13 in

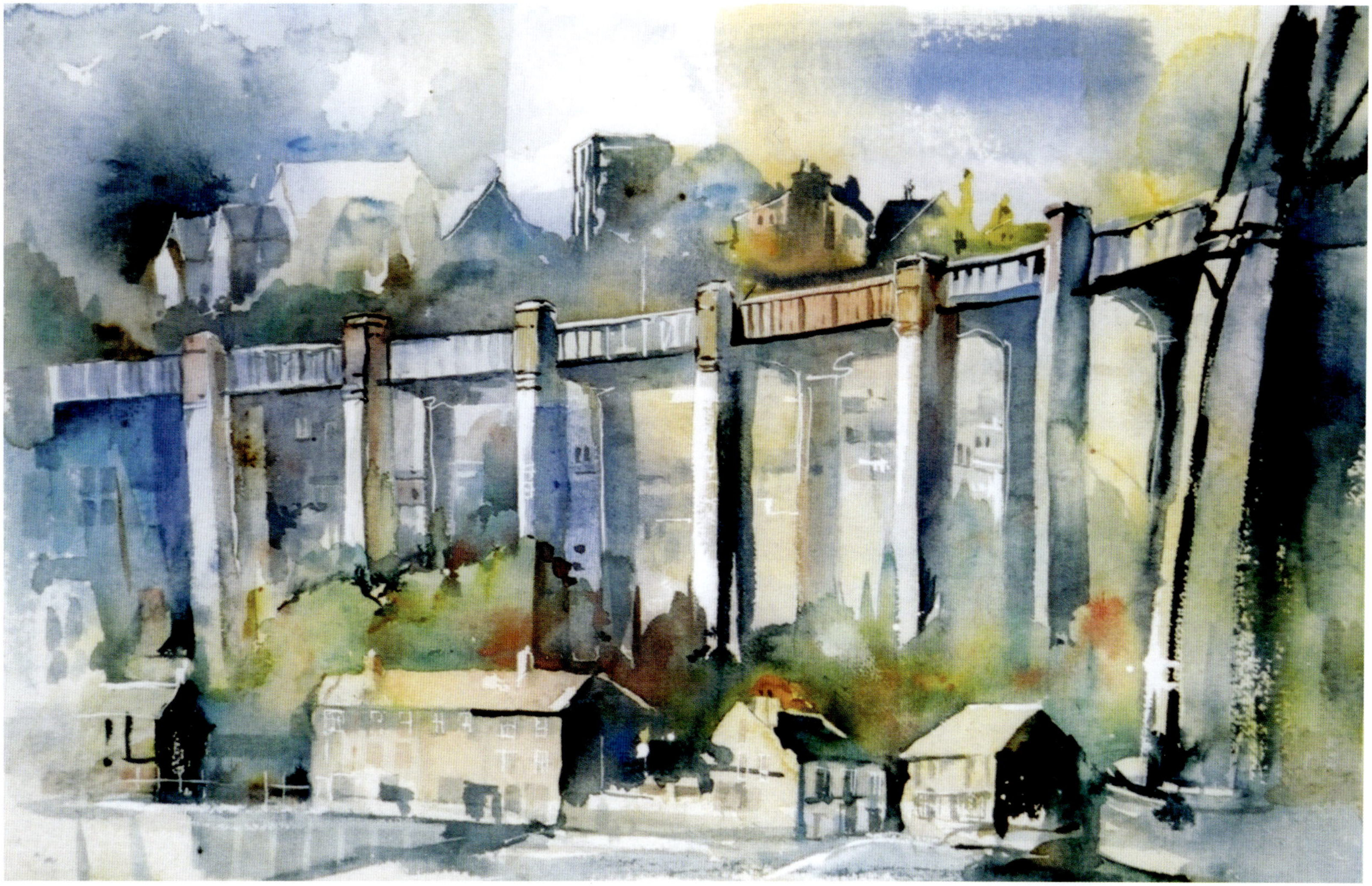

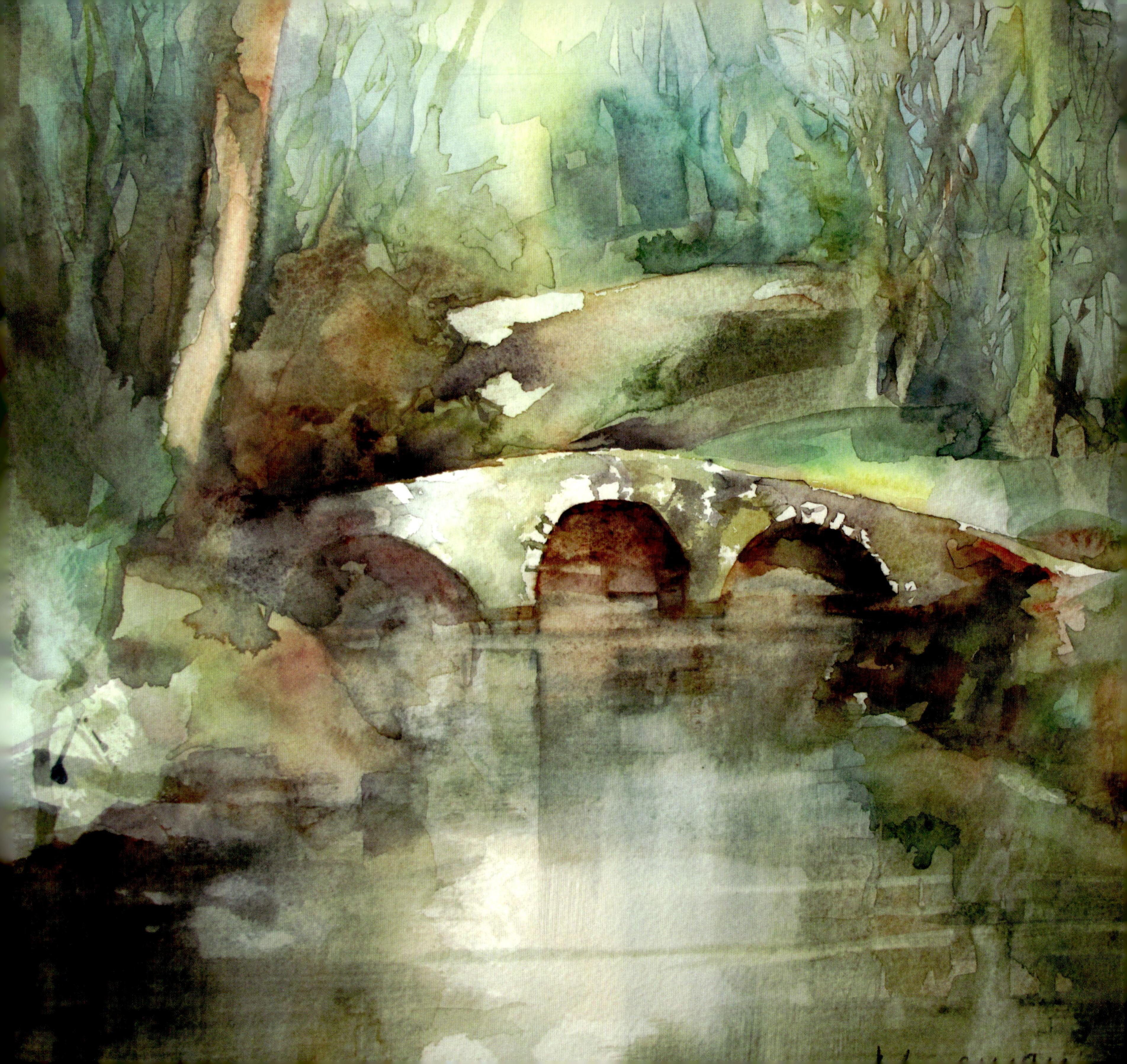

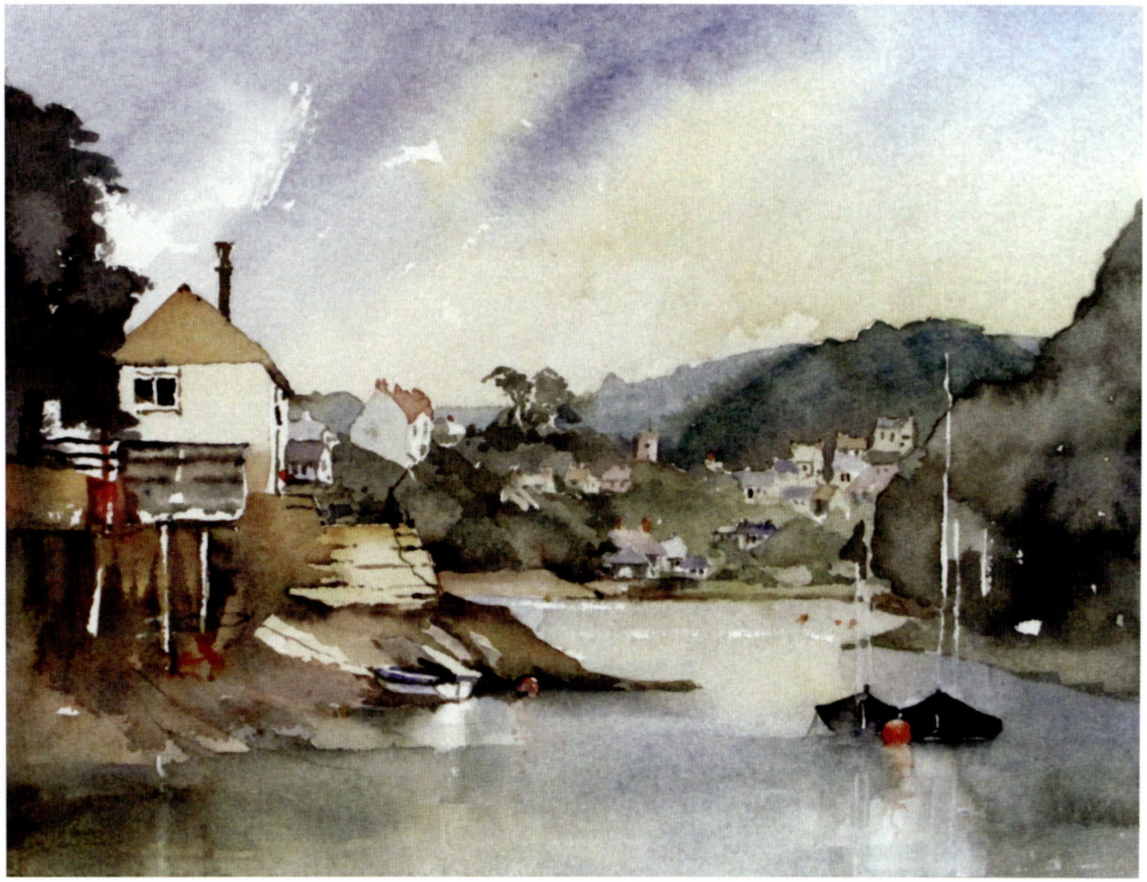

The Yealm, watercolour, 15 x 11 in

Dreamy Green, watercolour, 16 x 14 in

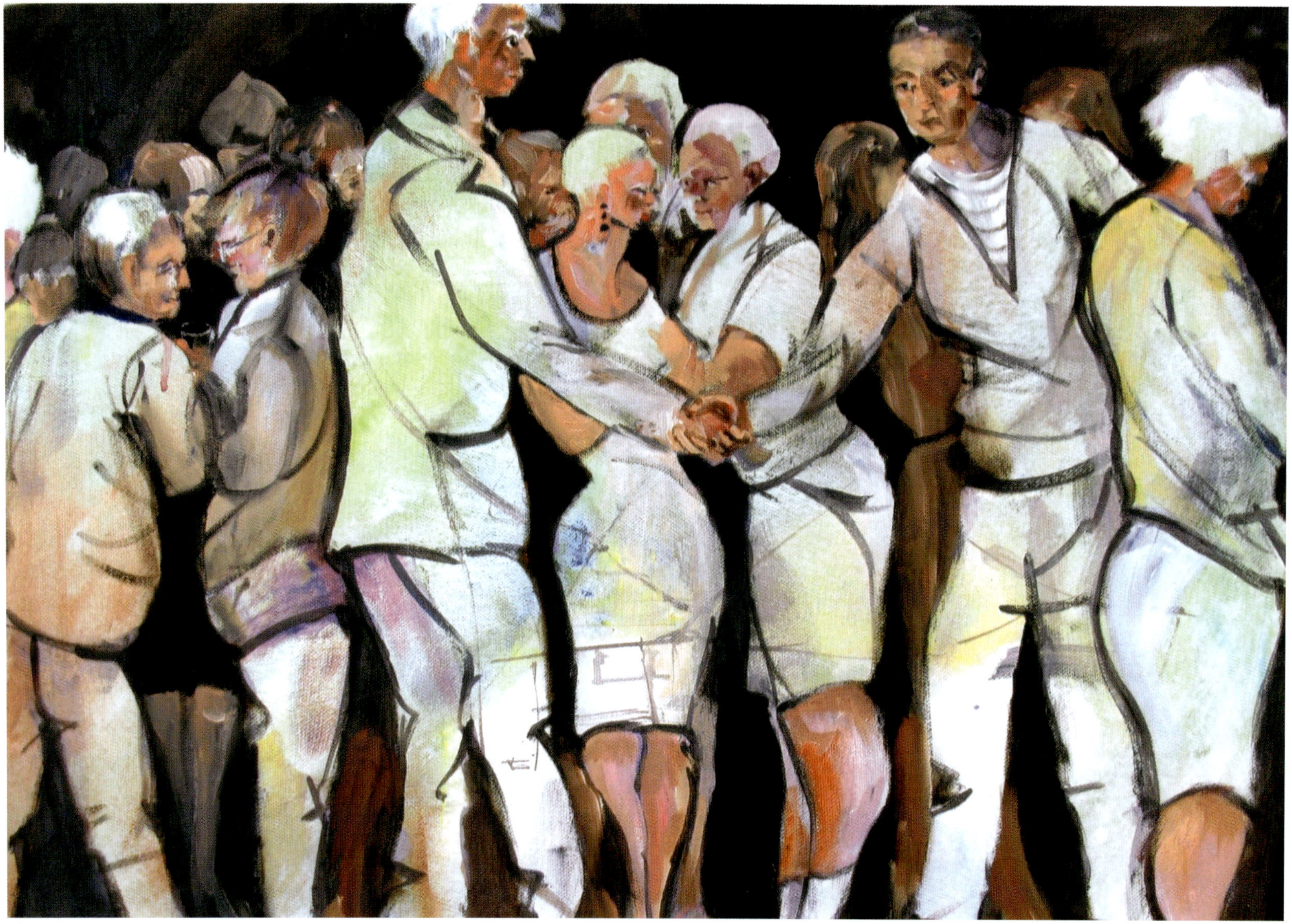

Head and Shoulders Above the Rest,
watercolour, 23 x 14 in

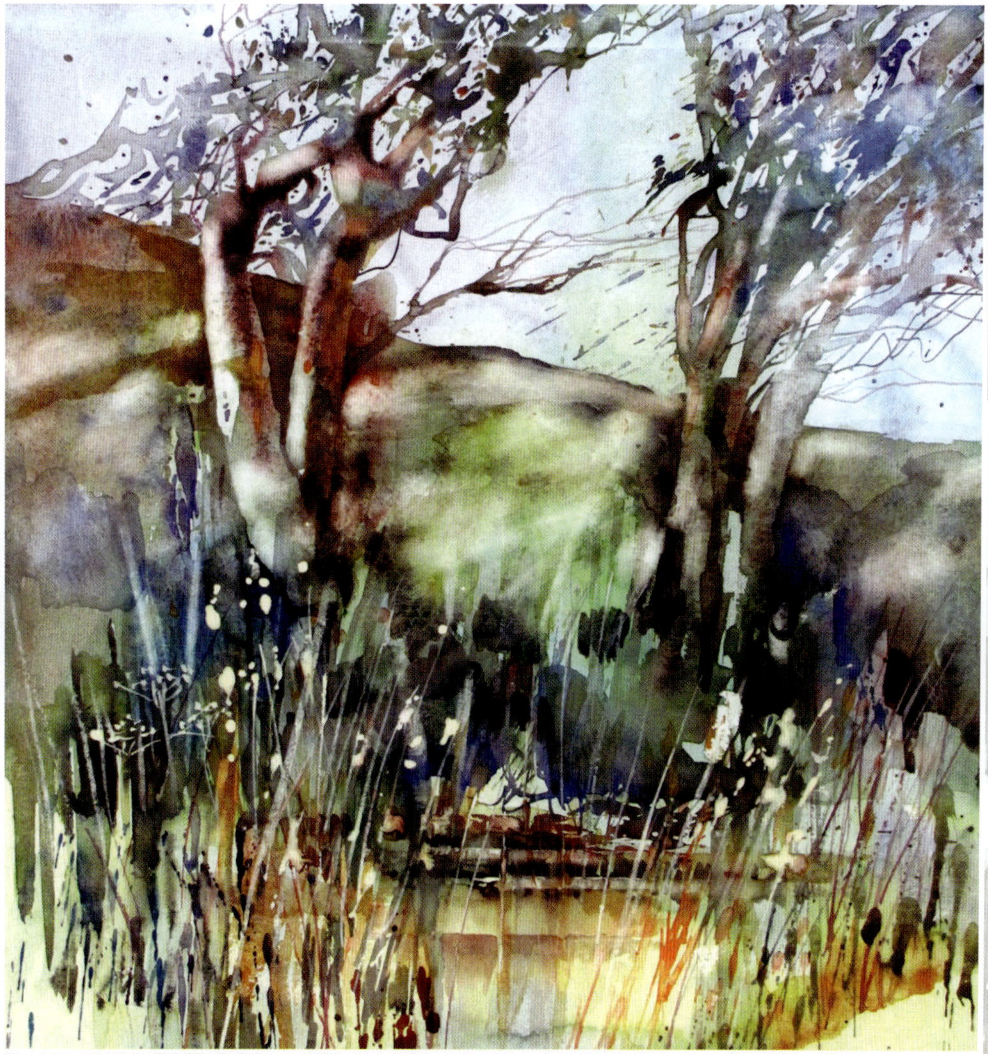

The Way the Wind Blows, watercolour, 14 x 18 in

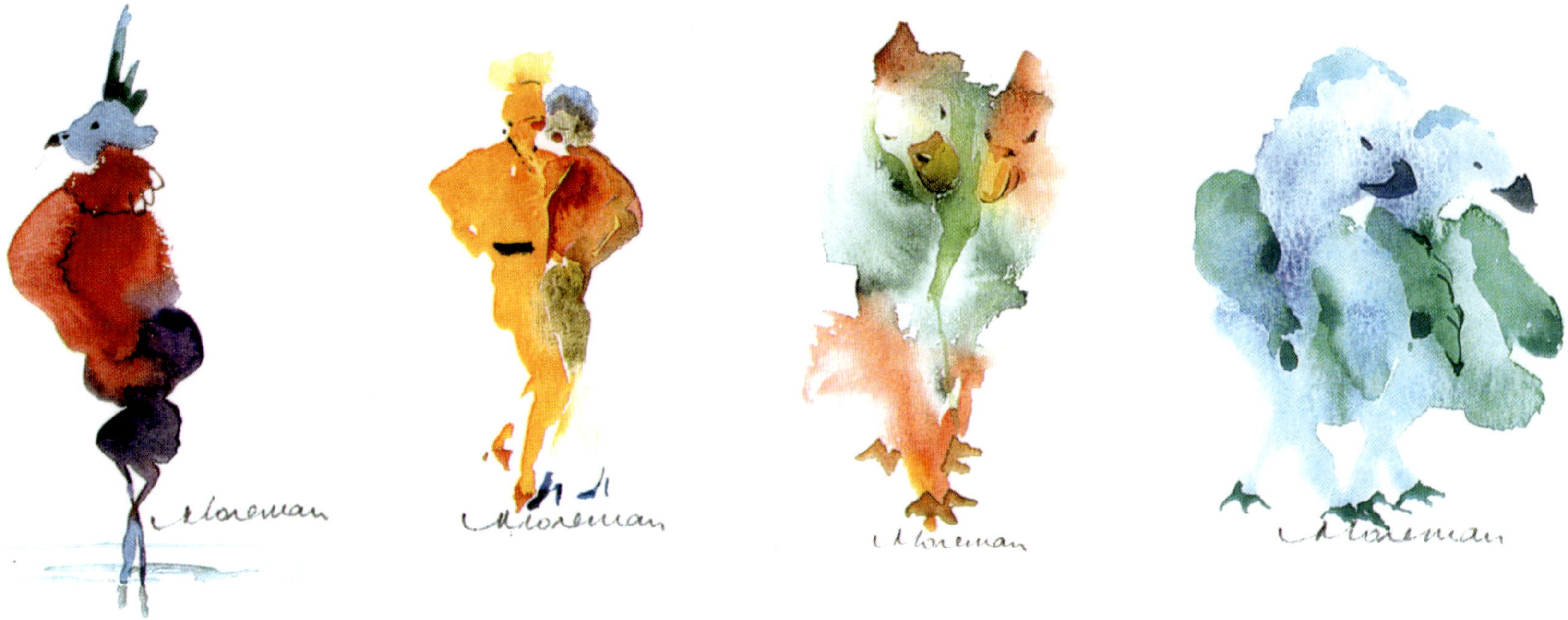

Doodle Birds, watercolour, 2 x 4 in

I made a collection of animals which all started just with a blob of paint.

Farmer's Gate, acrylic, 16 x 13 in

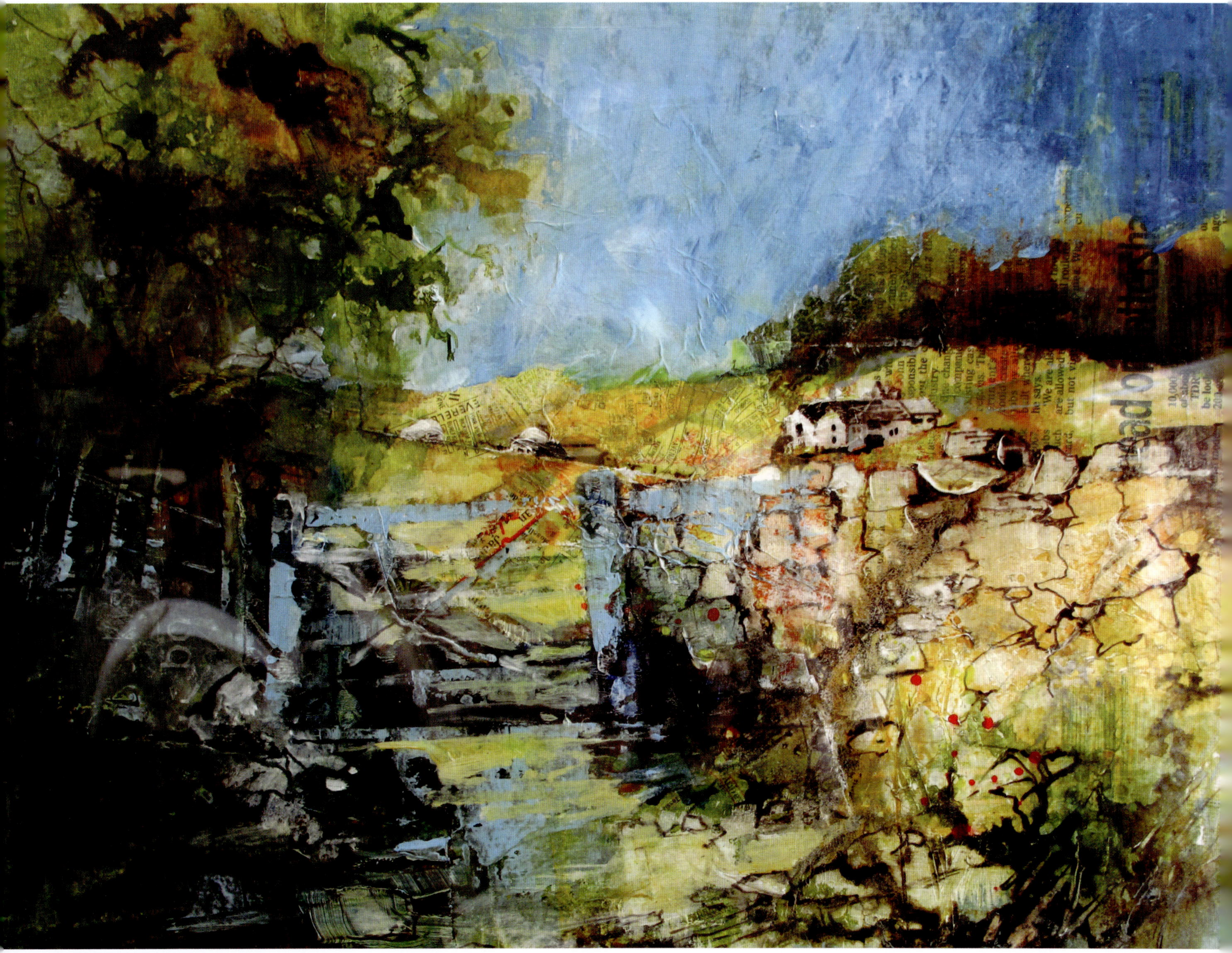

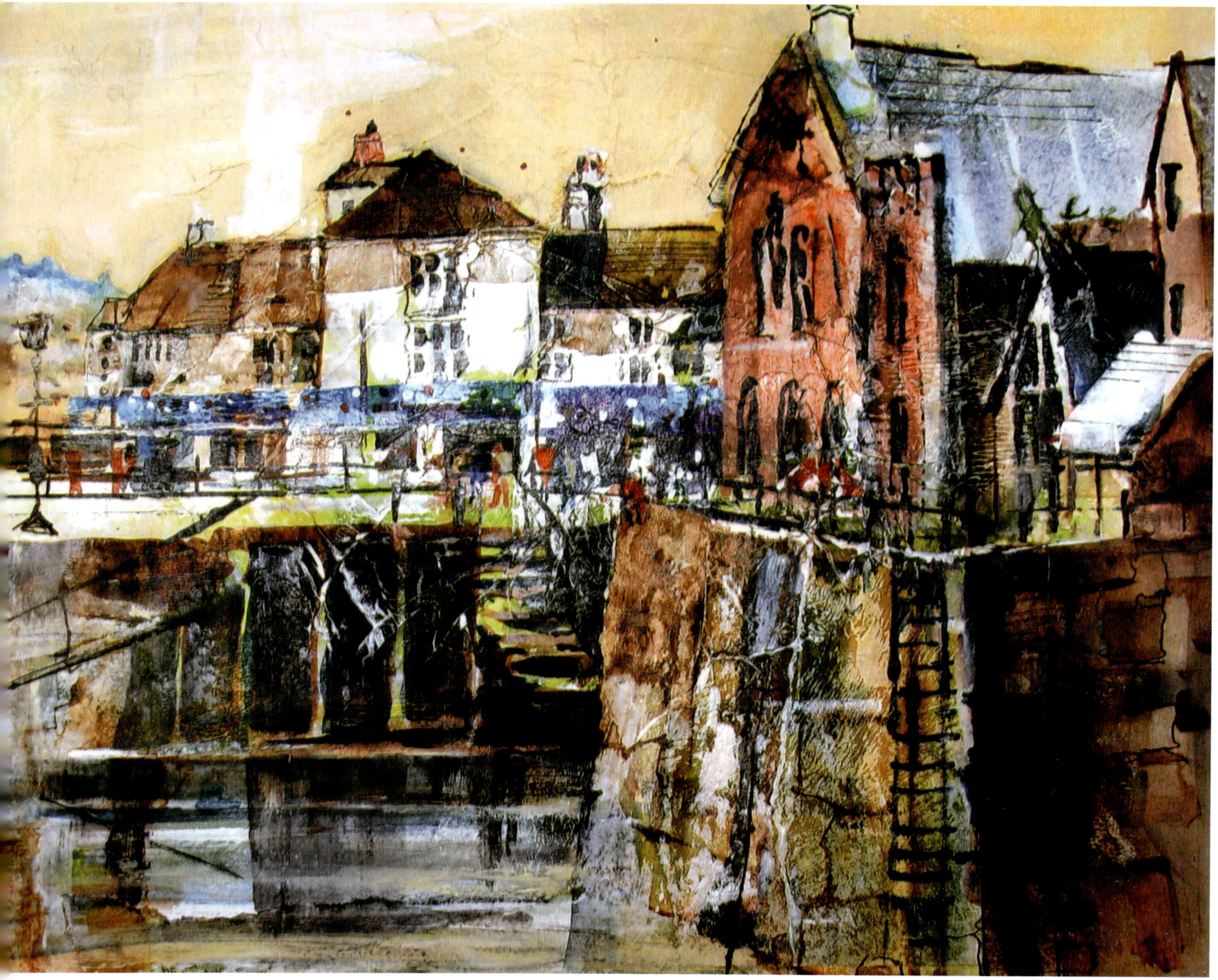

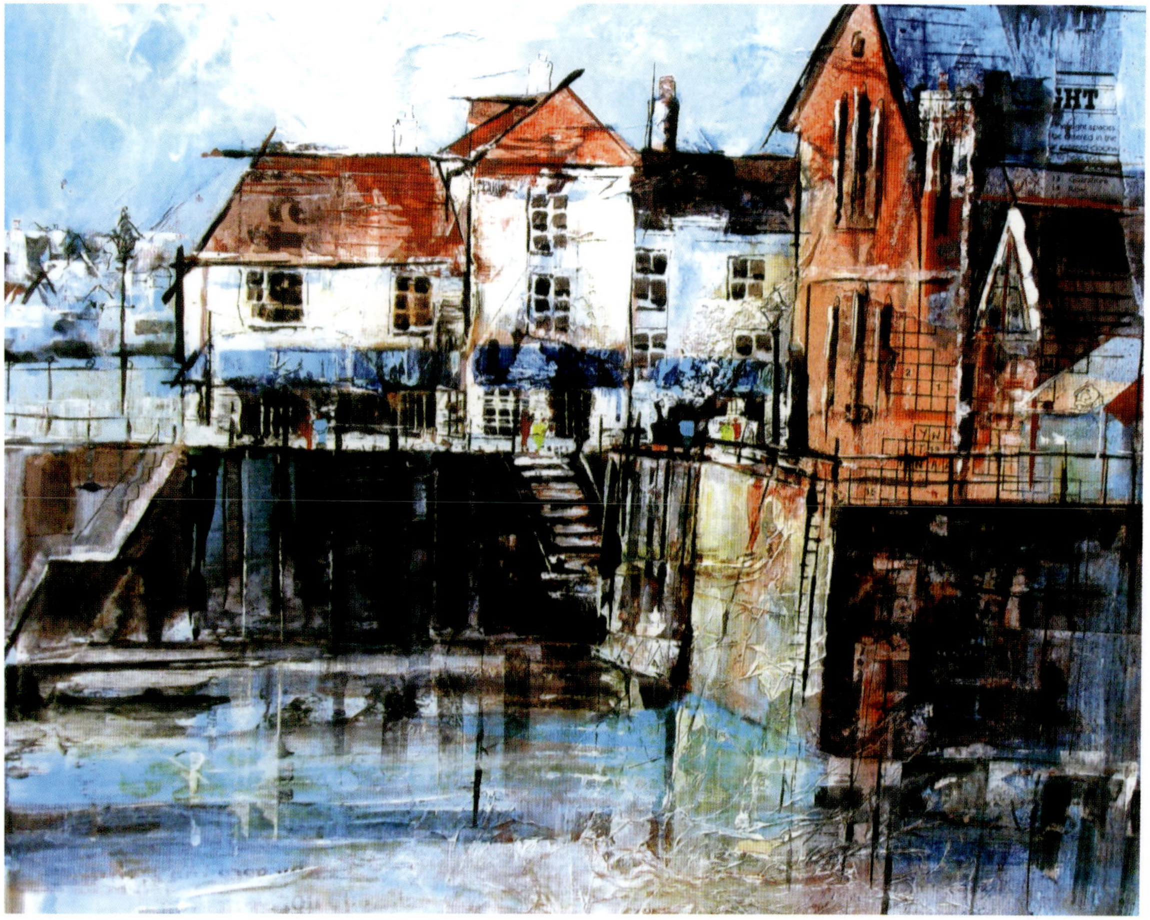

Cornish Harbour II, mixed media, 12 x 9 in

Cornish Harbour I, mixed media, 18 x 14 in

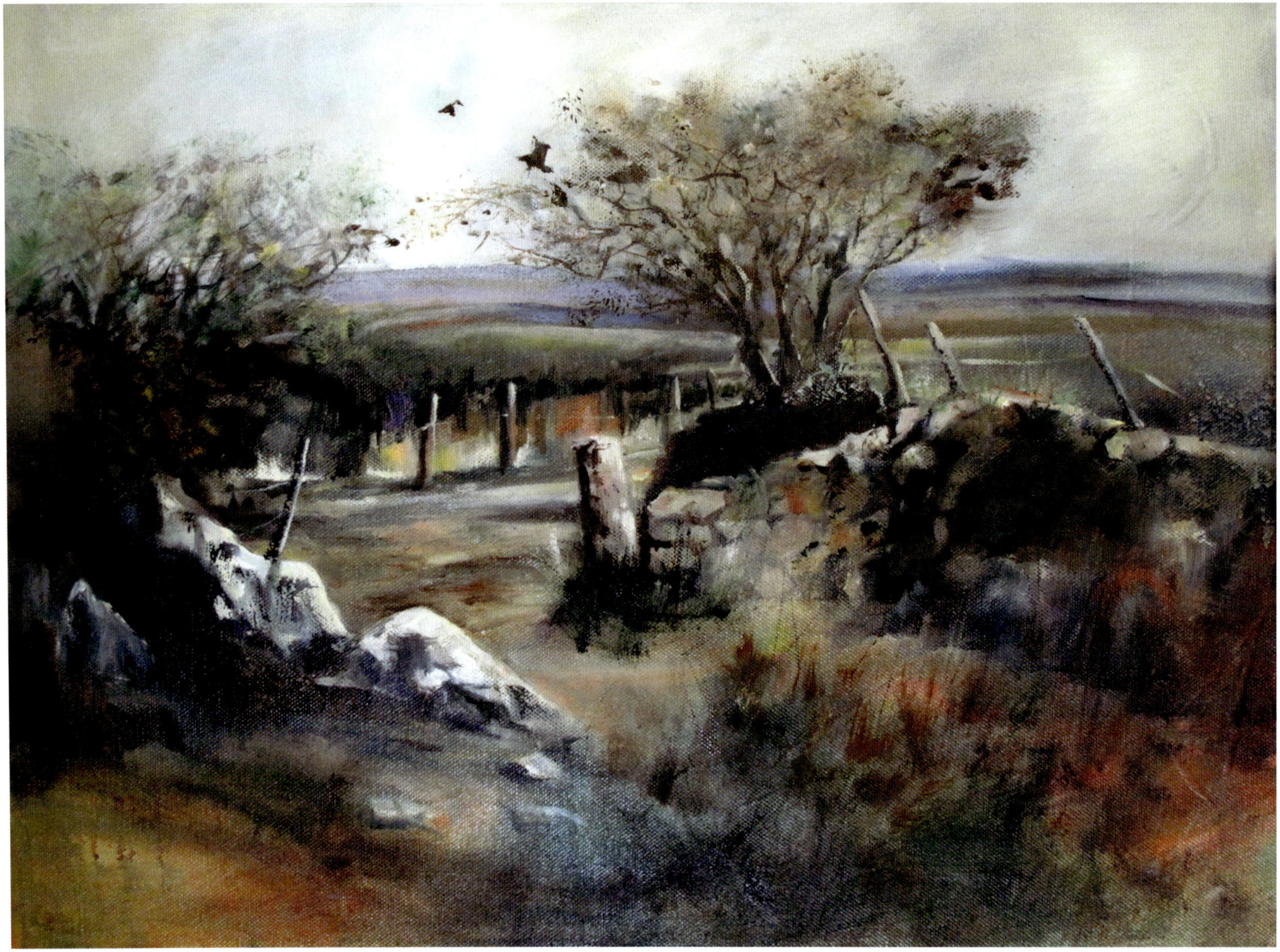

Moorland Way, mixed media, 15 x 12 in

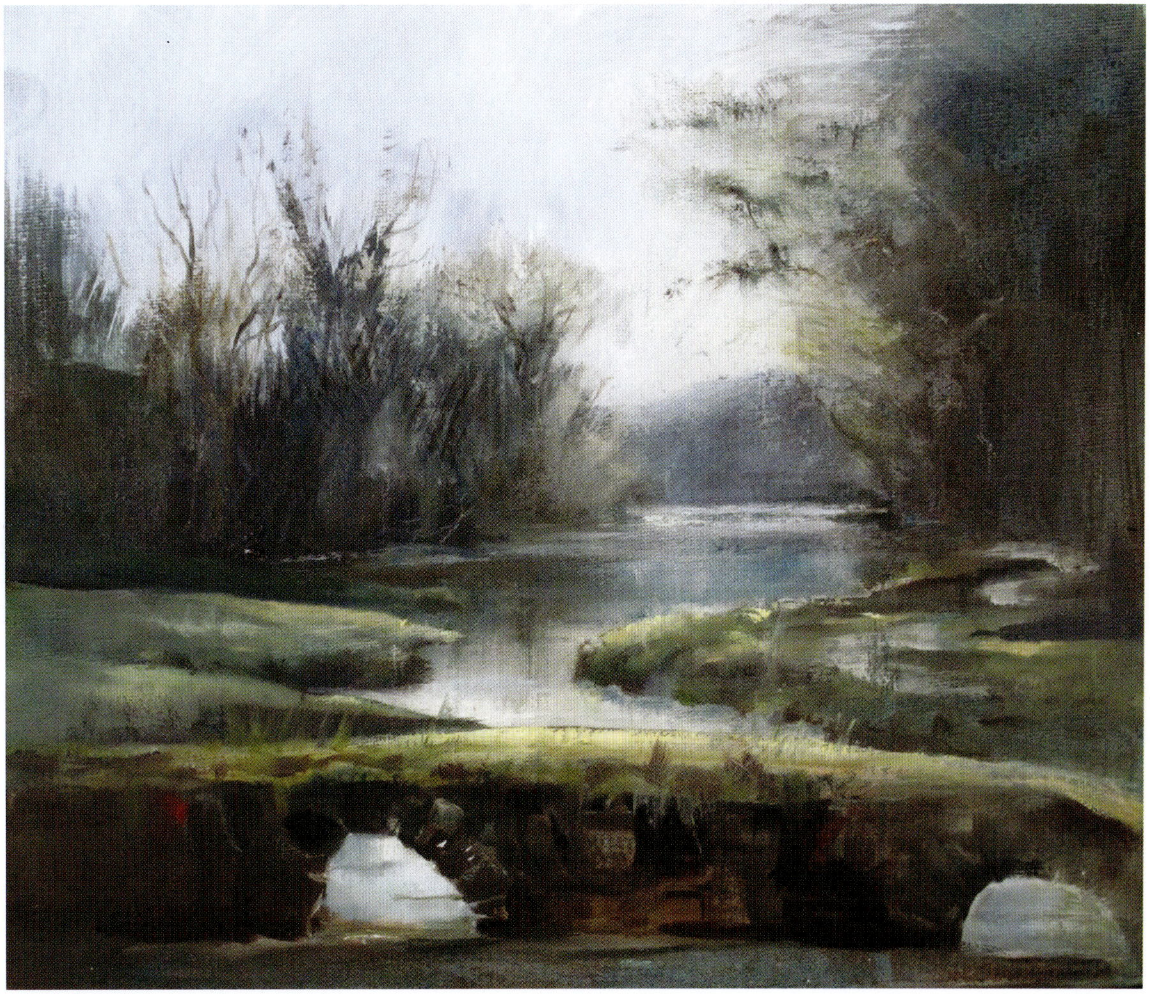

Cofflete Creek, oil, 12 x 10 in

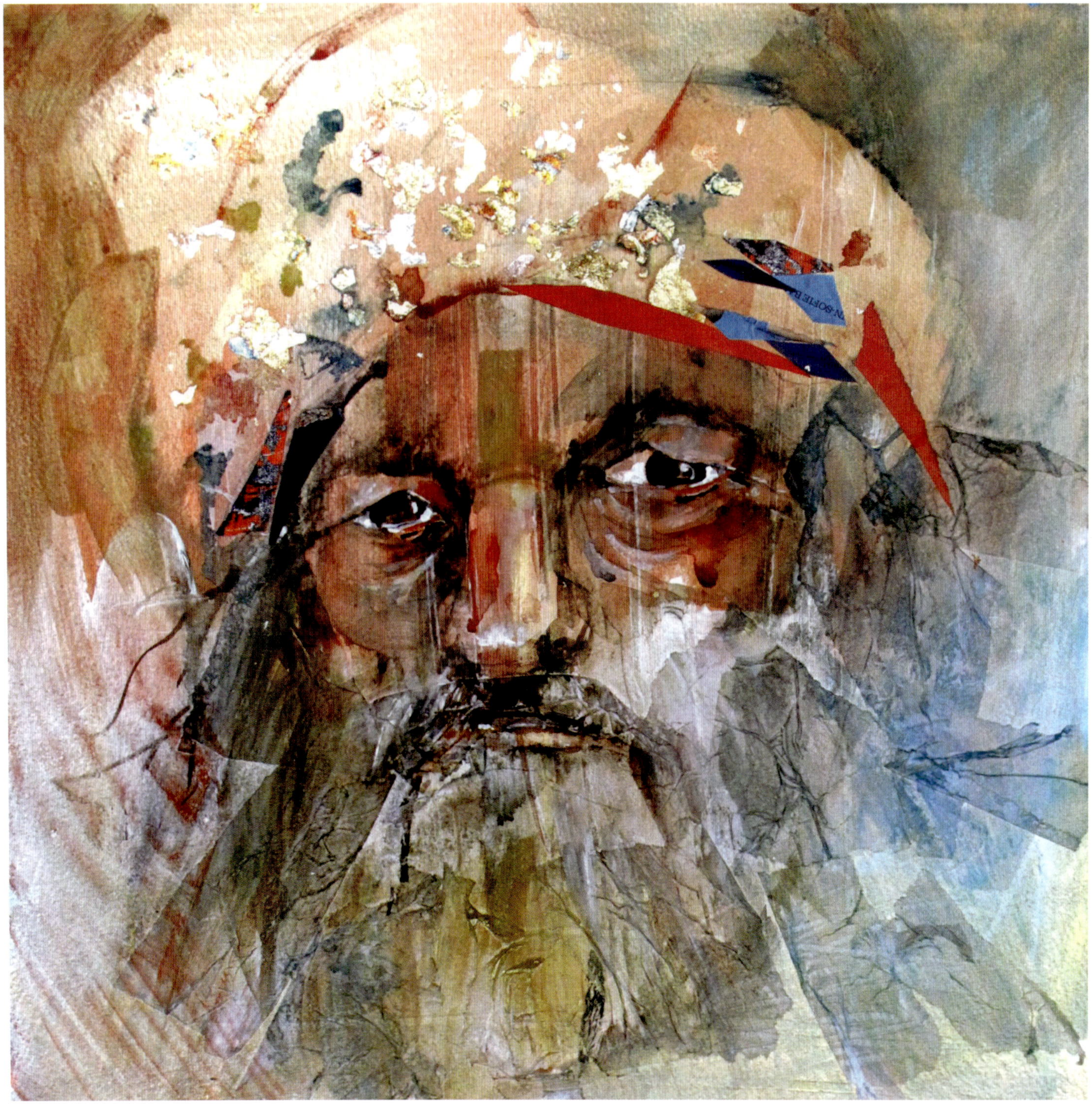

Portrait of a Painter,
acrylic, 17 x 21 in

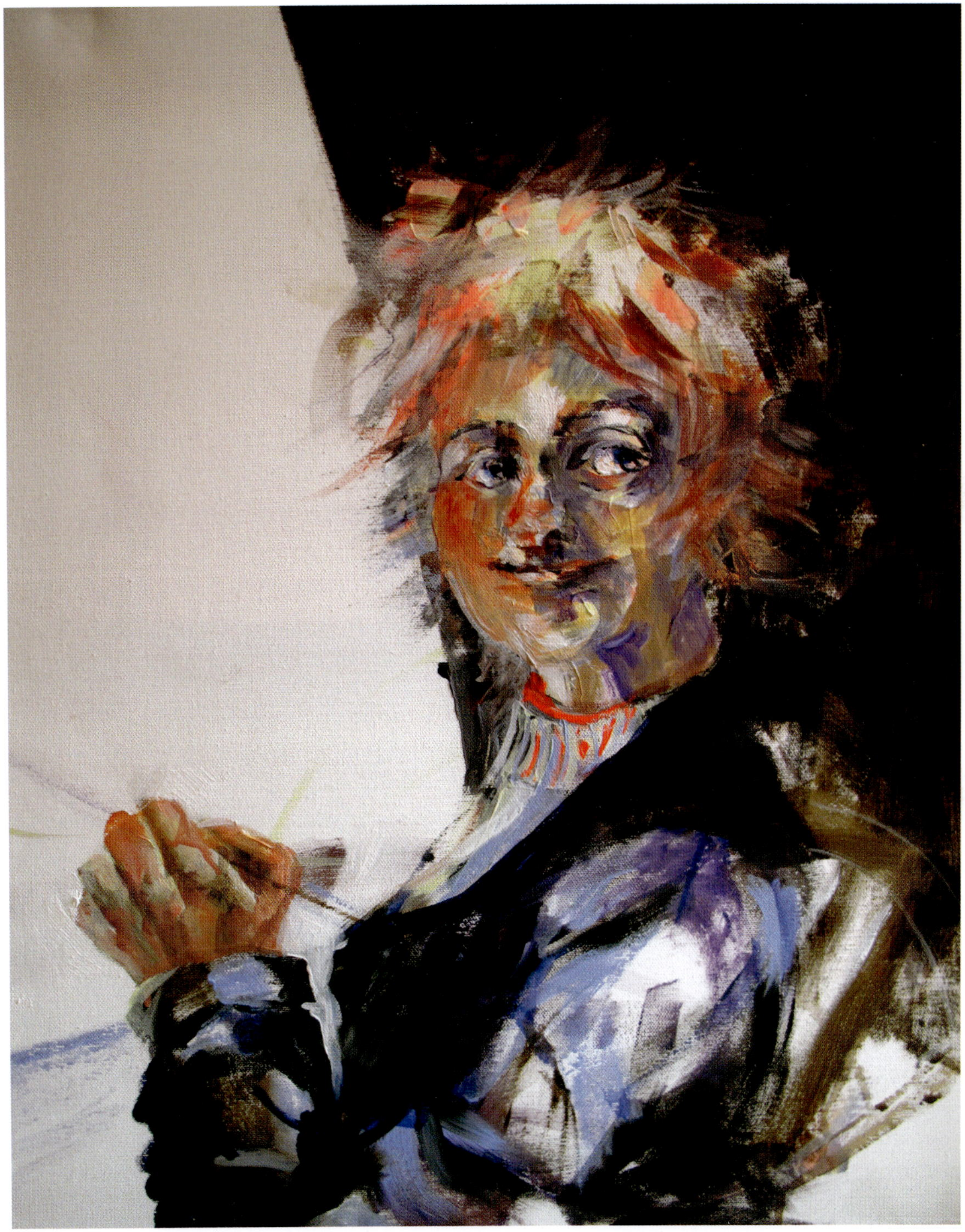

Rodney The Sage,
collage, 16 x 16 in

Mainly an exercise in using tissue paper as collage.

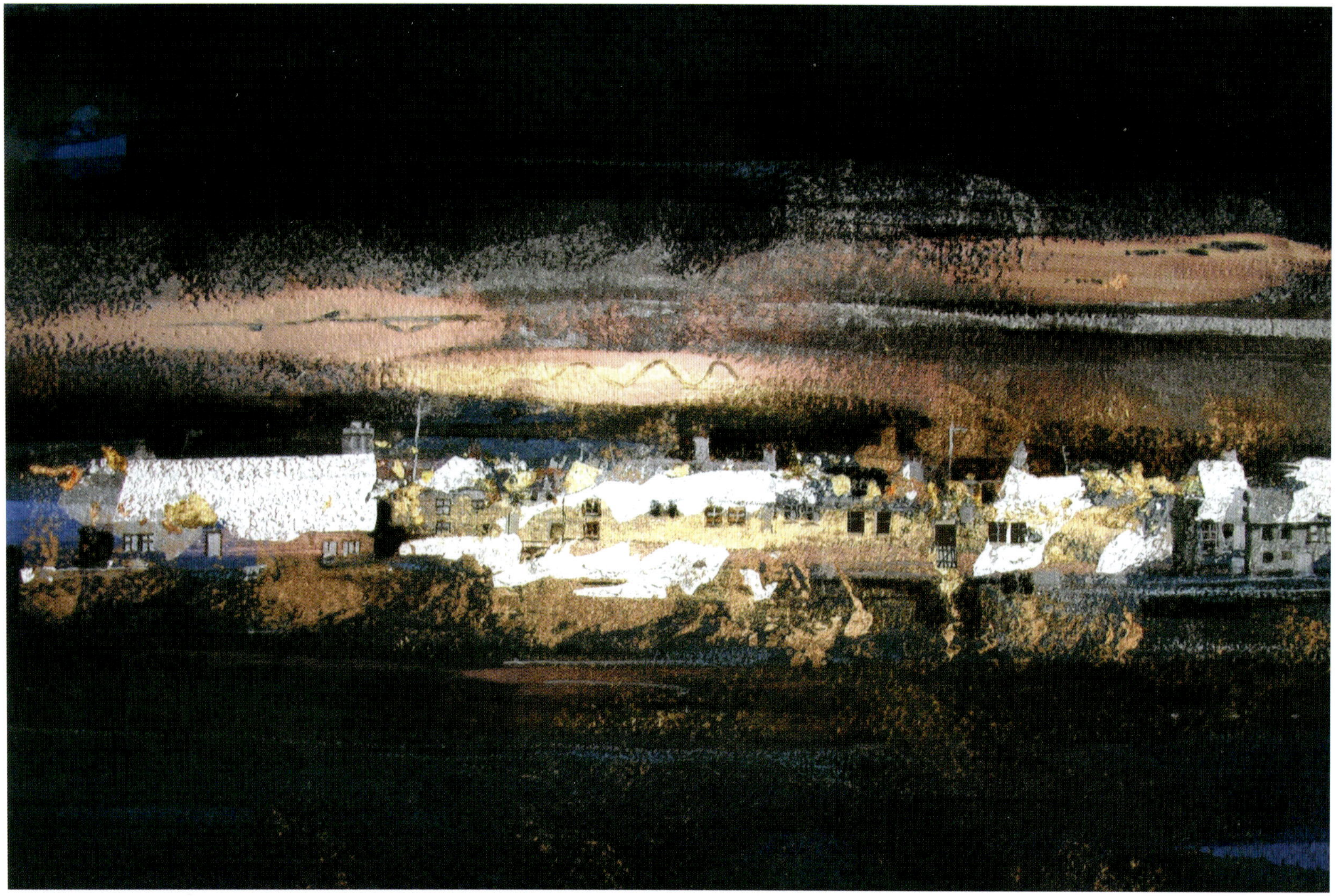

Golden Skies, mixed media, 16 x 12 in

This began life as a calligraphy project using gold and silver laid on a dark background, but became something else.

The Foreshore, Saltash, mixed media, 16 x 12 in

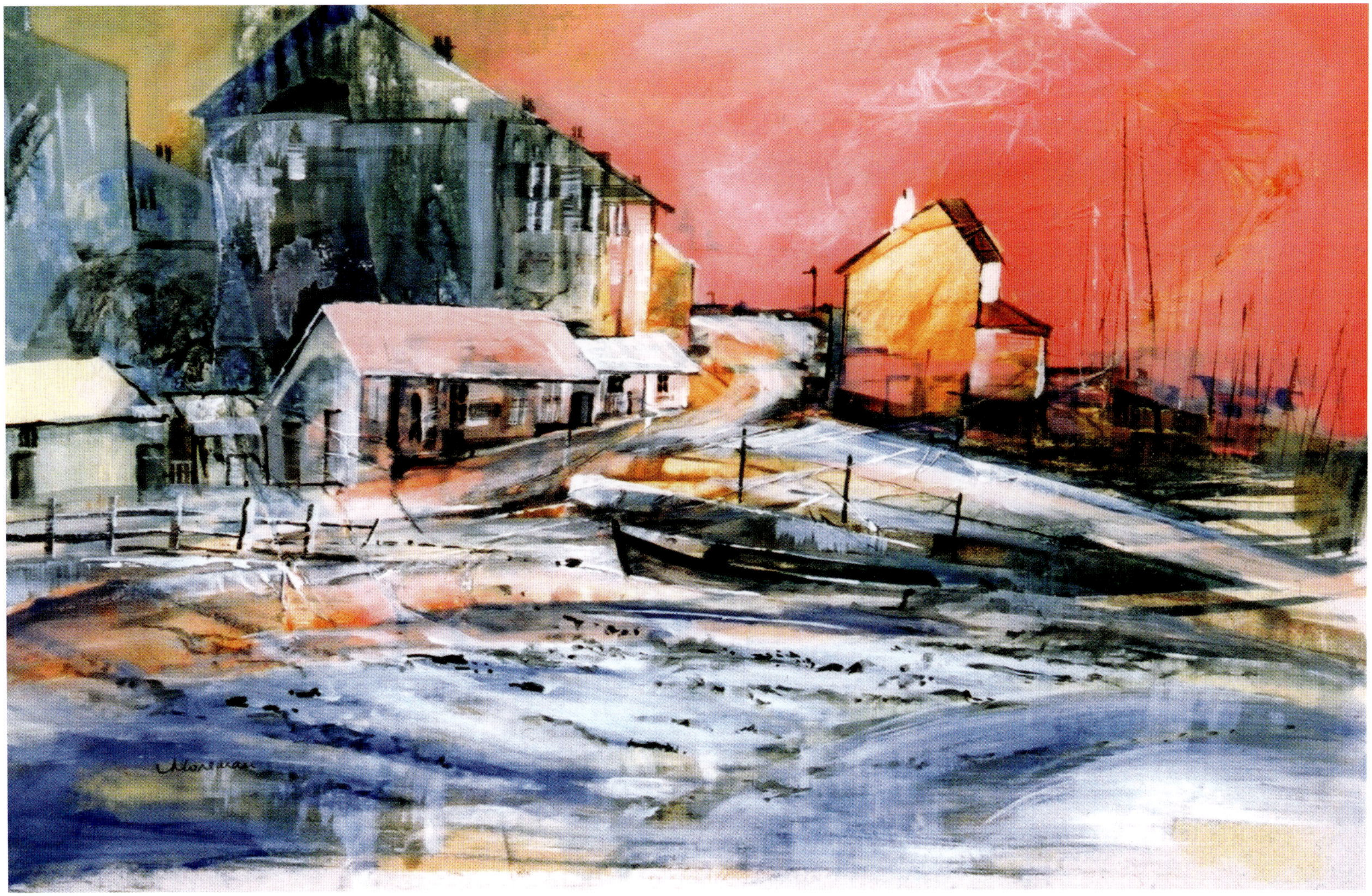

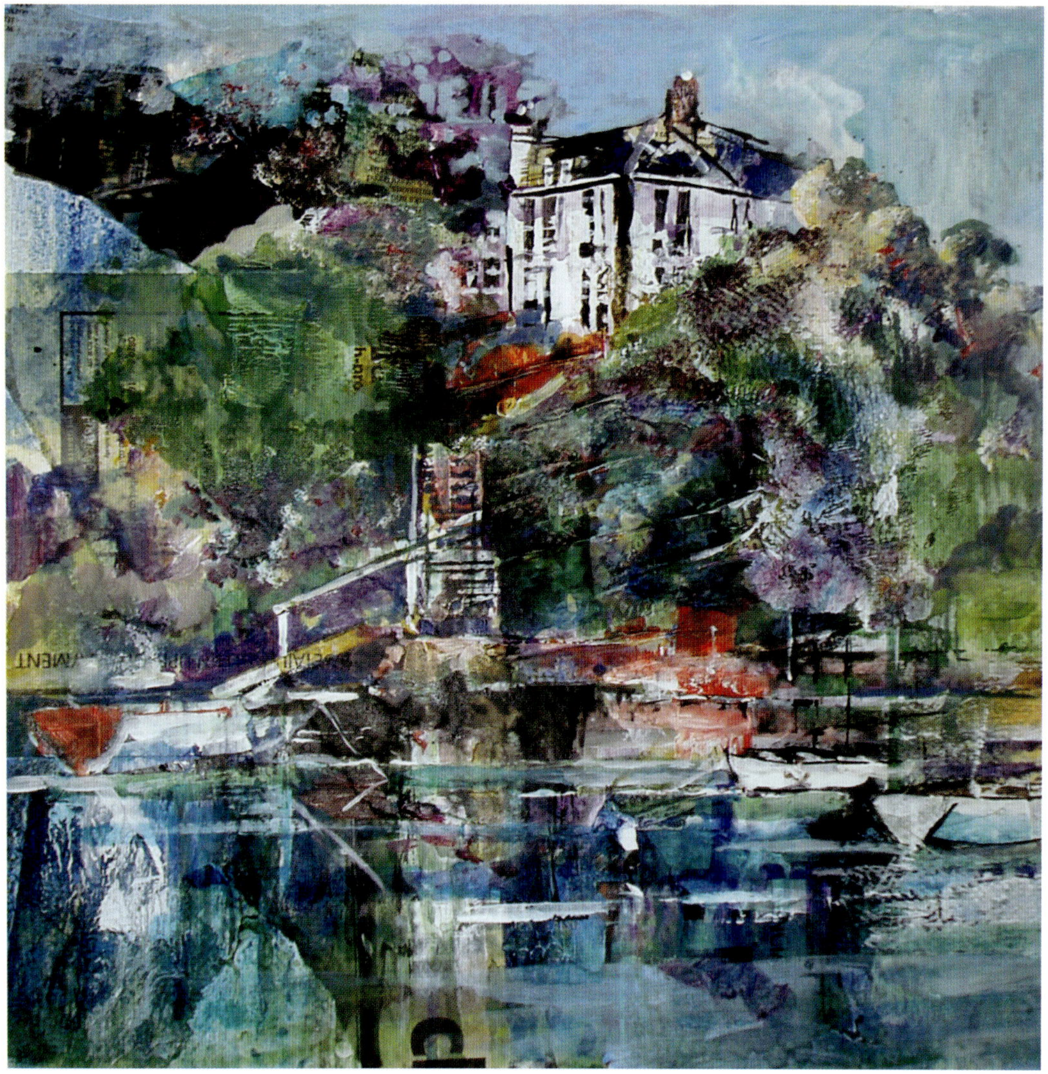

The Yealm Hotel, mixed media, 12 x 10 in

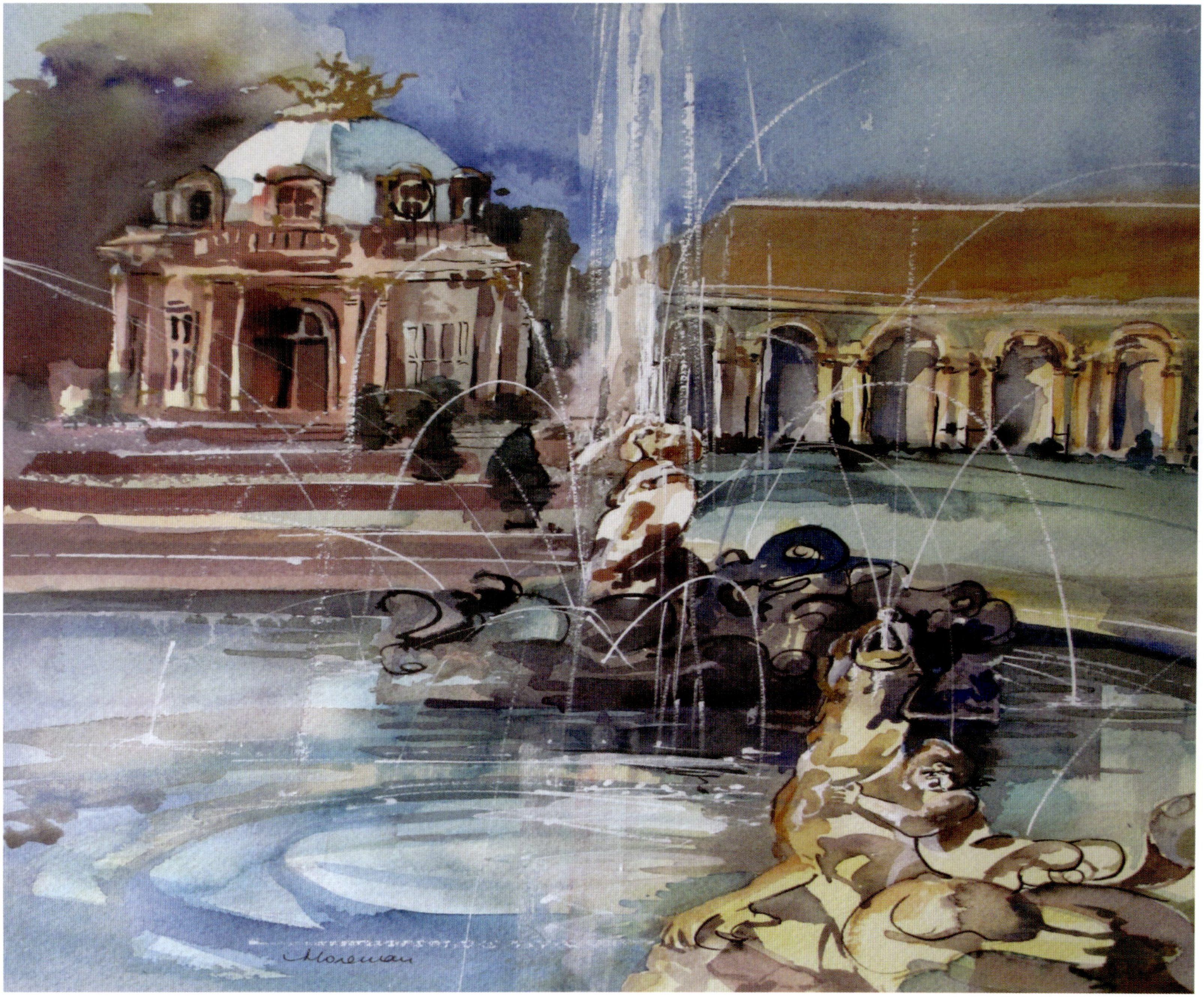

Bayreuth, Germany, watercolour, 14 x 13 in

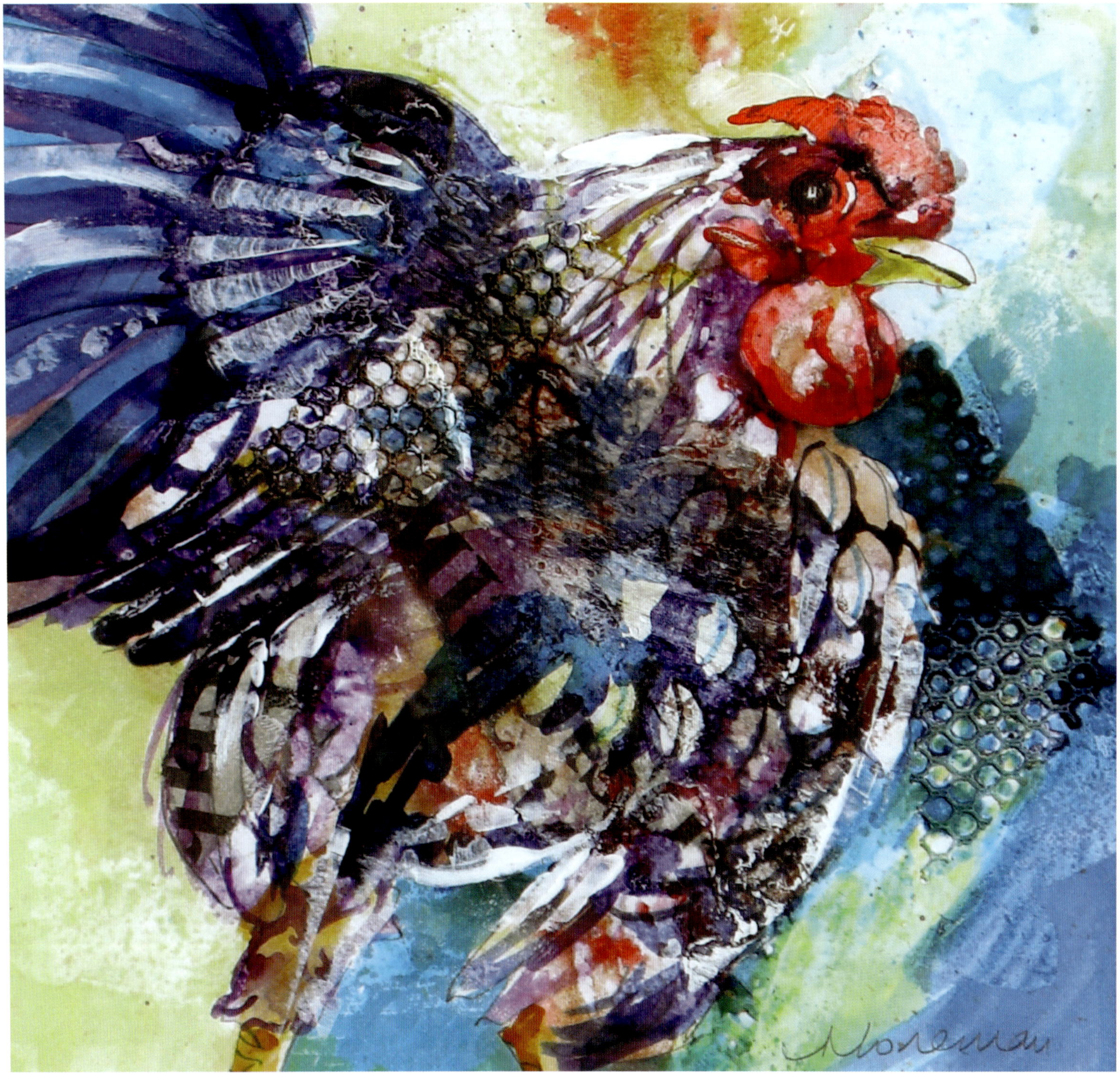

Dustbathing,
mixed media, 10 x 10 in

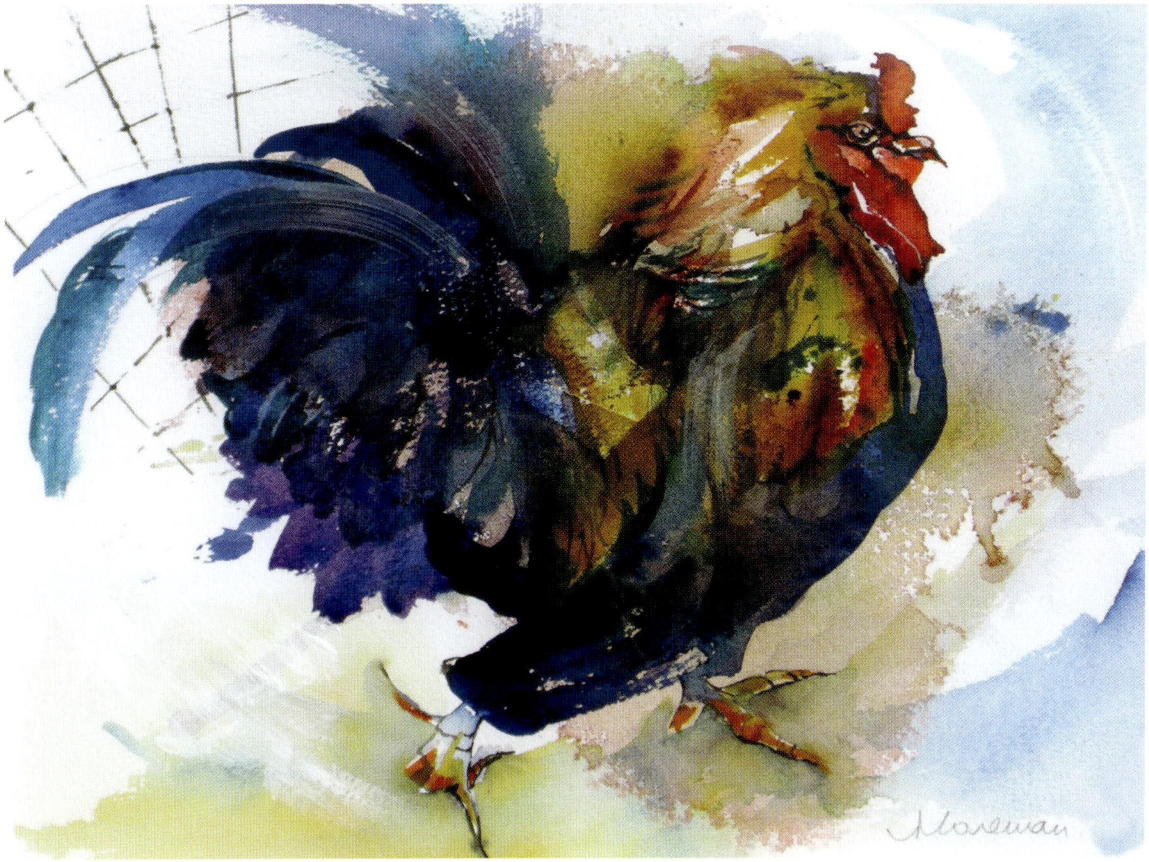

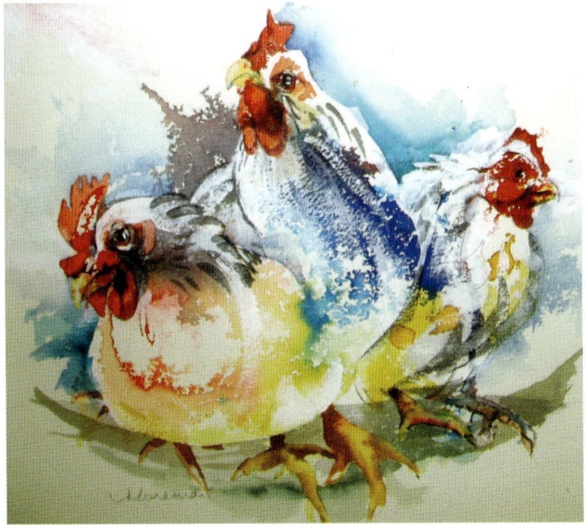

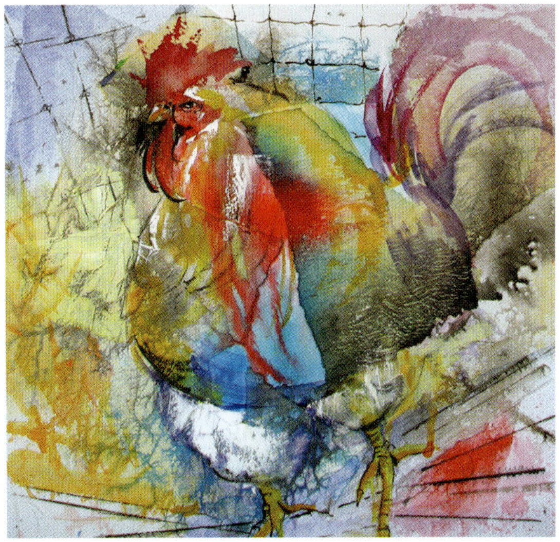

Above: *Strutting,*
watercolour and ink, 14 x 12 in

Far left: *Hen Friends,*
watercolour, 10 x 10 in

Left: *The Cockerel,*
watercolour and ink, 10 x 10 in

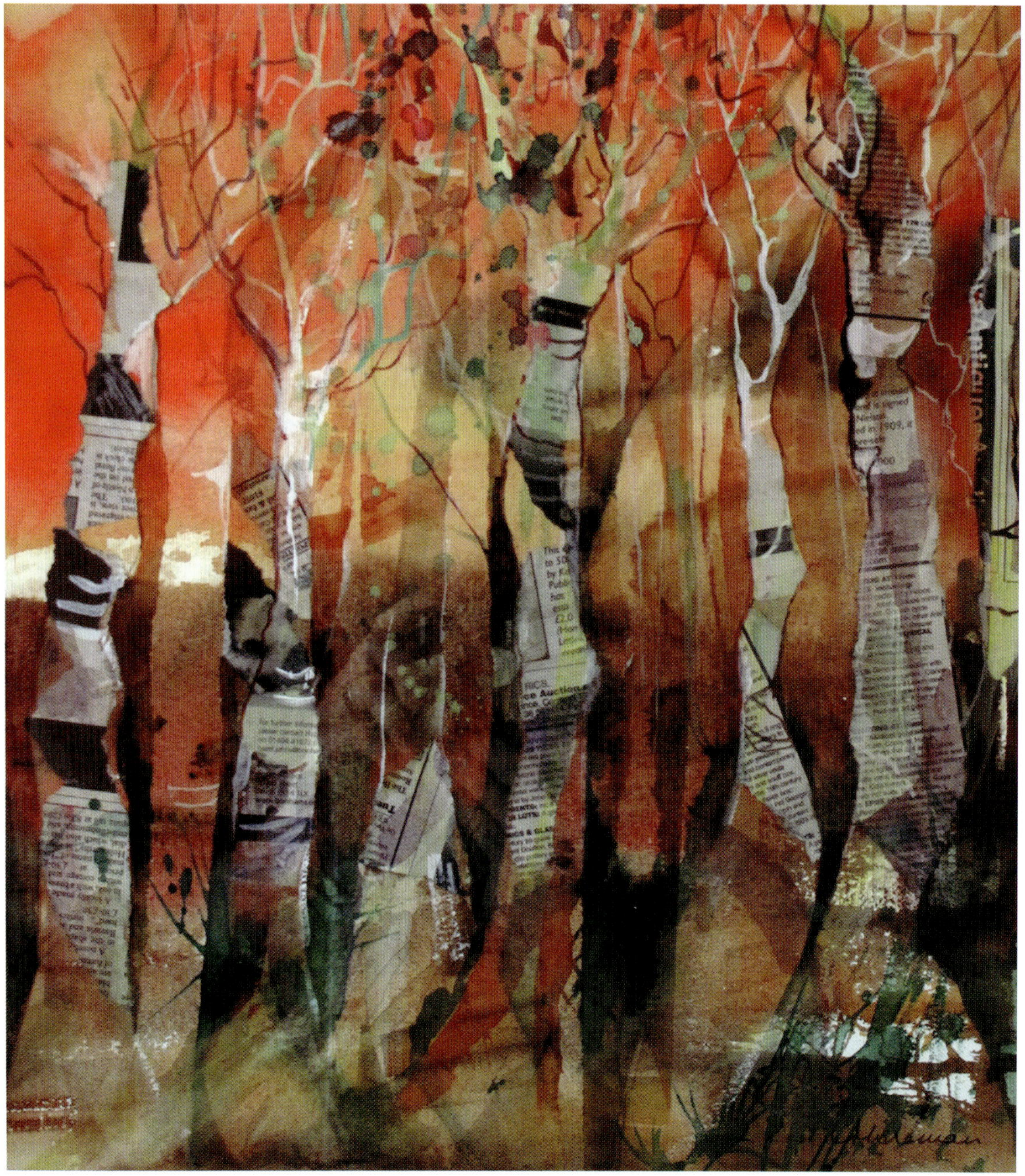

Birches, collage, 13 x 17 in

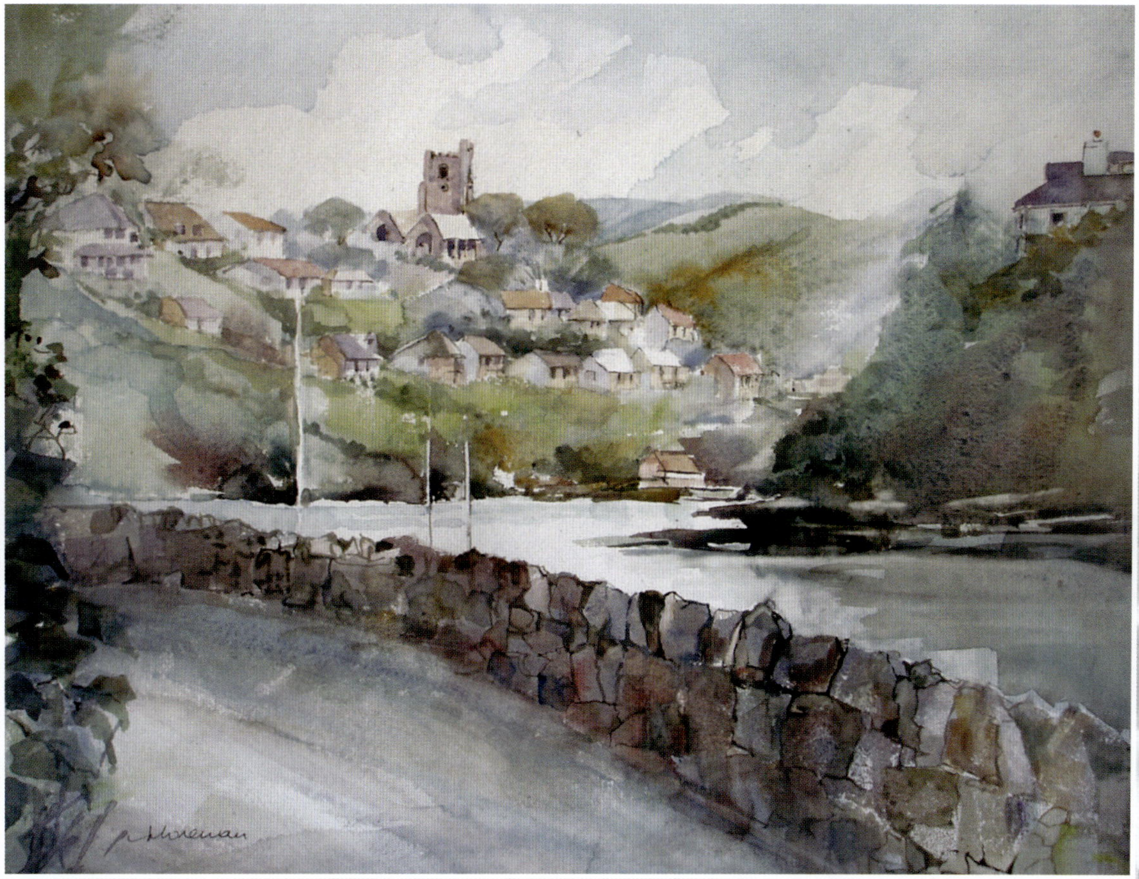

The Creek, Newton Ferrers, watercolour, 14 x 11 in

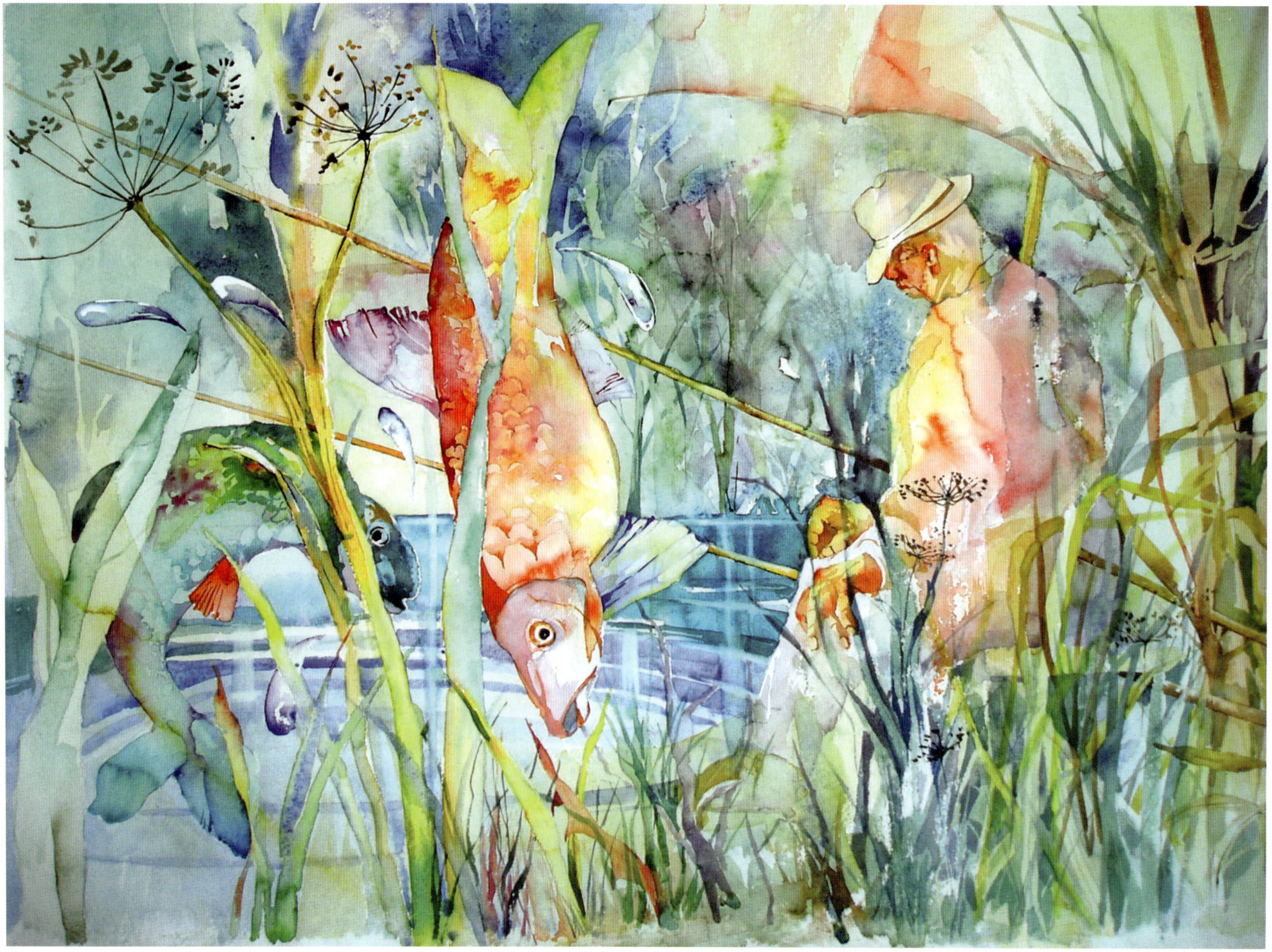

The Complacent Angler, watercolour, 24 x 19 in

Sometimes angling seems to be about just getting away from it all.

The Yellow House,
mixed media, 14 x 17 in

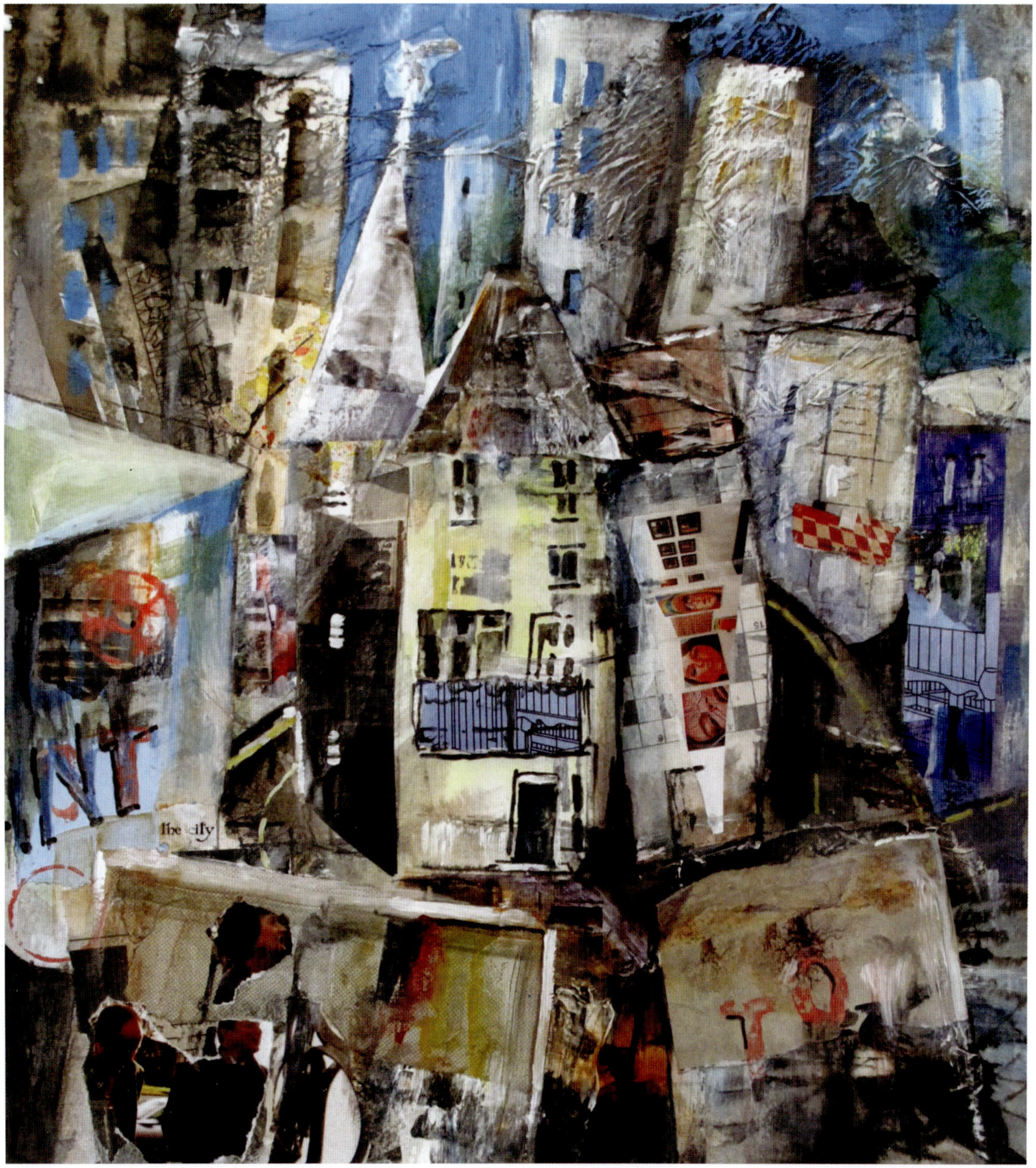

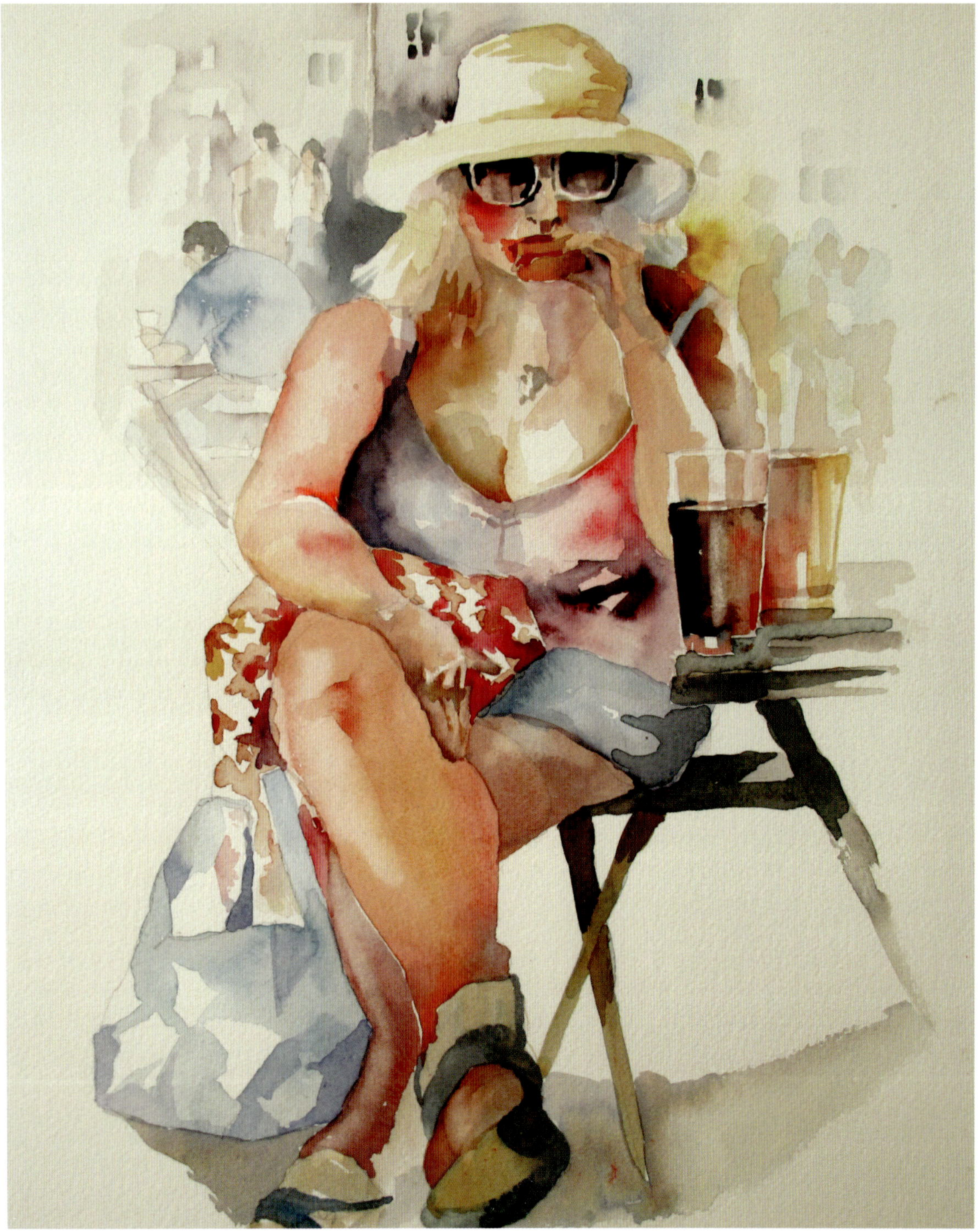

Drinks in the Sun,
watercolour, 15 x 21 in

Ziz, watercolour, 6 x 13 in

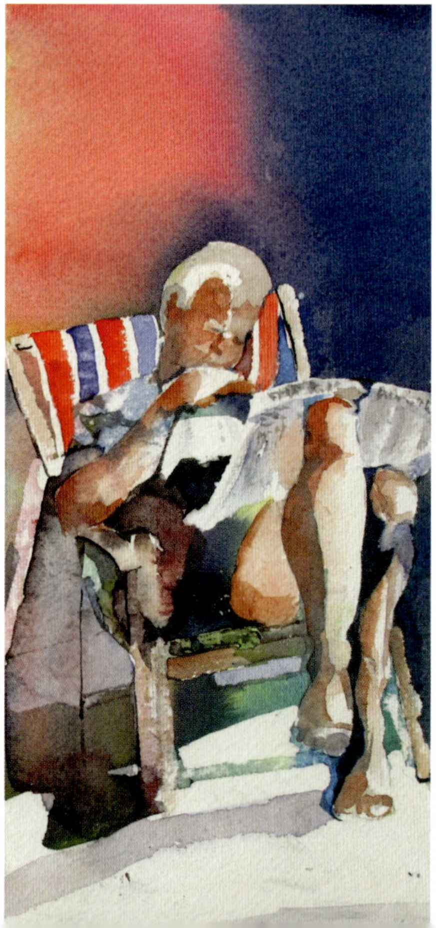

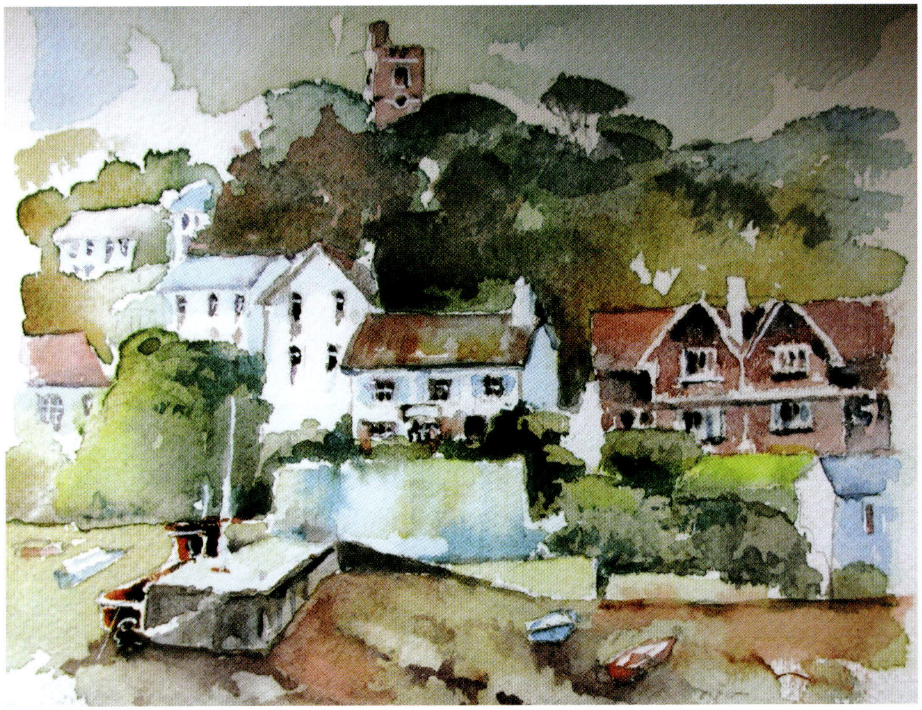

Low Tide at the Swan,
watercolour, 14 x 12 in

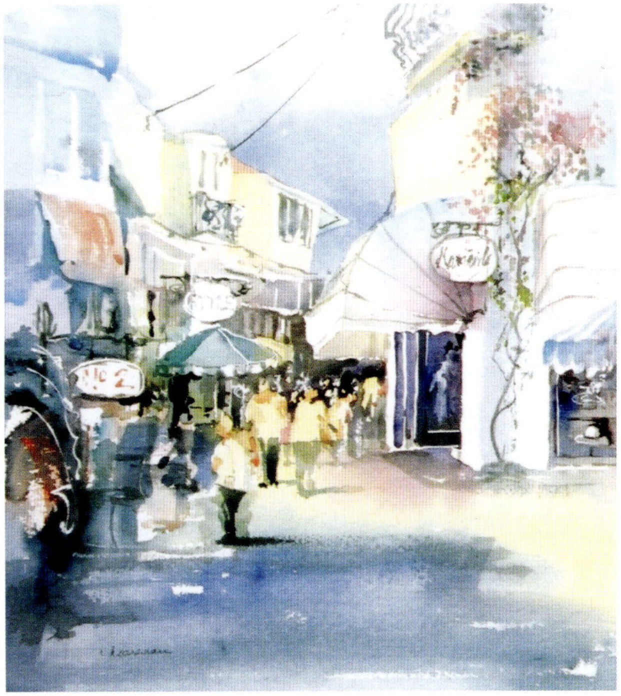

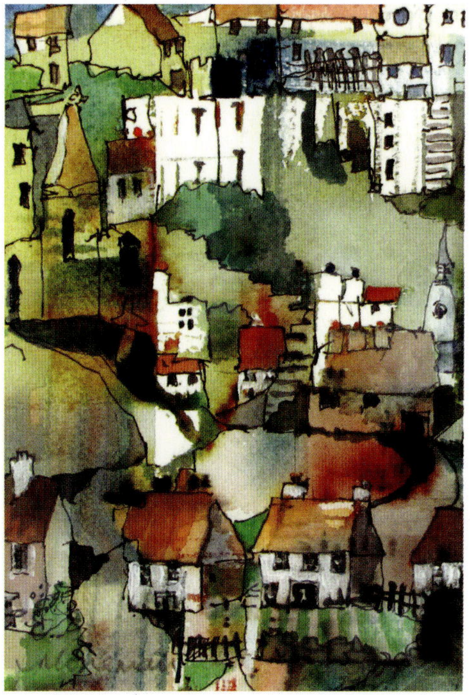

Right: *Bougainvillea, Spain,*
watercolour, 12 x 13 in

Far right: *Hillside Cottages,*
watercolour and ink, 7 x 11 in

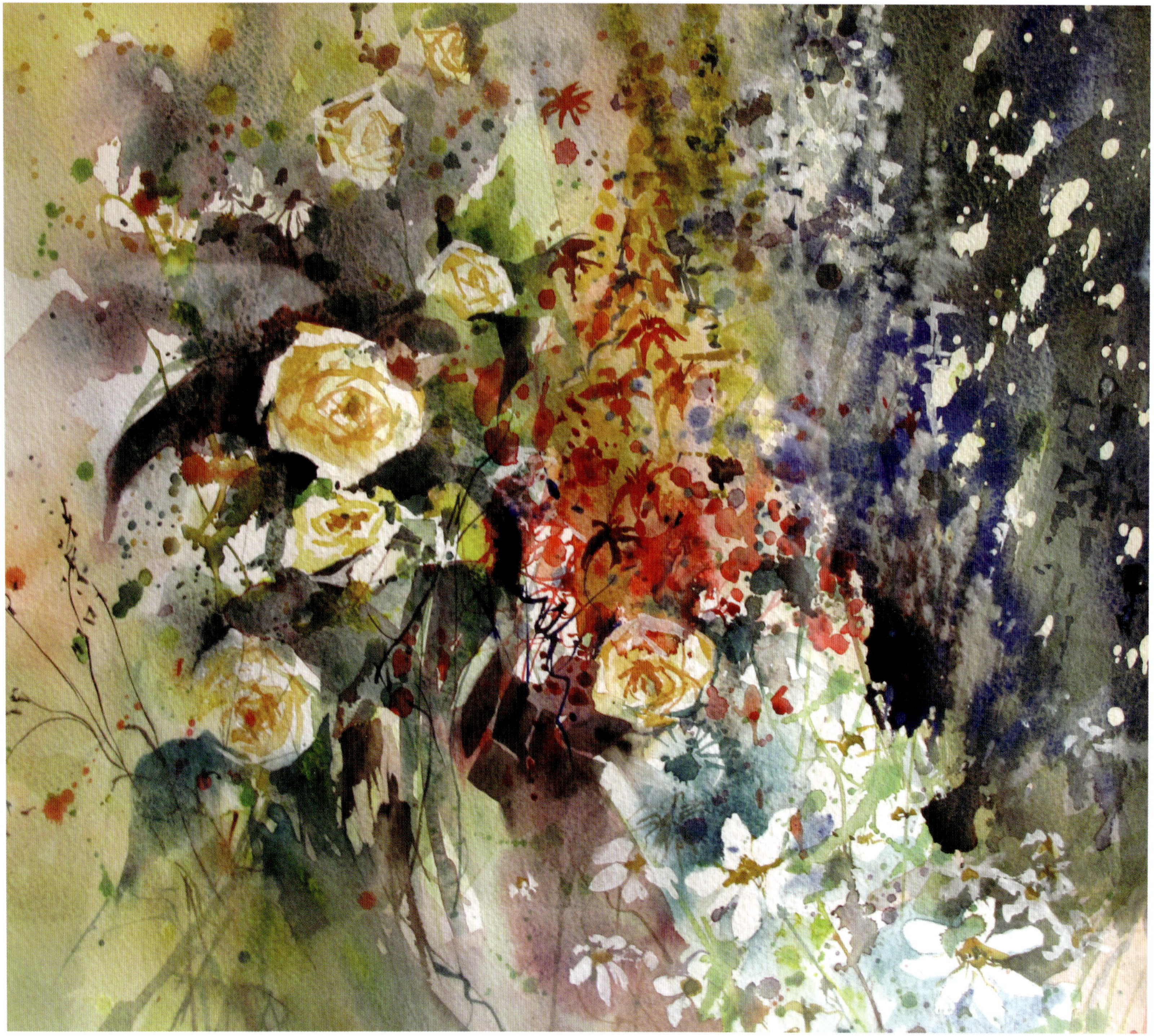

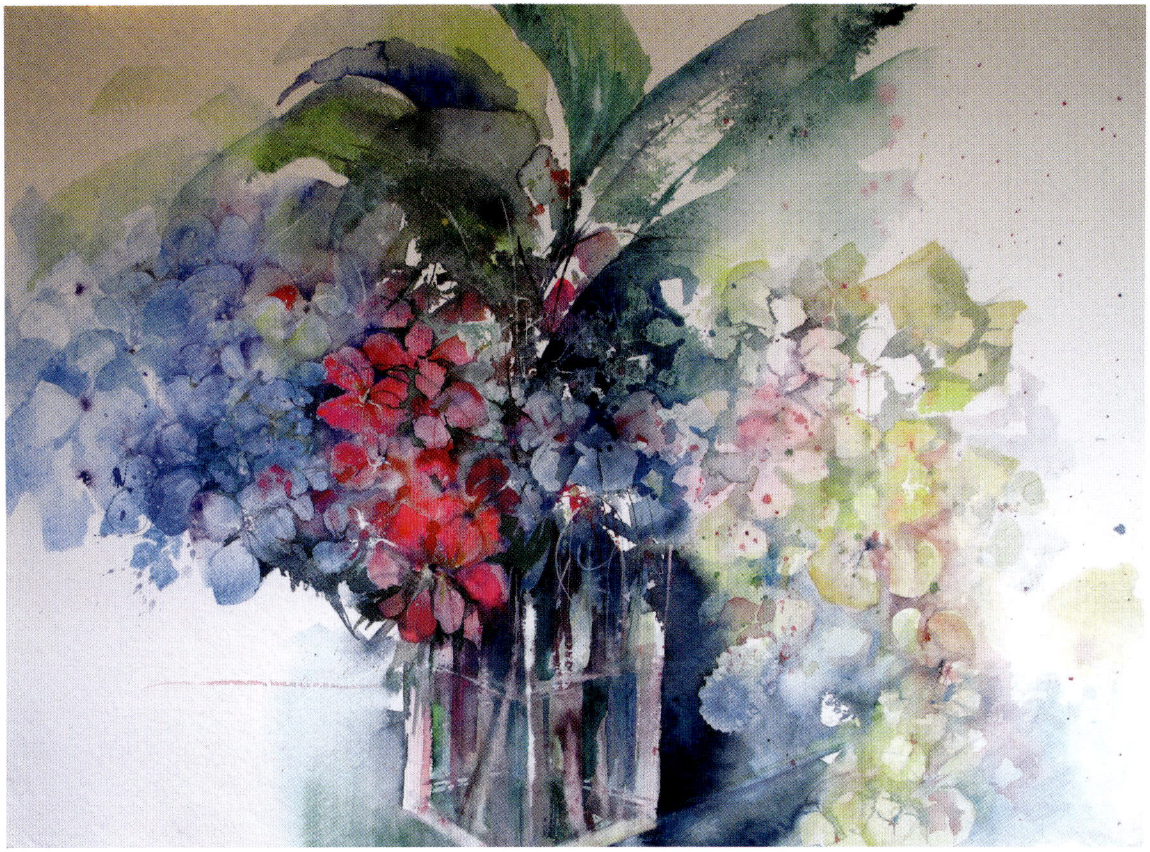

Hydrangeas, watercolour, 28 x 21 in

Cascade, watercolour, 14 x 14 in

Beach Huts I, watercolour and ink, 10 x 10 in

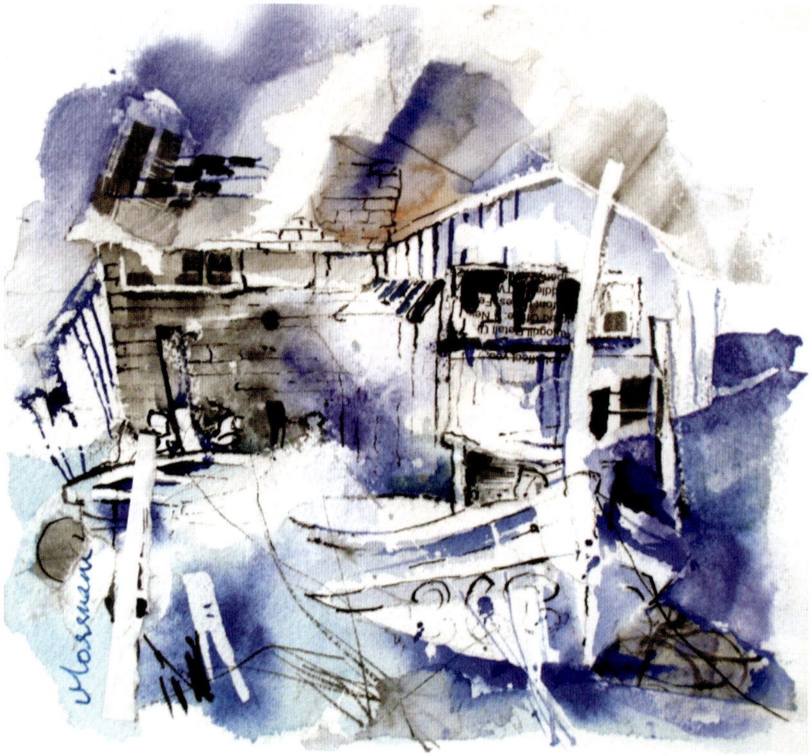

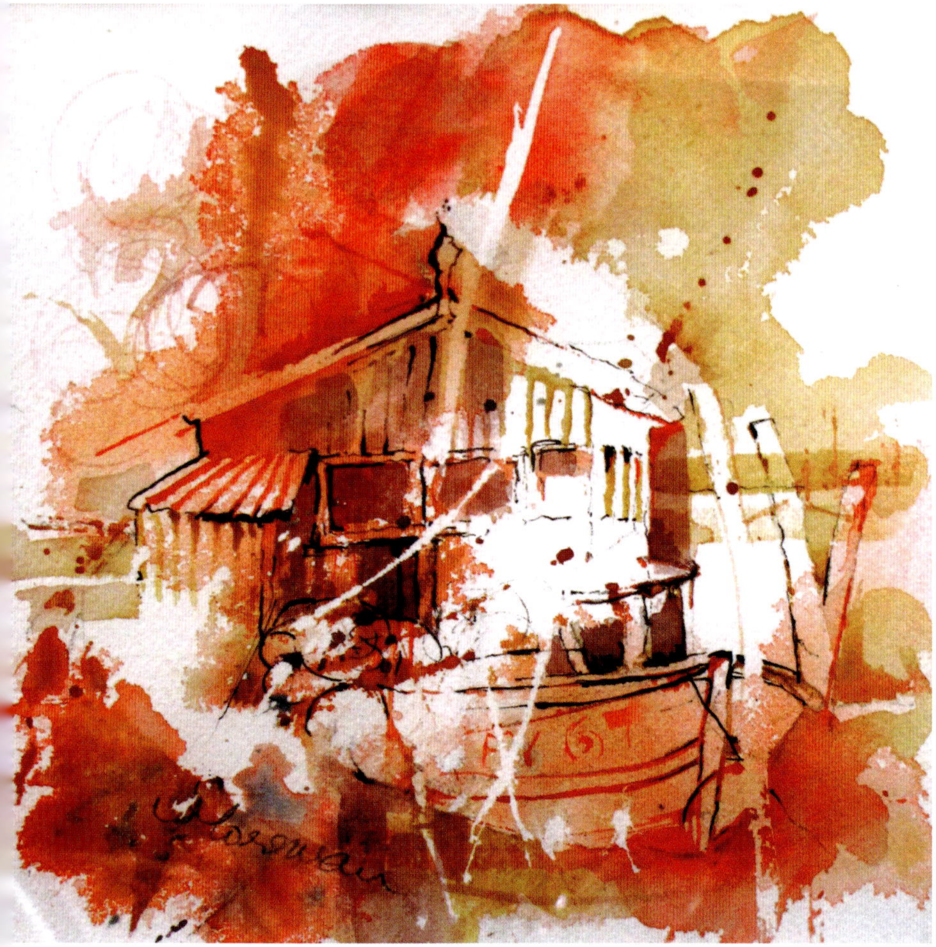

Beach Huts II, watercolour and ink, 10 x 10 in

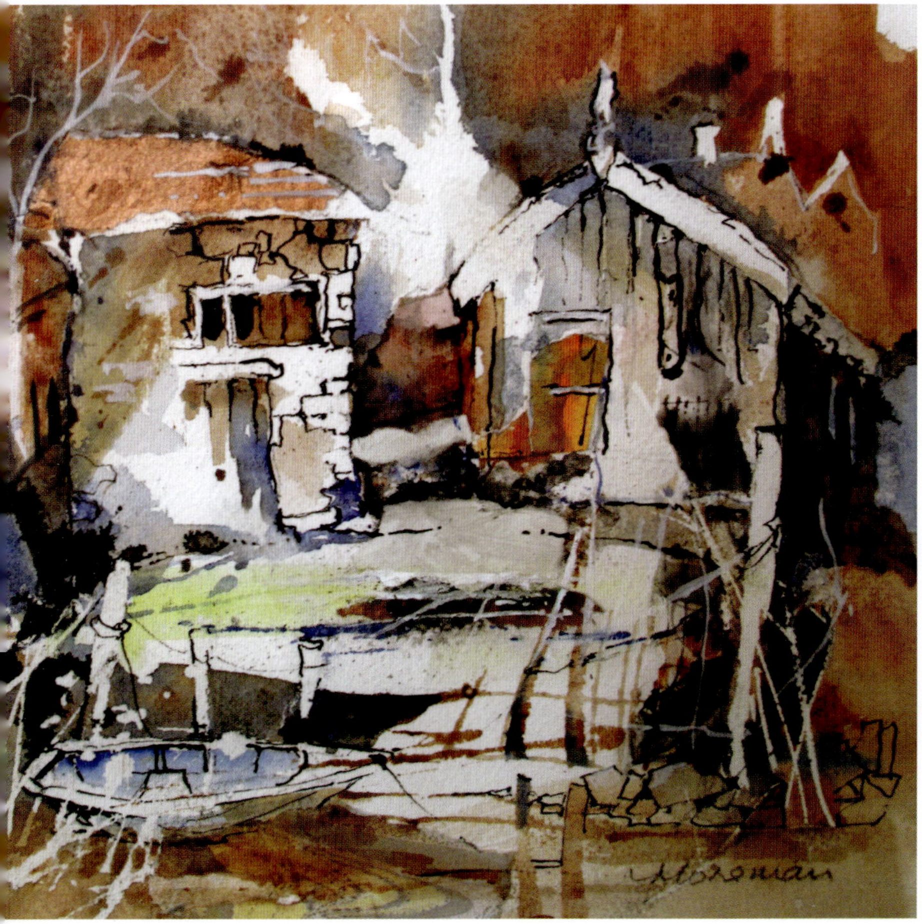

Beach Huts III, watercolour and ink, 10 x 10 in

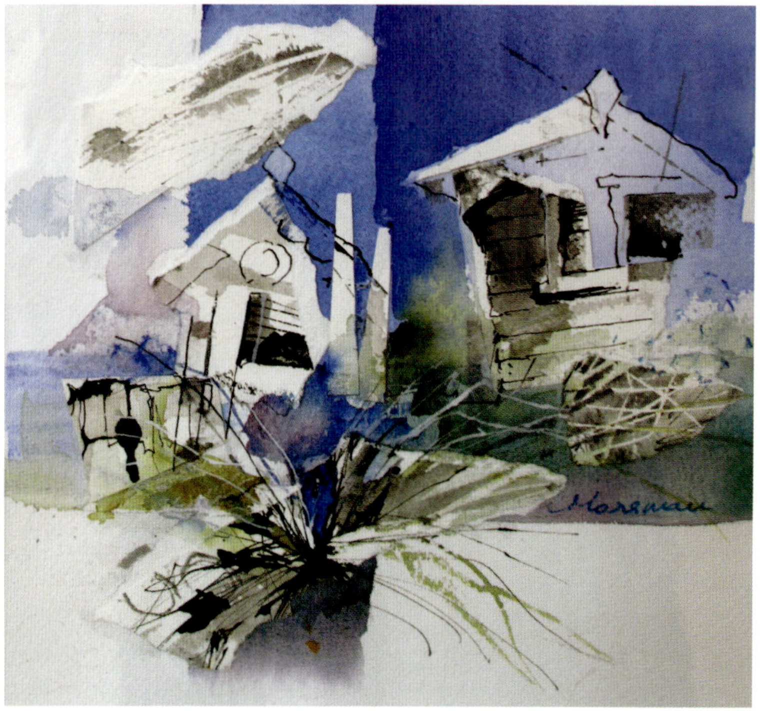

Beach Huts IV, watercolour and ink, 10 x 10 in

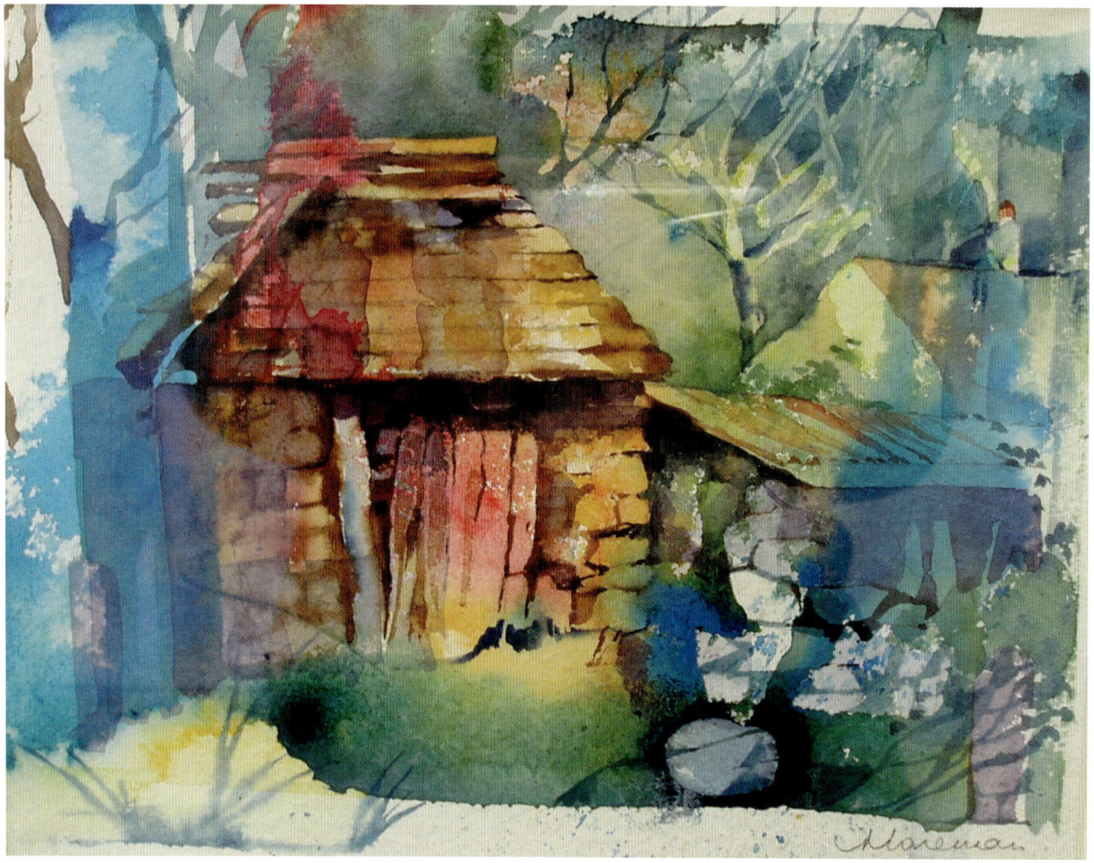

Outhouse, watercolour, 12 x 9 in

The Fat Lady Sings, collage, 16 x 11 in

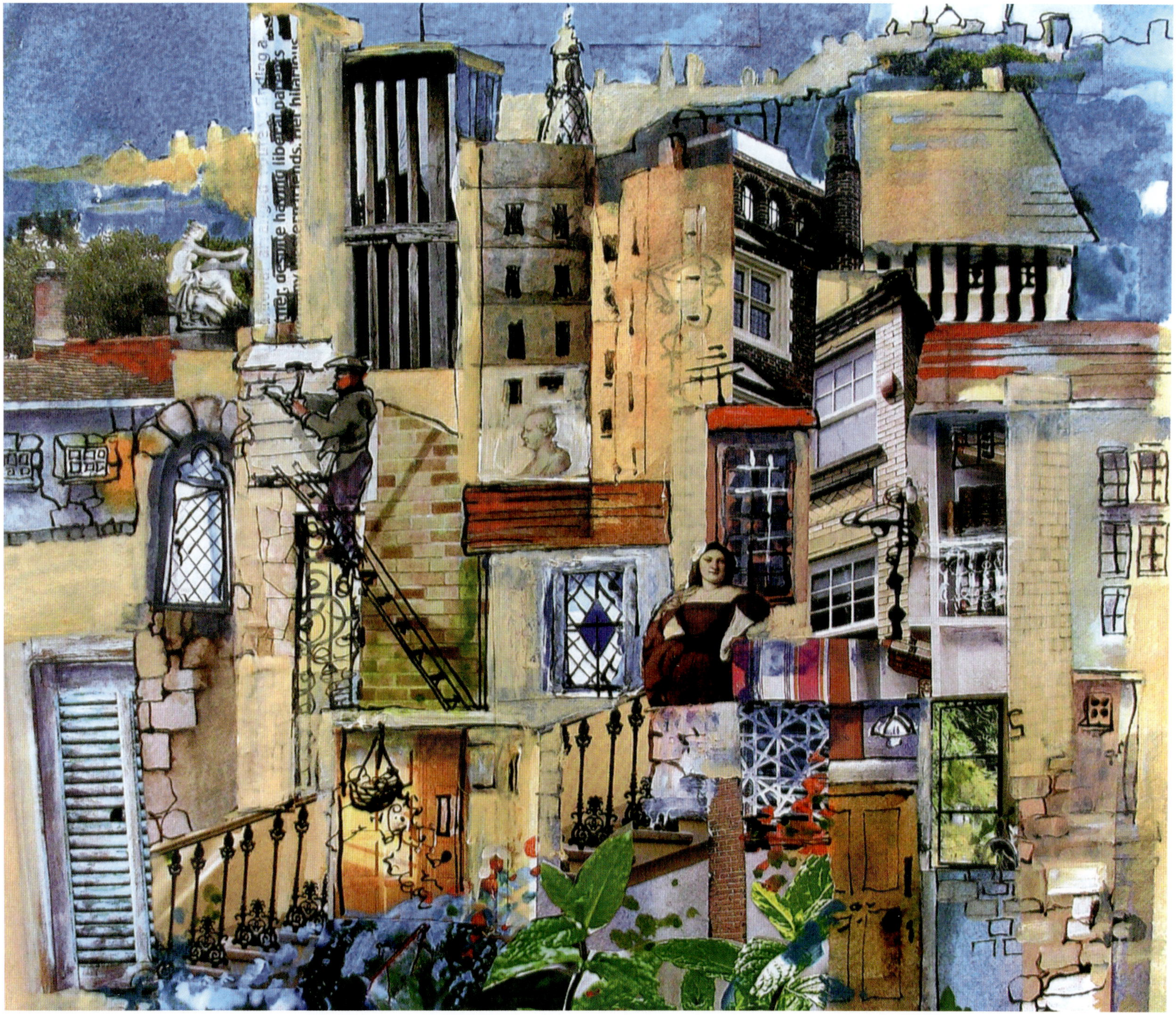

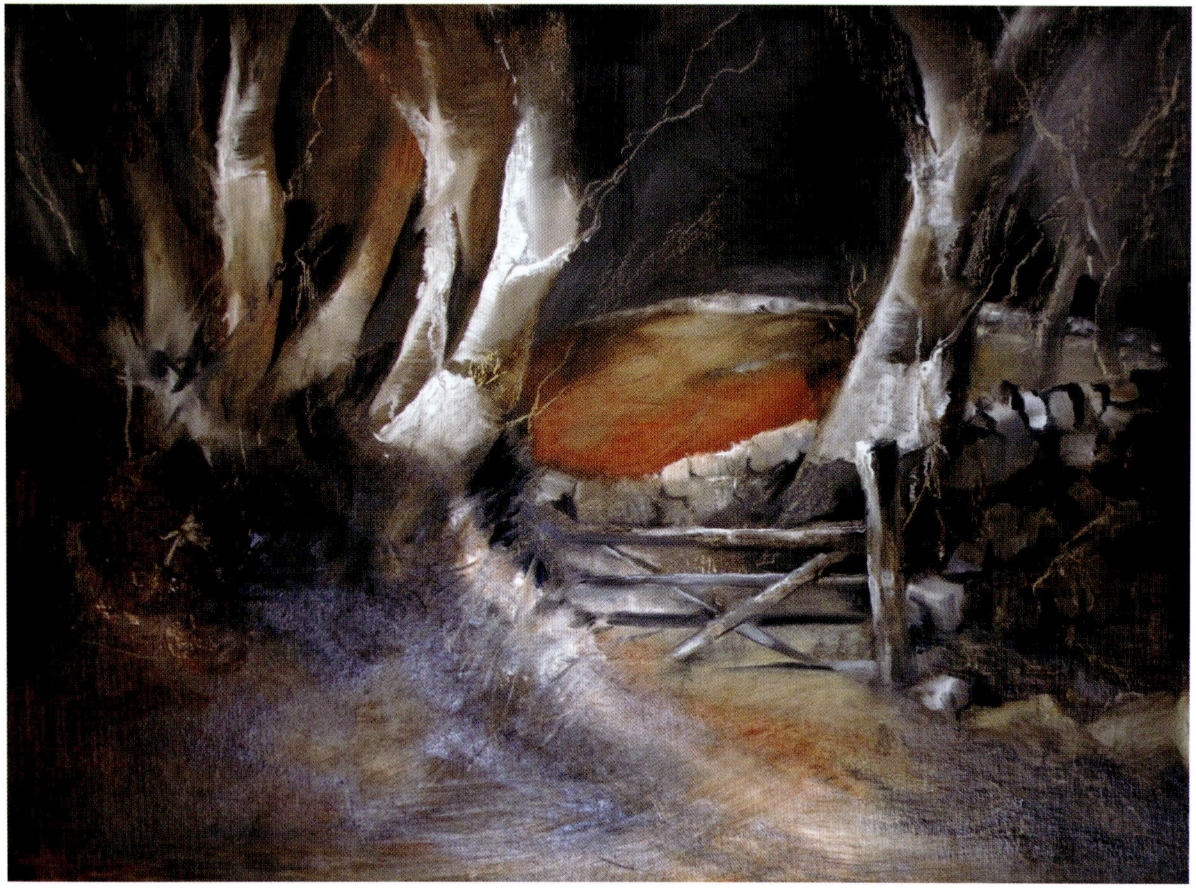

Hunter's Moon, acrylic, 17 x 13 in

Leaning Trees, collage and watercolour, 14 x 11 in

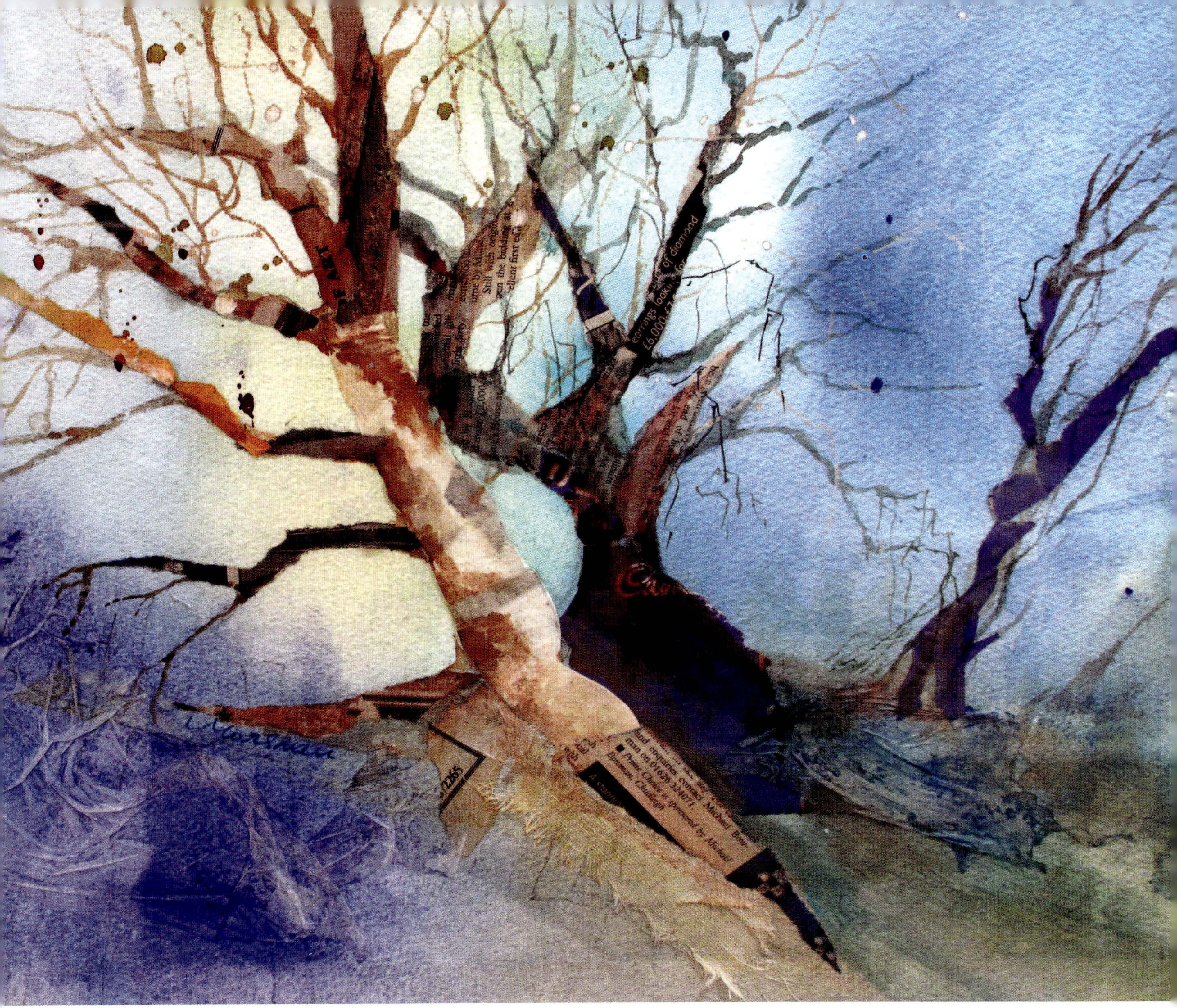

and enquiries contact Michael Bow-
man on 01626 324071.
Prime Choice is sponsored by Michael
Bowman, Chudleigh

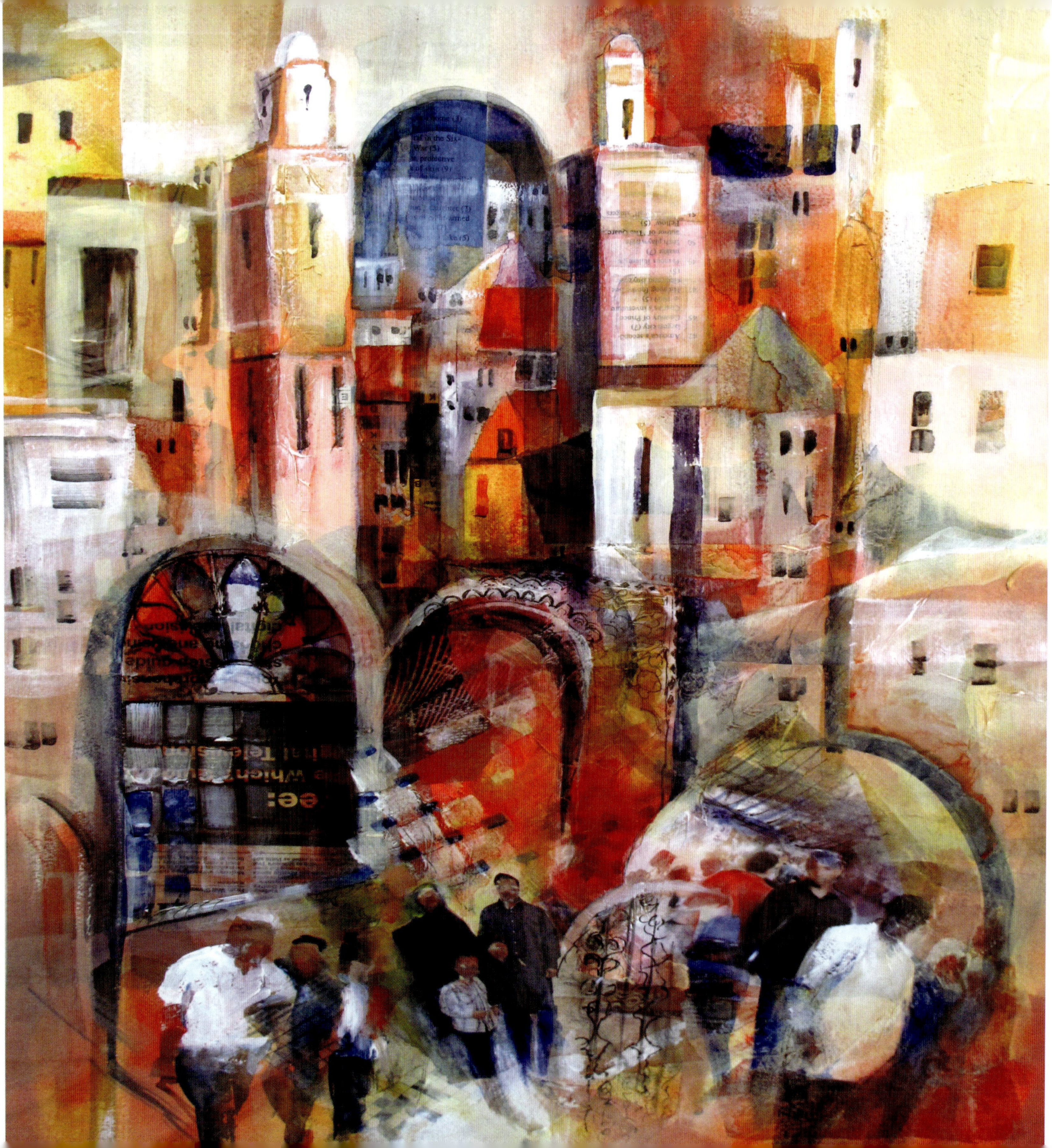

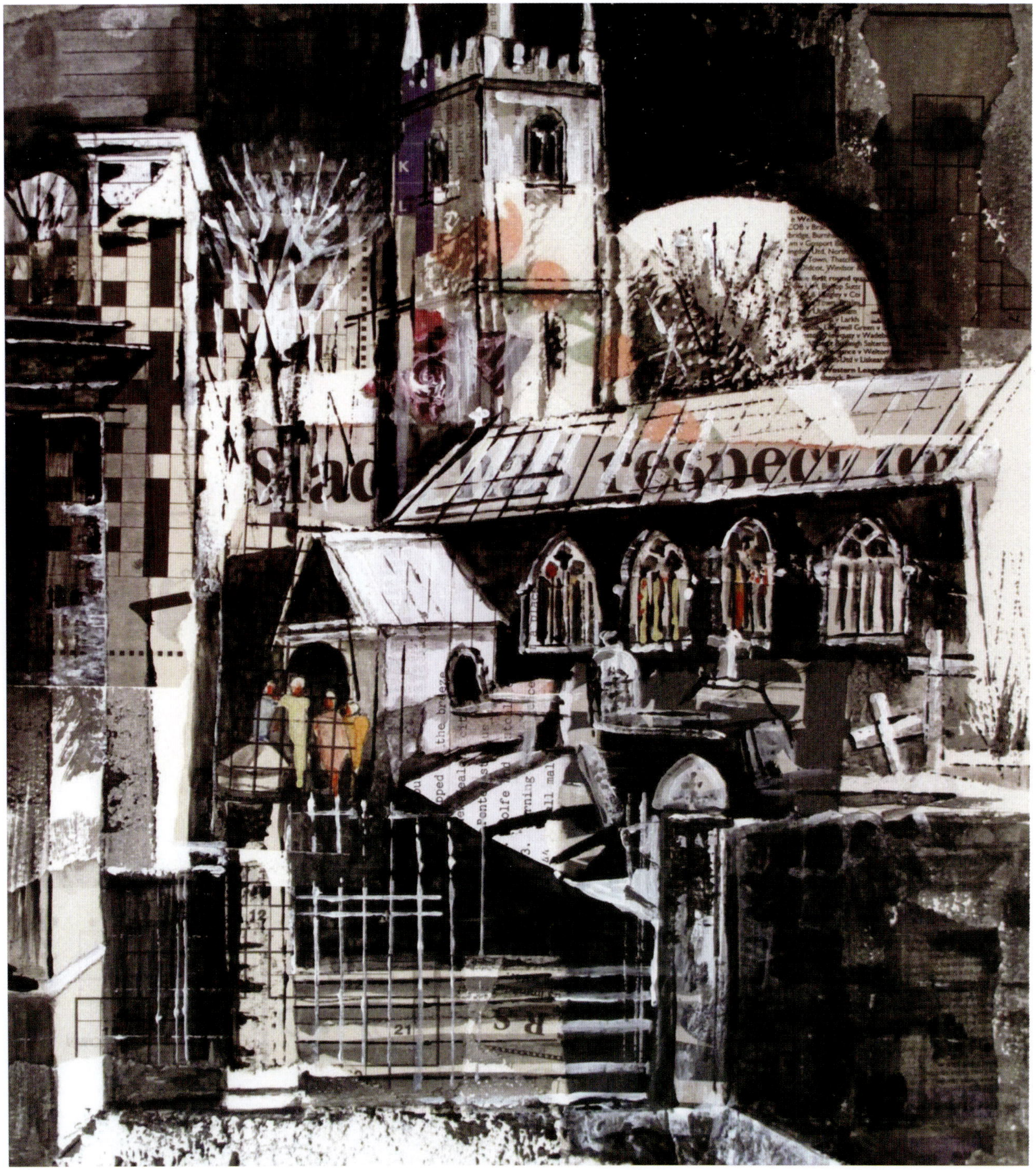

Midnight Mass,
collage and watercolour,
13 x 18 in

Opposite:
Medina, Fès,
mixed media,
17 x 27 in

Overleaf:
The Enchanted Wood,
mixed media,
12 x 12 in

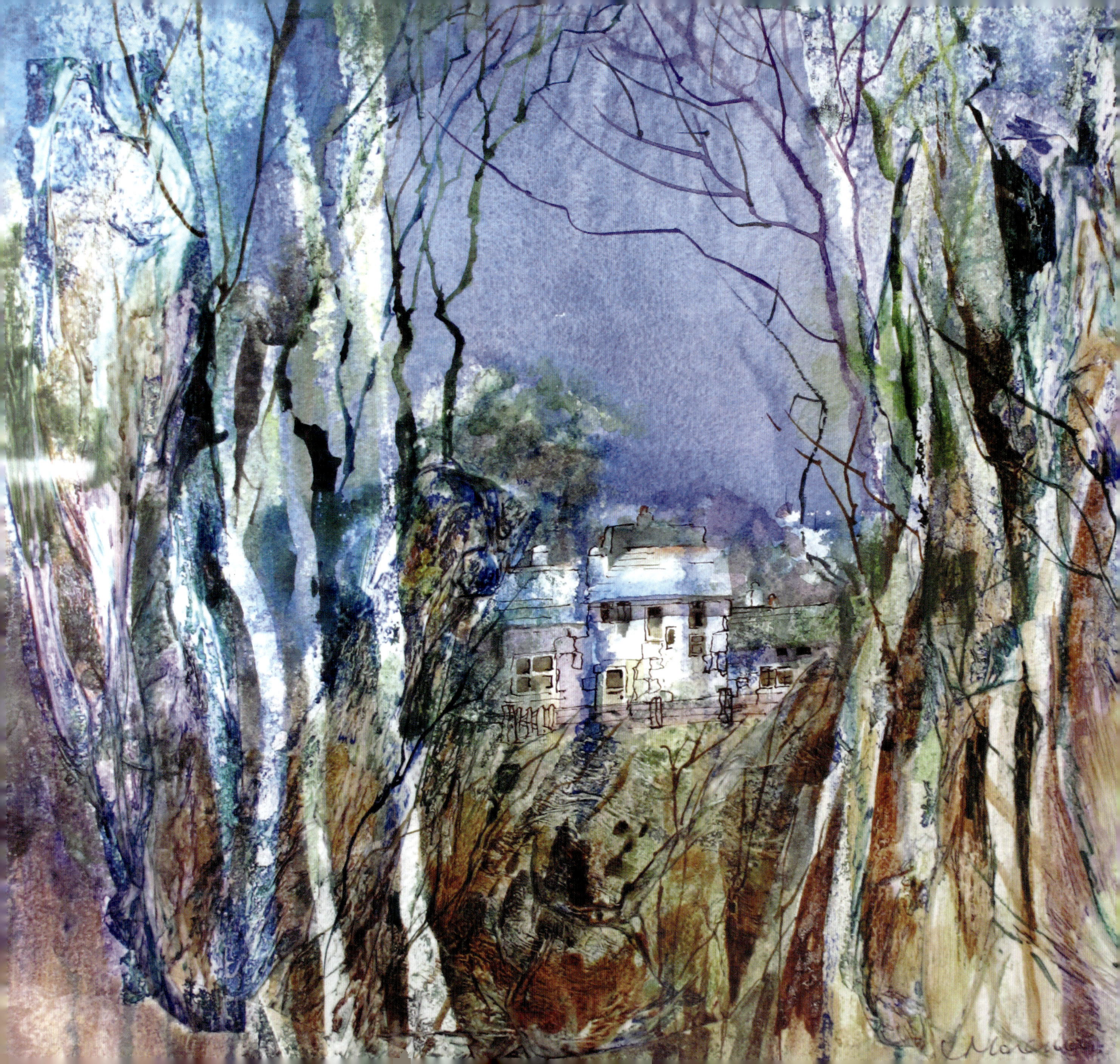